# THE GLORY THAT WAS GREECE:

## *FIRST FLORILEGIUM*

# THE GLORY THAT WAS GREECE:

## *FIRST FLORILEGIUM*

EDITED BY

**JEFFREY C. KALB, JR.**

*HONORS HISTORY SERIES, VOLUME 2*

# TABLE OF CONTENTS

i

# TABLE OF CONTENTS
## (CONTINUED)

# TABLE OF CONTENTS
## (CONTINUED)

# TABLE OF CONTENTS
## (CONTINUED)

# TABLE OF CONTENTS
## (CONTINUED)

## THE ATHÉNIAN EMPIRE; AGE OF PÉRICLES (479 - 431 B.C.)

### XVI.  The Growth of the Athénian Empire

# TABLE OF CONTENTS
## (CONTINUED)

# INTRODUCTION TO THE *HONORS HISTORY SERIES*

## *To the Parent, Teacher, and Student:*

The value of historical instruction is threefold: First, it allows the student to locate himself within the broader story of humanity. Second, it instructs him through concrete examples of virtue and vice, wisdom and foolishness. Third, it transmits to the student whatever elements of previous cultures are worthy of adoption or imitation.

The *Honors History Series* is a projected five-course study in which the flowers of the historical record are examined for their cultural value and moral lessons. In the first course, students are immersed in the aesthetic and investigative spirit of the ancient Greeks. In the second, they observe the Roman political, military, and legal genius. In the third course, they study the rise and flourishing of Christendom. In the fourth, students follow the political, intellectual, and cultural development of Europe from the Age of Exploration to modern times. Finally, they explore the distinctive history, character, and government of their own American nation. In discovering their ancient and modern origins, students arrive at deeper self-knowledge and a better appreciation of their cultural patrimony. What is here called the Florilegium approach to history is no educational novelty, but rather the methodical application and intensification of what many excellent instructors have always practiced. It is best understood by contrasting it to the "textbook" and "great book" methods. These are the extremes of secondary education to which the Florilegium method is a mean. Consider first the strengths and weakness of these other two methods.

The "textbook" (or "lecture") method conveys the primary facts of history, as best as these have been ascertained, together with a coherent and temporally progressive interpretation of the whole subject. This method has the virtue of simplifying and clearly organizing the material for consumption by students. If done well, it can provide a framework for the student to meaningfully locate himself, the current culture, and his nation within the larger course of human events. The deficiencies of this system are also manifest to anyone who has examined a contemporary history textbook. Textbook authors naturally project into the past our present attitudes and biases, thereby unconsciously making ourselves the term, purpose, and meaning of all history. The consequent familiarity bores the student and vitiates genuine learning. Only a single perspective is presented, and quite often not the traditional one. In the worst case, the textbook becomes a mere platform for the authors to preach their own idiosyncratic values. By no means are these texts able carry the student beyond the horizon of our debased modern culture.

In response not only to the inherent weakness of such a method, but also its present abuse, the "great book" (or "tutorial") method is favored by many who attach signal importance to literary excellence and active rational inquiry. Great teachers of the past, it is said, have left behind for us profound works that even today inform and educate. Our education should therefore consist principally in reading and studying these texts. With rhetorical flourish, the image is presented of Thucydides and Plutarch, Livy and Tacitus, Hamilton and De Tocqueville, eagerly attending to the devouring intellects of our students. The real teachers, it is said, and with some truth, are these great minds. Practice, however, is unequal to the theory. Students are left without a common framework or timeline to unify these histories. Visual aids are discounted, making imaginative synthesis all the more difficult. Art and architecture are generally passed over in silence. Moreover, excepting perhaps one in a thousand, the minds of adolescents are unprepared to absorb lofty genius unaided. Common sense tells us that too little learning takes place, and experience confirms it. Ideas and aphorisms, poorly comprehended, are merely parroted. Minds obtain a veneer of learning which, when scratched, discloses a lack of depth, integration, and coordination. Indeed, early exposure to "great books" without adequate guidance can produce an allergy to all such reading or, worse yet, the presumption of having mastered what is still above one's understanding.

The excellence of the writing notwithstanding, much that is compassed by these authors is irrelevant to the student and tedious in its detail. Let it be granted than an author is insightful and elegant; nevertheless, his intent in writing will not likely conform to our intentions in educating. Much of the narration may have served well the original audience but has little value today to anyone but the professional historian. The funeral oration of Pericles, the death of Cæsar, the battle of Agincourt, and Edmund Burke's observations on the character of the American colonies can make indelible marks upon young minds. But endless parades of Athenian military skirmishes, Roman consuls, French dynastic squabbles, or New Deal legislation produce no improvement in the student. He would be wholly justified in asking, "Why am I studying this?" Finally, the moral standards of many significant authors depart radically from those we would impart to our students. We cannot surrender children to perverse and dangerous authors simply because the latter have been inscribed into a canon of *historically* important writers.

An effective answer to these difficulties is the Florilegium method. The ideal remains to read the best that has been written: the most significant, the most beautiful, the most edifying. Yet even the greatest of authors cannot maintain himself perpetually on that high plane of wisdom; for lesser authors, brilliance is the exception rather than the rule. Given the limited time of the student and the mountain of cultural material available to the instructor, a selection process is inevitable. To demand that historical records be read in their entirety is to guarantee that much of serious value is kept entirely out of view. The *Florilegium* excerpts and collates what is worthy of the student's time, thereby increasing his cultural exposure. With proper help and encouragement as an adolescent, he will acquire a taste for such reading, in which case he may, as an adult already proficient in the necessary intellectual tools, read these same works in their entirety.

To address the remaining weaknesses of the "great book" method, the readings are indexed to concise *Outlines*, thereby supplying a framework in which they may hang together coherently. The *Outlines* also supply the visual helps that are necessary to better appreciate the history of a bygone era or the culture of a foreign people. A pronunciation guide is appended as an aid to mastery. The student will typically read each chapter of the *Outlines*, mastering names, dates, and facts to be tested by the instructor. He will then read the corresponding passages of the *Florilegium* to perfect and deepen his understanding. The *Florilegium* serves as a starting point for discussion and written essays. It is not intended to convey easily tested historical fact of the sort presented in the *Outlines*, but rather the historical, cultural, and simply human perspective that students should obtain before becoming adults. All the while, students are steeped in fine English. For the student preparing for higher learning and an intellectually engaged life, this is a method of study more fruitful than either the "textbook" or "great book" method.

*Beatae Mariae Semper Virgini*
*Mediatrici, Coredemptrici, et Advocatae*

Jeffrey C. Kalb, Jr.
*Honors History Series* Editor

# CHAPTER I.

## THE BEGINNINGS OF HISTORY

The Subject-Matter of History, I.—Early Condition of Mankind, II.—Divisions of the Human Race, III.

## I. THE SUBJECT-MATTER OF HISTORY

### The Purpose of Historical Studies

Cæsar once, seeing some wealthy strangers at Rome, carrying up and down with them in their arms and bosoms young puppy-dogs and monkeys, embracing and making much of them, took occasion not unnaturally to ask whether the women in their country were not accustomed to bear children; by that prince-like reprimand gravely reflecting upon persons who spend and lavish upon brute beasts that affection and kindness which nature has implanted in us to be bestowed on those of our own kind. With like reason may we blame those who misuse that love of inquiry and observation which nature has implanted in our souls, by expending it on objects unworthy of the attention either of their eyes or their ears, while they disregard such as are excellent in themselves, and would do them good... For as that color is most suitable to the eye whose freshness and pleasantness stimulates and strengthens the sight, so a man ought to apply his intellectual perception to such objects as, with the sense of delight, are apt to call it forth, and allure it to its own proper good and advantage.

Such objects we find in the acts of virtue, which also produce in the minds of mere readers about them, an emulation and eagerness that may lead them on to imitation. In other things there does not immediately follow upon the admiration and liking of the thing done, any strong desire of doing the like...

He who busies himself in mean occupations produces, in the very pains he takes about things of little or no use, an evidence against himself of his negligence and indisposition to what is really good. Nor did any generous and ingenuous young man, at the sight of the statue of Júpiter at Pisa, ever desire to be a Phídias, or, on seeing that of Júno at Árgos, long to be a Polyclítus, or feel induced by his pleasure in their poems to wish to be an Anácreon or Philítas or Archílochus. For it does not necessarily follow, that, if a piece of work please for its gracefulness, therefore he that wrought it deserves our admiration. Whence it is that neither do such things really profit or advantage the beholders, upon the sight of which no zeal arises for the imitation of them, nor any impulse or inclination, which may prompt any desire or endeavor of doing the like. But virtue... can so affect men's minds as to create at once both admiration of the things done and desire to imitate the doers of them. The goods of fortune we would possess and would enjoy; those of virtue we long to practice and exercise; we are content to receive the former from others, the latter we wish others to experience from us. Moral good is a practical stimulus; it is no sooner seen, than it inspires an impulse to practice; and does not influence the mind and character by a mere imitation which we look at, but, by the statement of the fact, creates a moral purpose which we form.

– Plútarch, *Life of Péricles* (translated by John Dryden)

### The Benefits of Historical Study

For it is an excellent thing to be able to use the ignorant mistakes of others as warning examples for the correction of error, and, when we confront the various vicissitudes of life, instead of having to investigate what is being done now, to be able to imitate the successes which have been achieved

1

in the past. Certainly all men prefer in their counsels the oldest men to those who are younger, because of the experience which has accrued to the former through the lapse of time; but it is a fact that such experience is as far surpassed by the understanding which is gained from history, as history excels in the multitude of facts at its disposal. For this reason, the acquisition of a knowledge of history is of the greatest utility for every conceivable circumstance of life. For it endows the young with the wisdom of the aged, while for the old it multiplies the experience which they already possess; citizens in private station it qualifies for leadership, and the leaders it incites, through the immortality of the glory which it confers, to undertake the noblest deeds; soldiers it makes more ready to face dangers in defense of their country because of the public encomiums which they will receive after death, and wicked men it turns aside from their impulse towards evil through the everlasting opprobrium to which it will condemn them.

In general, then, it is because of that commemoration of good deeds which history accords men that some of them have been induced to become the founders of cities, that others have been led to introduce laws which encompass man's social life with security, and that many have aspired to discover new sciences and arts in order to benefit the race of men.

— Diodórus Sículus, *Library of History*, I.1-2 (translated by C. H. Oldfather)

## History and Literacy

History also contributes to the power of speech, and a nobler thing than that may not easily be found. For it is this that makes the Greeks superior to the barbarians, and the educated to the uneducated, and, furthermore, it is by means of speech alone that one man is able to gain ascendancy over the many. In general, the impression made by every measure that is proposed corresponds to the power of the speaker who presents it, and we describe great and humane men as "worthy of speech," as though therein they had won the highest prize of excellence. And when speech is resolved into its several kinds, we find that—whereas poetry is more pleasing than profitable, and codes of law punish but do not instruct, and similarly, all the other kinds either contribute nothing to happiness or else contain a harmful element mingled with the beneficial, while some of them actually pervert the truth—history alone, since in it word and fact are in perfect agreement, embraces in its narration all the other qualities as well as the useful. For it is ever to be seen urging men to justice, denouncing those who are evil, lauding the good, laying up, in a word, for its readers a mighty store of experience.

— Diodórus Sículus, *Library of History*, I.2 (translated by C. H. Oldfather)

## True Portrait in Biography

For as we would wish that a painter who is to draw a beautiful face in which there is yet some imperfection, should neither wholly leave out, nor yet too pointedly express what is defective—because the latter would deform it, and the former spoil the resemblance—so, since it is hard, or indeed perhaps impossible, to show the life of a man wholly free from blemish, in all that is excellent we must follow truth exactly, and give it fully. Any lapses or faults that occur through human passions or political necessities we may regard as the shortcomings of some particular virtue, rather than as the natural effects of vice. We may be content, without introducing them curiously and officiously into our narrative, if it be but out of tenderness to the weakness of nature, which has never succeeded in producing any human character so perfect in virtue as to be pure from all admixture and open to no criticism.

– Plútarch, *Life of Címon* (translated by John Dryden)

# CHAPTER II.

## THE FAR EASTERN COUNTRIES — CHÍNA AND ÍNDIA

Chína and the Chínese, I.—Índia and the Híndus, II.

## I. CHÍNA AND THE CHÍNESE

### Sayings of Lao-Tse (Lao-Tse)

When merit has been achieved, do not take it to yourself; for if you do not take it to yourself, it shall never be taken from you.

By many words wit is exhausted; it is better to preserve a mean.

Keep behind, and you shall be put in front; keep out, and you shall be kept in.

He who grasps more than he can hold would be better without any; he who strikes with a sharp point, will not himself be safe for long.

Good words shall gain you honor in the marketplace; but good deeds shall gain you friends among men.

To see oneself is to be clear of sight.

He who knows how to shut, uses no bolts,—yet you cannot open; he who knows how to bind, uses no ropes,—yet you cannot undo.

He who does not desire power nor value wealth,—though his wisdom be as a fool's, shall be esteemed among men.

He who, conscious of being strong, is content to be weak,—he shall be a cynosure of men.

A great principle cannot be divided.

The empire is a divine trust; it may not be ruled. He who rules ruins; he who holds it by force, loses it.

Mighty is he who conquers himself.

If you would contract, you must first expand. If you would weaken, you must first strengthen. If you would take, you must first give.

Fishes cannot be taken from water; the instruments of government cannot be delegated to others.

If the Way prevails on earth, horses will be used for agriculture; if not, war-horses will breed in camp.

To the good I would be good. To the not-good I would also be good,—in order to make them good.

In governing men and in serving God, there is nothing like moderation.

Govern a great nation as you would cook a small fish.

Recompense injury with kindness.

Desire not to desire, and you will not value things difficult to obtain.

*– Sayings of Lao-Tse* (translated by Herbert Allen Giles)

# Excerpts of the Ánalects (School of Confúcius)

The Master said, "If the scholar be not grave, he will not call forth any veneration, and his learning will not be solid."

The Master said, "He who aims to be a man of complete virtue in his food does not seek to gratify his appetite, nor in his dwelling place does he seek the appliances of ease; he is earnest in what he is doing, and careful in his speech; he frequents the company of men of principle that he may be rectified:—such a person may be said indeed to love to learn."

The Master said, "I will not be afflicted at men's not knowing me; I will be afflicted that I do not know men."

The Master said, "He who exercises government by means of his virtue may be compared to the north polar star, which keeps its place and all the stars turn towards it."

The Master said, "Yu, shall I teach you what knowledge is? When you know a thing, to hold that you know it; and when you do not know a thing, to allow that you do not know it;—this is knowledge."

The Master said, "Those who are without virtue cannot abide long either in a condition of poverty and hardship, or in a condition of enjoyment. The virtuous rest in virtue; the wise desire virtue."

The Master said, "A scholar, whose mind is set on truth, and who is ashamed of bad clothes and bad food, is not fit to be discoursed with."

The Master said, "The superior man, in the world, does not set his mind either for anything, or against anything; what is right he will follow."

The Master said, "The superior man thinks of virtue; the small man thinks of comfort. The superior man thinks of the sanctions of law; the small man thinks of favors which he may receive."

The Master said, "When we see men of worth, we should think of equaling them; when we see men of a contrary character, we should turn inwards and examine ourselves."

The Master said, "They who know the truth are not equal to those who love it, and they who love it are not equal to those who delight in it."

The Master said, "I do not open up the truth to one who is not eager to get knowledge, nor help out anyone who is not anxious to explain himself. When I have presented one corner of a subject to anyone, and he cannot from it learn the other three, I do not repeat my lesson."

The Master said, "I am not one who was born in the possession of knowledge; I am one who is fond of antiquity, and earnest in seeking it there."

The Master said, "Learn as if you could not reach your object, and were always fearing also lest you should lose it..."

The Master said, "When a prince's personal conduct is correct, his government is effective without the issuing of orders. If his personal conduct is not correct, he may issue orders, but they will not be followed."

The Master said, "Can there be love which does not lead to strictness with its object? Can there be loyalty which does not lead to the instruction of its object?"

The Master said, "Those whose courses are different cannot lay plans for one another."

The Master said, "In language it is simply required that it convey the meaning."

— Confúcius, *Ánalects* (translated by James Legge)

## Dhammapáda (Búddha)

The best of ways is the eightfold; the best of truths the four words; the best of virtues passionlessness; the best of men he who has eyes to see.

This is the way, there is no other that leads to the purifying of intelligence. Go on this way! Everything else is the deceit of Mára (the tempter).

If you go on this way, you will make an end of pain! The way was preached by me, when I had understood the removal of the thorns (in the flesh).

You yourself must make an effort. The Tathágatas (Búddhas) are only preachers. The thoughtful who enter the way are freed from the bondage of Mára.

"All created things perish," he who knows and sees this becomes passive in pain; this is the way to purity.

"All created things are grief and pain," he who knows and sees this becomes passive in pain; this is the way that leads to purity.

"All forms are unreal," he who knows and sees this becomes passive in pain; this is the way that leads to purity.

He who does not rouse himself when it is time to rise, who, though young and strong, is full of sloth, whose will and thought are weak, that lazy and idle man will never find the way to knowledge.

Watching his speech, well restrained in mind, let a man never commit any wrong with his body! Let a man but keep these three roads of action clear, and he will achieve the way which is taught by the wise.

Through zeal knowledge is gotten, through lack of zeal knowledge is lost; let a man who knows this double path of gain and loss thus place himself that knowledge may grow.

Cut down the whole forest, not a tree only! Danger comes out of the forest. When you have cut down both the forest and its undergrowth, then, Bhíkshus, you will be rid of the forest and free!

So long as the love of man towards women, even the smallest, is not destroyed, so long is his mind in bondage, as the calf that drinks milk is to its mother.

Cut out the love of self, like an autumn lotus, with thy hand! Cherish the road of peace. Nirvána has been shown by Búddha.

"Here I shall dwell in the rain, here in winter and summer," thus the fool meditates, and does not think of his death.

Death comes and carries off that man, praised for his children and flocks, his mind distracted, as a flood carries off a sleeping village.

Sons are no help, nor a father, nor relations; there is no help from kinsfolk for one whom death has seized.

A wise and good man who knows the meaning of this, should quickly clear the way that leads to Nirvána.

– Búddha, *Dhammapáda*, XX. (translated by Friedrich Max Müller)

# CHAPTER III.

## THE MESOPOTÁMIAN COUNTRIES -  ASSÝRIA AND BABYLÓNIA

The Early Babylónian or "Chaldéan" Empire, I.—The Assýrian Empire, II.—The Later Babylónian Empire, III.

## I. THE EARLY BABYLÓNIAN OR "CHALDÉAN" EMPIRE

### Excerpt from the Code of Hammurábi

The king who ruleth among the kings of the cities am I. My words are well considered; there is no wisdom like unto mine. By the command of Shamásh, the great judge of heaven and earth, let righteousness go forth in the land: by the order of Márduk, my lord, let no destruction befall my monument. In Eságila, which I love, let my name be ever repeated; let the oppressed, who has a case at law, come and stand before this my image as king of righteousness; let him read the inscription, and understand my precious words: the inscription will explain his case to him; he will find out what is just, and his heart will be glad, so that he will say:

> "Hammurábi is a ruler, who is as a father to his subjects, who holds the words of Márduk in reverence, who has achieved conquest for Márduk over the north and south, who rejoices the heart of Márduk, his lord, who has bestowed benefits for ever and ever on his subjects, and has established order in the land."

When he reads the record, let him pray with full heart to Márduk, my lord, and Zárpanit, my lady; and then shall the protecting deities and the gods, who frequent Eságila, graciously grant the desires daily presented before Márduk, my lord, and Zárpanit, my lady.

In future time, through all coming generations, let the king, who may be in the land, observe the words of righteousness which I have written on my monument; let him not alter the law of the land which I have given, the edicts which I have enacted; my monument let him not mar. If such a ruler have wisdom, and be able to keep his land in order, he shall observe the words which I have written in this inscription; the rule, statute, and law of the land which I have given; the decisions which I have made will this inscription show him; let him rule his subjects accordingly, speak justice to them, give right decisions, root out the miscreants and criminals from this land, and grant prosperity to his subjects.

Hammurábi, the king of righteousness, on whom Shamásh has conferred right am I. My words are well considered; my deeds are not equaled; to bring low those that were high; to humble the proud, to expel insolence. If a succeeding ruler considers my words, which I have written in this my inscription, if he do not annul my law, nor corrupt my words, nor change my monument, then may Shamásh lengthen that king's reign, as he has that of me, the king of righteousness, that he may reign in righteousness over his subjects. If this ruler do not esteem my words, which I have written in my inscription, if he despise my curses, and fear not the curse of the god, if he destroy the law which I have given, corrupt my words, change my monument, efface my name, write his name there, or on account of the curses commission another so to do, that man, whether king or ruler, or commoner, no matter what he be, may the great god, Ánu, the father of the gods, who has ordered my rule, withdraw from him the glory of royalty, break his scepter, curse his destiny.

– Hammurábi, *Code of Hammurábi* (translated by Leonard William King)

## An Inscription of Tíglath-Piléser I.

Tíglath Piléser the powerful king; supreme King of Lash-Ánan; King of the four regions; King of all Kings; Lord of Lords; the supreme; Monarch of Monarchs; the illustrious Chief who under the auspices of the Sun god, being armed with the scepter and girt with the girdle of power over mankind, rules over all the people of Bel; the mighty Prince whose praise is blazoned forth among the Kings: the exalted sovereign, whose servants Áshur has appointed to the government of the country of the four regions (and) has made his name celebrated to posterity; the conqueror of many plains and mountains of the Upper and Lower Country; the conquering hero, the terror of whose name has overwhelmed all regions; the bright constellation who, according to his power has warred against foreign countries (and) under the auspices of Bel, there being no equal to him, has subdued the enemies of Áshur.

Áshur (and) the great gods, the guardians of my kingdom, who gave government and laws to my dominions, and ordered an enlarged frontier to their territory, having committed to (my) hand their valiant and warlike servants, I have subdued the lands and the peoples and the strong places, and the Kings who were hostile to Áshur; and I have reduced all that was contained in them. With a host of kings I have fought ... and have imposed on them the bond of servitude. There is not to me a second in war, nor an equal in battle. I have added territory to Assýria and peoples to her people. I have enlarged the frontier of my territories and subdued all the lands contained in them.

– Tíglath-Piléser I., Inscription (translated by Sir H. Rawlinson)

## III. THE LATER BABYLÓNIAN OR "CHALDÉAN" EMPIRE

## The Hanging Gardens of Bábylon

Bábylon itself also is situated in a plain. The wall is 385 stádia in circumference, and 32 feet in thickness. The height of the space between the towers is 50, and of the towers 60 cúbits. The roadway upon the walls will allow chariots with four horses when they meet to pass each other with ease. Whence, among the seven wonders of the world, are reckoned this wall and the hanging garden: the shape of the garden is a square, and each side of it measures four pléthra. It consists of vaulted terraces, raised one above another, and resting upon cube-shaped pillars. These are hollow and filled with earth to allow trees of the largest size to be planted. The pillars, the vaults, and the terraces are constructed of baked brick and asphalt.

The ascent to the highest story is by stairs, and at their side are water engines, by means of which persons, appointed expressly for the purpose, are continually employed in raising water from the Euphrátes into the garden. For the river, which is a stádium in breadth, flows through the middle of the city, and the garden is on the side of the river.

– Strábo, *Geography*, XVI.1.5 (translated by H. L. Jones)

## The Motive for the Hanging Gardens

After fortifying the city on this grand scale and adorning the gateways in a manner worthy of their sanctity, he constructed a second palace adjoining that of his father. It would perhaps be tedious to describe the towering height and general magnificence of this building; it need only be remarked that, notwithstanding its immense and imposing proportions, it was completed in fifteen days. Within this palace he erected lofty stone terraces, in which he closely reproduced mountain scenery, completing the resemblance by planting them with all manner of trees and constructing the so-called hanging garden; because his wife, having been brought up in Média, had a passion for mountain surroundings.

– Joséphus, *Against Ápion*, I.19 (translated by H. St. J. Thackeray)

## The Temple of Júpiter Bélus

And here I may not omit to tell the use to which the mold dug out of the great moat was turned, nor the manner wherein the wall was wrought. As fast as they dug the moat the soil which they got from the cutting was made into bricks, and when a sufficient number were completed, they baked the bricks in kilns. Then they set to building, and began with bricking the borders of the moat, after which they proceeded to construct the wall itself, using throughout for their cement hot bitumen, and interposing a layer of wattled reeds at every thirtieth course of the bricks. On the top, along the edges of the wall, they constructed buildings of a single chamber facing one another, leaving between them room for a four-horse chariot to turn. In the circuit of the wall are a hundred gates, all of brass, with brazen lintels and side-posts. The bitumen used in the work was brought to Bábylon from the Is, a small stream which flows into the Euphrátes at the point where the city of the same name stands, eight days' journey from Bábylon. Lumps of bitumen are found in great abundance in this river.

The city is divided into two portions by the river which runs through the midst of it. This river is the Euphrátes, a broad, deep, swift stream, which rises in Arménia, and empties itself into the Erythræan sea. The city wall is brought down on both sides to the edge of the stream: thence, from the corners of the wall, there is carried along each bank of the river a fence of burnt bricks. The houses are mostly three and four stories high; the streets all run in straight lines, not only those parallel to the river, but also the cross streets which lead down to the waterside. At the river end of these cross streets are low gates in the fence that skirts the stream, which are, like the great gates in the outer wall, of brass, and open on the water.

The outer wall is the main defense of the city. There is, however, a second inner wall, of less thickness than the first, but very little inferior to it in strength. The center of each division of the town was occupied by a fortress. In the one stood the palace of the kings, surrounded by a wall of great strength and size: in the other was the sacred precinct of Júpiter Bélus, a square enclosure two furlongs each way, with gates of solid brass; which was also remaining in my time. In the middle of the precinct there was a tower of solid masonry, a furlong in length and breadth, upon which was raised a second tower, and on that a third, and so on up to eight. The ascent to the top is on the outside, by a path which winds round all the towers. When one is about half-way up, one finds a resting-place and seats, where persons are wont to sit some time on their way to the summit. On the topmost tower there is a spacious temple, and inside the temple stands a couch of unusual size, richly adorned, with a golden table by its side.

—Heródotus, *History*, I.179-181 (translated by George Rawlinson)

# CHAPTER IV.

## THE HITHER ÓRIENT—ÉGYPT, PHŒNÍCIA, AND ÁSIA MÍNOR

Ancient Égypt and its Civilization, I.—Phœnícia and Ancient Commerce, II.—Nations of Ásia Mínor, III.

## I. ANCIENT ÉGYPT AND ITS CIVILIZATION

### The Egýptian Book of the Dead

If [these] words be recited by the spirit when he shall come to the Seven Árits, and as he entereth the doors, he shall neither be turned back nor repulsed before Osíris, and he shall be made to have his being among the blessed spirits, and to have dominion among the ancestral followers of Osíris. If these things be done for any spirit he shall have his being in that place like a lord of eternity in one body with Osíris, and at no place shall any being contend against him.

– *Papýrus of Áni* (translated by E. A. Wallace Budge)

### A Description of Égypt

The Egýptians, they said, were the first to discover the solar year, and to portion out its course into twelve parts. They obtained this knowledge from the stars. (To my mind they contrive their year much more cleverly than the Greeks, for these last every other year intercalate a whole month, but the Egýptians, dividing the year into twelve months of thirty days each, add every year a space of five days besides, whereby the circuit of the seasons is made to return with uniformity.) The Egýptians, they went on to affirm, first brought into use the names of the twelve gods, which the Greeks adopted from them; and first erected altars, images, and temples to the gods; and also first engraved upon stone the figures of animals... And they told me that the first man who ruled over Égypt was Min, and that in his time all Égypt, except the Thebáic canton, was a marsh, none of the land below Lake Mœris then showing itself above the surface of the water. This is a distance of seven days' sail from the sea up the river.

The following is the general character of the region. In the first place, on approaching it by sea, when you are still a day's sail from the land, if you let down a sounding-line you will bring up mud, and find yourself in eleven fathoms' water, which shows that the soil washed down by the stream extends to that distance... From the coast inland as far as Heliópolis the breadth of Égypt is considerable, the country is flat, without springs, and full of swamps... As one proceeds beyond Heliópolis up the country, Égypt becomes narrow, the Arábian range of hills, which has a direction from north to south, shutting it in upon the one side, and the Líbyan range upon the other. The former ridge runs on without a break, and stretches away to the sea called the Erythræan; it contains the quarries whence the stone was cut for the pýramids of Mémphis: and this is the point where it ceases its first direction, and bends away in the manner above indicated... Such are the chief features of this range. On the Líbyan side, the other ridge whereon the pýramids stand is rocky and covered with sand; its direction is the same as that of the Arábian ridge in the first part of its course. Above Heliópolis, then, there is no great breadth of territory for such a country as Égypt, but during four days' sail Égypt is narrow; the valley between the two ranges is a level plain, and seemed to me to be, at the narrowest point, not more than two hundred furlongs across from the Arábian to the Líbyan hills. Above this point Égypt again widens.

– Heródotus, *History*, II.4-8 (translated by George Rawlinson)

## The Rise and Fall of the Nile

Concerning the nature of the river, I was not able to gain any information either from the priests or from others. I was particularly anxious to learn from them why the Nile, at the commencement of the summer solstice, begins to rise, and continues to increase for a hundred days, and why, as soon as that number is past, it forthwith retires and contracts its stream, continuing low during the whole of the winter until the summer solstice comes round again. On none of these points could I obtain any explanation from the inhabitants, though I made every inquiry, wishing to know what was commonly reported; they could neither tell me what special virtue the Nile has which makes it so opposite in its nature to all other streams, nor why, unlike every other river, it gives forth no breezes from its surface.

— Heródotus, *History*, II.19 (translated by George Rawlinson)

## Egýptian Religion

When they write or calculate, instead of going, like the Greeks, from left to right, they move their hand from right to left; and they insist, notwithstanding, that it is they who go to the right, and the Greeks who go to the left. They have two quite different kinds of writing, one of which is called sacred [hieroglýphic], the other common [demótic].

They are religious to excess, far beyond any other race of men, and use the following ceremonies: They drink out of brazen cups, which they scour every day; there is no exception to this practice. They wear linen garments, which they are specially careful to have always fresh washed. They practice circumcision for the sake of cleanliness, considering it better to be cleanly than comely. The priests shave their whole body every other day, that no lice or other impure thing may adhere to them when they are engaged in the service of the gods. Their dress is entirely of linen, and their shoes of the papýrus plant: it is not lawful for them to wear either dress or shoes of any other material. They bathe twice every day in cold water, and twice each night; besides which they observe, so to speak, thousands of ceremonies. They enjoy, however, not a few advantages. They consume none of their own property, and are at no expense for anything; but every day bread is baked for them of the sacred grain, and a plentiful supply of beef and of goose's flesh is assigned to each, and also a portion of wine made from the grape. Fish they are not allowed to eat; and beans—which none of the Egýptians ever sow, or eat, if they come up of their own accord, either raw or boiled—the priests will not even endure to look on, since they consider it unclean. Instead of a single priest, each god has the attendance of a college, at the head of which is a chief priest; when one of these dies, his son is appointed in his room.

Male kine are reckoned to belong to [the god] Épaphus and are therefore tested in the following manner: One of the priests appointed for the purpose searches to see if there is a single black hair on the whole body, since in that case the beast is unclean. He examines him all over, standing on his legs, and again laid upon his back; after which he takes the tongue out of his mouth, to see if it be clean in respect of the prescribed marks (what they are I will mention elsewhere); he also inspects the hairs of the tail, to observe if they grow naturally. If the animal is pronounced clean in all these various points, the priest marks him by twisting a piece of papýrus round his horns, and attaching thereto some sealing-clay, which he then stamps with his own signet-ring. After this the beast is led away; and it is forbidden, under the penalty of death, to sacrifice an animal which has not been marked in this way.

The following is their manner of sacrifice: They lead the victim, marked with their signet, to the altar where they are about to offer it, and setting the wood alight, pour a libation of wine upon the altar in front of the victim, and at the same time invoke the god. Then they slay the animal, and cutting off his head, proceed to flay the body. Next they take the head, and heaping imprecations on it, if there is a marketplace and a body of Greek traders in the city, they carry it there and sell it instantly; if, however, there are no Greeks among them, they throw the head into the river. The imprecation is to this effect: They pray that if any evil is impending either over those who sacrifice, or over universal Égypt, it may be made to fall upon that head. These practices, the imprecations upon the heads, and the libations of wine, prevail all over Égypt, and extend to victims of all sorts; and hence the Egýptians will never eat the head of any animal.

The disemboweling and burning are, however, different in different sacrifices. I will mention the mode in use with respect to the goddess whom they regard as the greatest, and honor with the chiefest festival. When they have flayed their steer they pray, and when their prayer is ended they take the paunch of the animal out entire, leaving the intestines and the fat inside the body; they then cut off the legs, the ends of the loins, the shoulders, and the neck; and having so done, they fill the body of the steer with clean bread, honey, raisins, figs, frankincense, myrrh, and other aromatics. Thus filled, they burn the body, pouring over it great quantities of oil. Before offering the sacrifice they fast, and while the bodies of the victims are being consumed they beat themselves. Afterwards, when they have concluded this part of the ceremony, they have the other parts of the victim served up to them for a repast.

— Heródotus, *History*, II.36-40 (translated by George Rawlinson)

## The Worship of Animals in Égypt

As regards the consecration of animals in Égypt, the practice naturally appears to many to be extraordinary and worthy of investigation. For the Egýptian venerate certain animals exceedingly, not only during their lifetime but even after their death, such as cats, mongooses and dogs, and, again, hawks and the birds which they call "íbis," as well as wolves and crocodiles and a number of other animals of that kind, and the reasons for such worship we shall undertake to set forth, after we have first spoken briefly about the animals themselves.

In the first place, for each kind of animal that is accorded this worship there has been consecrated a portion of land which returns a revenue sufficient for their care and sustenance; moreover, the Egýptians make vows to certain gods on behalf of their children who have been delivered from an illness, in which case they shave off their hair and weigh it against silver or gold, and then give the money to the attendants of the animals mentioned. These cut up flesh for the hawks and calling them with a loud cry toss it up to them, as they swoop by, until they catch it, while for the cats and mongooses they break up bread into milk and calling them with a clucking sound set it before them, or else they cut up fish caught in the Nile and feed the flesh to them raw; and in like manner each of the other kinds of animals is provided with the appropriate food. And as for the various services which these animals require, the Egýptians not only do not try to avoid them or feel ashamed to be seen by the crowds as they perform them, but on the contrary, in the belief that they are engaged in the most serious rites of divine worship, they assume airs of importance, and wearing special insignia make the rounds of the cities and the countryside. And since it can be seen from afar in the service of what animals they engaged, all who meet them fall down before them and render them honor.

When one of these animals dies they wrap it in fine linen and then, wailing and beating their breasts, carry it off to be embalmed; and after it has been treated with cedar oil and such spices as have the quality of imparting a pleasant odor and of preserving the body for a long time, they lay it away in a consecrated tomb. And whoever intentionally kills one of these animals is put to death, unless it be a cat or an íbis that he kills; but if he kills one of these, whether intentionally or unintentionally, he is certainly put to death, for the common people gather in crowds and deal with the perpetrator most cruelly, sometimes doing this without waiting for a trial. And because of their fear of such a punishment any who have caught sight of one of these animals lying dead withdraw to a great distance and shout with lamentations and protestations that they found the animal already dead. So deeply implanted also in the hearts of the common people is their superstitious regard for these animals and so unalterable are the emotions cherished by every man regarding the honor due to them that once, at the time when Ptólemy their king had not as yet been given by the Rómans the appellation of "friend" and the people were exercising all zeal in courting the favor of the embassy from Ítaly which was then visiting Égypt and, in their fear, were intent upon giving no cause for complaint or war, when one of the Rómans killed a cat and the multitude rushed in a crowd to his house, neither the officials sent by the king to beg the man off nor the fear of Rome which all the people felt were enough to save the man from punishment, even though his act had been an accident. And this incident we relate, not from hearsay, but we saw it with our own eyes on the occasion of the visit we made to Égypt.

But if what has been said seems to many incredible and like a fanciful tale, what is to follow will appear far more extraordinary. Once, they say, when the inhabitants of Égypt were being hard pressed by a famine, many in their need laid hands upon their fellows, yet not a single man was even accused of having partaken of the sacred animals. Furthermore, whenever a dog is found dead in any house, every inmate of it shaves his entire body and goes into mourning, and what is more astonishing than this, if any wine or grain or any other thing necessary to life happens to be stored in the building where one of these animals has expired, they would never think of using it thereafter for any purpose.

– Diodórus Sículus, *Library of History*, I.83-84 (translated by C. H. Oldfather)

## Egýptian Embalming Practices

There are a set of men in Égypt who practice the art of embalming and make it their proper business. These persons, when a body is brought to them, show the bearers various models of corpses, made in wood, and painted so as to resemble nature. The most perfect is said to be after the manner of him whom I do not think it religious to name in connection with such a matter; the second sort is inferior to the first, and less costly; the third is the cheapest of all. All this the embalmers explain, and then ask in which way it is wished that the corpse should be prepared. The bearers tell them, and having concluded their bargain, take their departure, while the embalmers, left to themselves, proceed to their task. The mode of embalming, according to the most perfect process, is the following: They take first a crooked piece of iron, and with it draw out the brain through the nostrils, thus getting rid of a portion, while the skull is cleared of the rest by rinsing with drugs; next they make a cut along the flank with a sharp Ethiópian stone, and take out the whole contents of the abdomen, which they then cleanse, washing it thoroughly with palm wine, and again frequently with an infusion of pounded aromatics. After this they fill the cavity with the purest bruised myrrh, with cassia, and every other sort of spicery except frankincense, and sew up the opening. Then the body is placed in natrum for seventy days and covered entirely over. After the expiration of that space of time, which must not be exceeded, the body is washed, and wrapped round, from head to foot, with bandages of fine linen cloth, smeared over with gum, which is used generally by the Egýptians in the place of glue, and in this state it is given back to the relations, who enclose it in a wooden case which they have had made for the purpose, shaped into the figure of a man. Then fastening the case, they place it in a sepulchral chamber, upright against the wall. Such is the most costly way of embalming the dead.

If persons wish to avoid expense, and choose the second process, the following is the method pursued: Syringes are filled with oil made from the cedar tree, which is then, without any incision or disemboweling, injected into the abdomen. The passage by which it might be likely to return is stopped, and the body laid in natrum the prescribed number of days. At the end of the time the cedar oil is allowed to make its escape; and such is its power that it brings with it the whole stomach and intestines in a liquid state. The natrum meanwhile has dissolved the flesh, and so nothing is left of the dead body but the skin and the bones. It is returned in this condition to the relatives, without any further trouble being bestowed upon it.

The third method of embalming, which is practiced in the case of the poorer classes, is to clear out the intestines with an enema, and let the body lie in natrum the seventy days, after which it is at once given to those who come to fetch it away.

— Heródotus, *History*, II.86-88 (translated by George Rawlinson)

## The Pýramid of Chéops

Till the death of Rhampsinítus, the priests said, Égypt was excellently governed, and flourished greatly; but after him Chéops succeeded to the throne and plunged into all manner of wickedness. He closed the temples, and forbade the Egýptians to offer sacrifice, compelling them instead to labor, one and all, in his service. Some were required to drag blocks of stone down to the Nile from the quarries in the Arábian range of hills; others received the blocks after they had been conveyed in boats across the river and drew them to the range of hills called the Líbyan. A hundred thousand men labored constantly and were relieved every three months by a fresh lot. It took ten years' oppression of the people to make the causeway for the conveyance of the stones, a work not much inferior, in my judgment, to the pýramid itself. This causeway is five furlongs in length, ten fathoms wide, and in height, at the highest part, eight fathoms. It is built of polished stone and is covered with carvings of animals. To make it took ten years, as I said, or rather to make the causeway, the works on the mound where the pýramid stands, and the underground chambers, which Chéops intended as vaults for his own use: these last were built on a sort of island, surrounded by water introduced from the Nile by a canal. The pýramid itself was twenty years in building. It is a square, eight hundred feet each way, and the height the same, built entirely of polished stone, fitted together with the utmost care. The stones of which it is composed are none of them less than thirty feet in length.

The pýramid was built in steps, battlement-wise, as it is called, or, according to others, altar-wise. After laying the stones for the base, they raised the remaining stones to their places by means of machines formed of short wooden planks. The first machine raised them from the ground to the top of the first step. On this there was another machine, which received the stone upon its arrival, and conveyed it to the second step, whence a third machine advanced it still higher. Either they had as many machines as there were steps in the pýramid, or possibly they had but a single machine, which, being easily moved, was transferred from tier to tier as the stone rose; both accounts are given, and therefore I mention both. The upper portion of the pýramid was finished first, then the middle, and finally the part which was lowest and nearest the ground. There is an inscription in Egýptian characters on the pýramid which records the quantity of radishes, onions, and garlic consumed by the laborers who constructed it; and I perfectly well remember that the interpreter who read the writing to me said that the money expended in this way was 1600 talents of silver. If this then is a true record, what a vast sum must have been spent on the iron tools used in the work, and on the feeding and clothing of the laborers, considering the length of time the work lasted, which has already been stated, and the additional time—no small space, I imagine—which must have been occupied by the quarrying of the stones, their conveyance, and the formation of the underground apartments.

— Heródotus, *History*, II.124-125 (translated by George Rawlinson)

## The Lábyrinth and Lake Mœris

To bind themselves yet more closely together, it seemed good to them to leave a common monument. In pursuance of this resolution they made the Lábyrinth which lies a little above Lake Mœris, in the neighborhood of the place called the city of crocodiles. I visited this place, and found it to surpass description; for if all the walls and other great works of the Greeks could be put together in one, they would not equal, either for labor or expense, this Lábyrinth; and yet the temple of Éphesus is a building worthy of note, and so is the temple of Sámos. The pýramids likewise surpass description and are severally equal to a number of the greatest works of the Greeks, but the Lábyrinth surpasses the pýramids. It has twelve courts, all of them roofed, with gates exactly opposite one another, six looking to the north, and six to the south. A single wall surrounds the entire building. There are two different sorts of chambers throughout, half under ground, half above ground, the latter built upon the former; the whole number of these chambers is three thousand, fifteen hundred of each kind. The upper chambers I myself passed through and saw, and what I say concerning them is from my own observation; of the underground chambers I can only speak from report: for the keepers of the building could not be got to show them, since they contained (as they said) the sepulchers of the kings who built the Lábyrinth, and also those of the sacred crocodiles. Thus it is from hearsay only that I can speak of the lower chambers. The upper chambers, however, I saw with my own eyes, and found them to excel all other human productions; for the passages through the houses, and the varied windings of the paths across the courts excited in me infinite admiration as I passed from the courts into chambers, and from the chambers into colonnades, and from the colonnades into fresh houses, and again from these into courts unseen before. The roof was throughout of stone, like the walls; and the walls were carved all over with figures; every court was surrounded with a colonnade which was built of white stones exquisitely fitted together. At the corner of the Lábyrinth stands a pýramid, forty fathoms high, with large figures engraved on it, which is entered by a subterranean passage.

Wonderful as is the Lábyrinth, the work called the Lake of Mœris, which is close by the Lábyrinth, is yet more astonishing. The measure of its circumference is sixty schœnes, or three thousand six hundred furlongs, which is equal to the entire length of Égypt along the sea-coast. The lake stretches in its longest direction from north to south, and in its deepest parts is of the depth of fifty fathoms. It is manifestly an artificial excavation, for nearly in the center there stand two pýramids, rising to the height of fifty fathoms above the surface of the water, and extending as far beneath, crowned each of them with a colossal statue sitting upon a throne. Thus these pýramids are one hundred fathoms high, which is exactly a furlong (stádium) of six hundred feet: the fathom being six feet in length, or four cúbits, which is the same thing, since a cúbit measures six, and a foot four, palms. The water of the lake does not come out of the ground, which is here excessively dry, but is introduced by a canal from the Nile. The current sets for six months into the lake from the river, and for the next six months into the river from the lake. When it runs outward it returns a talent of silver daily to the royal treasury from the fish that are taken, but when the current is the other way the return sinks to one-third of that sum.

— Heródotus, *History*, II.148-149 (translated by George Rawlinson)


## II. PHŒNÍCIA AND ANCIENT COMMERCE


## A Series of Abductions

According to the Pérsians best informed in history, the Phœnícians began to quarrel. This people, who had formerly dwelt on the shores of the Erythrǽan Sea, having migrated to the Mediterránean and settled in the parts which they now inhabit, began at once, they say, to adventure on long voyages, freighting their vessels with the wares of Égypt and Assýria. They landed at many places on the coast, and among the rest at Árgos, which was then preeminent above all the states included now under the common name of Héllas. Here they exposed their merchandise, and traded with the natives for five or six days; at the end of which time, when almost everything was sold, there came down to the beach a number of women, and among them the daughter of the king, who was, they say, agreeing in this with the Greeks, Ío, the child of Ínachus. The women were standing by the stern of the ship intent upon their purchases, when

14

the Phœnícians, with a general shout, rushed upon them. The greater part made their escape, but some were seized and carried off. Ío herself was among the captives. The Phœnícians put the women on board their vessel and set sail for Égypt. Thus did Ío pass into Égypt, according to the Pérsian story, which differs widely from the Phœnícian: and thus commenced, according to their authors, the series of outrages.

At a later period, certain Greeks, with whose name they are unacquainted, but who would probably be Crétans, made a landing at Tyre, on the Phœnícian coast, and bore off the king's daughter, Európa. In this they only retaliated; but afterwards the Greeks, they say, were guilty of a second violence. They manned a ship of war, and sailed to Æa, a city of Cólchis, on the river Phásis; from whence, after dispatching the rest of the business on which they had come, they carried off Medéa, the daughter of the king of the land. The monarch sent a herald into Greece to demand reparation of the wrong, and the restitution of his child; but the Greeks made answer that, having received no reparation of the wrong done them in the seizure of Ío the Árgive, they should give none in this instance.

— Heródotus, *History*, II.1-2 (translated by George Rawlinson)

## III. NATIONS OF ÁSIA MÍNOR

## Crœsus and the Lýdian Empire

On the death of Alyáttes, Crœsus, his son, who was thirty-five years old, succeeded to the throne. Of the Greek cities, Éphesus was the first that he attacked. The Ephésians, when he laid siege to the place, made an offering of their city to Diána, by stretching a rope from the town wall to the temple of the goddess, which was distant from the ancient city, then besieged by Crœsus, a space of seven furlongs. They were, as I said, the first Greeks whom he attacked. Afterwards, on some pretext or other, he made war in turn upon every Iónian and Æólian state, bringing forward, where he could, a substantial ground of complaint; where such failed him, advancing some poor excuse.

In this way he made himself master of all the Greek cities in Ásia and forced them to become his tributaries; after which he began to think of building ships and attacking the islanders. Everything had been got ready for this purpose, when Bías of Priéne (or, as some say, Píttacus of Mytiléne) put a stop to the project. The king had made inquiry of this person, who was lately arrived at Sárdis, if there were any news from Greece; to which he answered, "Yes, sire, the islanders are gathering ten thousand horse, designing an expedition against thee and against thy capital." Crœsus, thinking he spake seriously, broke out, "Ah, might the gods put such a thought into their minds as to attack the sons of the Lýdians with cavalry!" "It seems, oh! king," rejoined the other, "that thou desirest earnestly to catch the islanders on horseback upon the mainland. Thou knowest well what would come of it. But what thinkest thou the islanders desire better, now that they hear thou art about to build ships and sail against them, than to catch the Lýdians at sea, and there revenge on them the wrongs of their brothers upon the mainland, whom thou holdest in slavery?" Crœsus was charmed with the turn of the speech; and thinking there was reason in what was said, gave up his shipbuilding and concluded a league of amity with the Iónians of the isles.

Crœsus afterwards, in the course of many years, brought under his sway almost all the nations to the west of the Hálys. The Lýcians and Cilícians alone continued free; all the other tribes he reduced and held in subjection. They were the following: the Lýdians, Phrýgians, Mýsians, Mariandýnians, Chalýbians, Paphlagónians, Thýnian and Bithýnian Thrácians, Cárians, Iónians, Dórians, Æólians and Pamphýlians.

— Heródotus, *History*, I.26-28 (translated by George Rawlinson)

# CHAPTER V.

## HÉLLAS AND THE HÉLLENES

### I. THE PLACE OF GREECE IN HISTORY

## The Uncertainty of Early Greek History

My first thought is one of intense astonishment at the current opinion that, in the study of primeval history, the Greeks alone deserve serious attention, that the truth should be sought from them, and that neither we nor any others in the world are to be trusted. In my view the very reverse of this is the case, if, that is to say, we are not to take idle prejudices as our guide, but to extract the truth from the facts themselves. For in the Greek world everything will be found to be recent, and dating, so to speak, from yesterday or the day before: I refer to the foundation of their cities, the invention of the arts, and the compilation of a code of laws; but the most recent, or nearly the most recent, of all their attainments is care in historical composition. On the contrary, as is admitted even by themselves, the Egýptians, the Chaldéans, and the Phœnícians—for the moment I omit to add our nation to the list—possess a very ancient and permanent record of the past. For all these nations inhabit countries which are least exposed to the ravages of the atmosphere, and they have been very careful to let none of the events in their history be forgotten, but always to have them enshrined in official records written by their greatest sages. The land of Greece, on the contrary, has experienced countless catastrophes, which have obliterated the memory of the past; and as one civilization succeeded another the men of each epoch believed that the world began with them. They were late in learning the alphabet and found the lesson difficult; for those who would assign the earliest date to its use pride themselves on having learnt it from the Phœnícians and Cádmus.

– Joséphus, *Against Ápion* I.2 (Translated by H. St. J. Thackeray)

### II. HÉLLAS, THE LAND OF THE GREEKS

## The Greek Picture of the Earth

We may learn both from the evidence of our senses and from experience that the inhabited world is an island; for wherever it has been possible for man to reach the limits of the earth, sea has been found, and this sea we call "Océanus." And wherever we have not been able to learn by the evidence of our sense, there reason points the way. For example, as to the eastern (Índian) side of the inhabited earth, and the western (Ibérian and Maurúsian) side, one may sail wholly around them and continue the voyage for a considerable distance along the northern and southern regions. As for the rest of the distance around the inhabited earth which has not been visited by us up to the present time (because of the fact that the navigators who sailed in opposite directions towards each other never met), it is not of very great extent, if we reckon from the parallel distances that have been traversed by us. It is unlikely that the Atlántic Ocean is divided into two seas, thus being separated by isthmuses so narrow and that prevent the circumnavigation; it is more likely that it is one confluent and continuous sea. For those who undertook circumnavigation, and turned back without having achieved their purpose, say that they were made to turn back, not because of any continent that stood in their way and hindered their further advance—inasmuch as the sea still continued open as before—but because of their destitution and loneliness. This theory accords better, too, with the behavior of the ocean, that, in respect of the ebb and flow of the tides. Everywhere, at all events, the same principle—or else one that does not vary much—accounts for the changes both of high tide and low tide, as would be the case if their movements were produced by one sea and were the result of one cause.

— Strábo, *Geography*, I.1.8 (translated by H. L. Jones)

## Geometry and Astronomy in Geography

All those who undertake to describe the distinguishing features of countries devote special attention to astronomy and geometry, in explaining matters of shape, of size, of distances between points, and of latitudes as well as matters of heat and cold, and, in general, the peculiarities of the atmosphere. Indeed, an architect in constructing a house, or an engineer in founding a city, would make provision for all these conditions; and all the more would they be considered by the man whose purview embraced the whole inhabited world, for they concern him more than anyone else. Within the area of small countries it involves no very great discrepancy if a given place be situated more towards the north, or more towards the south; but when the area is that of the whole round of the inhabited world, the north extends to the remote confines of Scýthia and Céltica, and the south to the remote confines of Ethiópia, and the difference between these two extremes is very great. The same thing holds true also as regards a man's living in Índia or Ibéria; the one country is in the far east, and the other is in the far west; indeed, they are, in a sense, the antipodes of each other, as we know.

Everything of this kind, since it is caused by the movement of the sun and the other stars as well as by their tendency towards the center, compels us to look to the vault of heaven, and to observe the phenomena of the heavenly bodies peculiar to our individual positions; and in these phenomena we see very great variations in the positions of inhabited place. So, if one is about to treat of the differences between countries, how can he discuss his subject correctly and adequately if he has paid no attention, even superficially, to any of these matters? For even if it be impossible in a treatise of this nature, because of its having a greater bearing on affairs of state, to make everything scientifically accurate, it will naturally be appropriate to do so, at least in so far as the man in public life is able to follow the thought.

Most of all, it seems to me, we need, as I have said, geometry and astronomy for a subject like geography; and the need of them is real indeed; for without such methods as they offer it is not possible accurately to determine our geometrical figures, latitudes, dimensions, and the other related things; but just as these sciences prove for us in other treatises all that has to do with the measurement of the earth as a whole and as I must in this treatise take for granted that the universe is sphere-shaped, and also that the earth's surface is sphere-shaped, and, what is more, I must take for granted the law that is prior to these two principles, namely that the bodies tend toward the center; and I need only indicate, in a brief and summary way, whether a proposition comes—if it really does—within the range of sense-perception or of intuitive knowledge.

Take, for example, the proposition that the earth is sphere-shaped: whereas the suggestion of this proposition comes to us mediately from the law that bodies tend toward the center and that each body inclines toward its own center of gravity, the suggestion comes immediately from the phenomena observed at sea and in the heavens; for our sense-perception and also our intuition can bear testimony in the latter case. For instance, it is obviously the curvature of the sea that prevents sailors from seeing distant lights at an elevation equal to that of the eye; however, if they are at a higher elevation than that of the eye, they become visible, even though they be at a greater distance from the eyes; and similarly if the eyes themselves are elevated, they see what was before invisible. This fact is noted by Hómer, also, for such is the meaning of the words: "With a quick glance ahead, being borne up on a great wave, [he saw the land very near]." So, also, when sailors are approaching land, the different parts of the shore become revealed progressively, more and more, and what at first appeared to be low-lying land grows gradually higher and higher. Again, the revolution of the heavenly bodies is evident on many grounds, but it is particularly evident from the phenomena of the sundial; and from these phenomena our intuitive judgment itself suggests that no such revolution could take place if the earth were rooted to an infinite depth. As regards the latitudes, they are treated in our discussion of the Inhabited Districts.

Now as for the matters which he regards as fundamental principles of his science, the geographer must rely upon the geometers who have measured the earth as a whole; and in their turn the geometers must rely upon the astronomers; and again, the astronomers upon the physicists. Physics is a kind of *Areté*; by *Areté* is meant a science that postulates nothing but depends upon itself and contains within itself its own principles as well as the proofs thereof. Now what we are taught by the physicists is as follows: The universe and the heavens are sphere-shaped. The tendency of the bodies that have weight is towards the center. And, having taken its position about this center in the form of a sphere, the earth remains homocentric with the heavens, as does also the axis through it, which axis extends also through the center of the heavens. The heavens revolve round both the earth and its axis from east to west; and along with the heavens revolve the fixed stars, with the same rapidity as the vault of the heavens. Now the fixed stars move along parallel circles, and the best-known parallel circles are the equator, the two tropics, and the arctic circles; whereas the planets and the sun and the moon move along certain oblique circles whose positions lie in the zodiac. Now the astronomers first accept these principles, either in whole or in part, and then work out the subsequent problems, namely, the movements of the heavenly bodies, their revolutions, their eclipses, their sizes, their respective distances, and a host of other things. And, in the same way, the geometers, in measuring the earth as a whole, adhere to the doctrines of the physicists and the astronomers, and, in their turn, the geographers adhere to those of the geometers.

– Strábo, *Geography*, I.1.13-14,20, II.5.2 (translated by H. L. Jones)


## III. THE HÉLLENES, THE PEOPLE OF HÉLLAS

### Iónian and Dórian Tribes

There have been many tribes in Greece, but those which go back to the earliest times are only as many in number as the Greek dialects which we have learned to distinguish. But though the dialects themselves are four in number, we may say that the Iónic is the same as the ancient Áttic, for the Áttic people of ancient times were called Iónians, and from that stock sprang those Iónians who colonized Ásia and used what is now called the Iónic speech; and we may say that the Dóric dialect is the same as the Æólic, for all the Greeks outside the Ísthmus, except the Athénians and the Megárians and the Dórians who live about Parnássus, are to this day still called Æólians. And it is reasonable to suppose that the Dórians too, since they were few in number and lived in a most rugged country, have, because of their lack of intercourse with others, changed their speech and their other customs to the extent that they are no longer a part of the same tribe as before. And this was precisely the case with the Athénians; that is, they lived in a country that was both thin-soiled and rugged, and for this reason, according to Thucýdides, their country remained free from devastation, and they were regarded as an indigenous people, who always occupied the same country, since no one drove them out of their country or even desired to possess it. This, therefore, as one may suppose, was precisely the cause of their becoming different both in speech and in customs, albeit they were few in number...

– Strábo, *Geography*, VIII.1.2 (translated by H. L. Jones)

# CHAPTER VI.

## THE OLDEST CIVILIZATION OF GREECE

The Legends of Early Greece, I.—Monuments of Ancient Greece; the Mycenǽan Age, II.
The Mycenǽan Civilization in Greece, III.

## I. LEGENDS OF EARLY GREECE

### Théseus and the Mínotaur

Not long after arrived the third time from Crete the collectors of the tribute, which the Athénians paid them upon the following occasion. Andrógeus having been treacherously murdered in the confines of Áttica, not only did Mínos, his father, put the Athénians to extreme distress by a perpetual war, but the gods also laid waste their country; both famine and pestilence lay heavy upon them, and even their rivers were dried up. Being told by the oracle that, if they appeased and reconciled Mínos, the anger of the gods would cease and they should enjoy rest from the miseries they labored under, they sent heralds, and with much supplication were at last reconciled, entering into an agreement to send to Crete every nine years a tribute of seven young men and as many virgins, as most writers agree in stating. The most poetical story adds that the Mínotaur destroyed them, or that, wandering in the Lábyrinth and finding no possible means of getting out, they miserably ended their lives there; and that this Mínotaur was (according to Eurípides): "A mingled form, where two strange shapes combined, And different natures, bull and man, were joined."

But Philóchorus says that the Crétans will by no means allow the truth of this, but say that the Lábyrinth was only an ordinary prison, having no other bad quality but that it secured the prisoners from escaping, and that Mínos, having instituted games in honor of Andrógeus, gave, as a reward to the victors, these youths, who in the mean time were kept in the Lábyrinth; and that the first that overcame in those games was one of the greatest power and command among them, named Táurus, a man of no merciful or gentle disposition, who treated the Athénians that were made his prize in a proud and cruel manner... This may show us how dangerous a thing it is to incur the hostility of a city that is mistress of eloquence and song. For Mínos was always ill spoken of and represented ever as a very wicked man in the Athénian theaters; neither did Hésiod help him by calling him "the most royal Mínos," nor Hómer, who styles him "Júpiter's familiar friend." The tragedians got the better and, from the vantage ground of the stage, showered down obloquy upon him as a man of cruelty and violence, whereas, in fact, he appears to have been a king and a lawgiver, and Rhadamánthus a judge under him, administering the statutes that he ordained.

Now when the time of the third tribute was come, and the fathers who had any young men for their sons were to proceed by lot to the choice of those that were to be sent, there arose fresh discontents and accusations against Ægéus among the people, who were full of grief and indignation that he, who was the cause of all their miseries, was the only person exempt from the punishment; adopting and settling his kingdom upon a bastard and foreign son, he took no thought, they said, of their destitution and loss, not of bastards, but lawful children. These things sensibly affected Théseus, who, thinking it only just not to disregard, but rather partake of, the sufferings of his fellow citizens, offered himself for one without any lot. All else were struck with admiration for the nobleness and with love for the goodness of the act; and Ægéus, after prayers and entreaties, finding him inflexible and not to be persuaded, proceeded to the choosing of the rest by lot. Hellánicus, however, tells us that the Athénians did not send the young men and virgins by lot, but that Mínos himself used to come and make his own choice, and pitched upon Théseus before all others; according to the conditions agreed upon between them, namely, that the Athénians should furnish them with a ship, and that the young men that were to sail with him should carry no weapon of war; but that if the Mínotaur was destroyed, the tribute should cease.

On the two former occasions of the payment of the tribute, entertaining no hopes of safety or return, they sent out the ship with a black sail, as to unavoidable destruction. But now, with Théseus encouraging his father and speaking greatly of himself, confident that he should kill the Mínotaur, Ægéus gave the pilot another sail, which was white, commanding him, as he returned, if Théseus were safe, to make use of that; but if not, to sail with the black one, and to hang out that sign of his misfortune...

The lot being cast, and Théseus having received out of the Prytanéum those upon whom it fell, he went to the Delphínium, and made an offering for them to Apóllo of his suppliant's badge, which was a bough of a consecrated olive tree, with white wool tied about it...

When he arrived at Crete, as most of the ancient historians as well as poets tell us, having a clue of thread given him by Ariádne, who had fallen in love with him, and being instructed by her how to use it so as to conduct him through the windings of the Lábyrinth, he escaped out of it and slew the Mínotaur, and sailed back, taking along with him Ariádne and the young Athénian captives. Pherecýdes adds that he bored holes in the bottoms of the Crétan ships to hinder their pursuit. Démon writes that Táurus, the chief captain of Mínos, was slain by Théseus at the mouth of the port, in a naval combat, as he was sailing out for Áthens. But Philóchorus gives us the story thus: That at the setting forth of the yearly games by king Mínos, Táurus was expected to carry away the prize, as he had done before; and was much grudged the honor... And as it was a custom in Crete that the women also should be admitted to the sight of these games, Ariádne, being present, was struck with admiration of the manly beauty of Théseus, and the vigor and address which he showed in the combat, overcoming all that encountered with him. Mínos, too, being extremely pleased with him, especially because he had overthrown and disgraced Táurus...

There are yet many other traditions about these things, and as many concerning Ariádne, all inconsistent with each other. Some relate that she hung herself, being deserted by Théseus. Others that she was carried away by his sailors to the isle of Náxos, and married to Œnárus, priest of Bácchus; and that Théseus left her because he fell in love with another...

When they were come near the coast of Áttica, so great was the joy for the happy success of their voyage, that neither Théseus himself nor the pilot remembered to hang out the sail which should have been the token of their safety to Ægéus, who, in despair at the sight, threw himself headlong from a rock, and perished in the sea...

— Plútarch, *Life of Théseus* (translated by John Dryden)


## II. MONUMENTS OF ANCIENT GREECE; THE MYCENÆAN AGE


## The End of Mycénæ

It was jealousy which caused the Árgives to destroy Mycénæ. For at the time of the Pérsian invasion the Árgives made no move, but the Mycenæans sent eighty men to Thermópylæ who shared in the achievement of the Lacedæmónians. This eagerness for distinction brought ruin upon them by exasperating the Árgives. There still remain, however, parts of the city wall, including the gate, upon which stand lions. These, too, are said to be the work of the Cyclópes, who made for Prœtus the wall at Tíryns.

— Strábo, *Geography*, II.16.5 (translated by H. L. Jones)

## The End of Tíryns

Going on from here and turning to the right, you come to the ruins of Tíryns. The Tirýnthians also were removed by the Árgives, who wished to make Árgos more powerful by adding to the population. The hero Tíryns, from whom the city derived its name, is said to have been a son of Árgus, a son of Zeus. The wall, which is the only part of the ruins still remaining, is a work of the Cyclópes made of unwrought stones, each stone being so big that a pair of mules could not move the smallest from its place to the slightest degree. Long ago small stones were so inserted that each of them binds the large blocks firmly together.

— Strábo, *Geography*, II.25.8 (translated by H. L. Jones)


## III. THE MYCENÆN CIVILIZATION IN GREECE

# King Mínos and the City of Cnóssos

There are several cities in Crete, but the greatest and most famous are three: Cnóssus, Górtyna and Cydýnia. The praises of Cnóssus are hymned above the rest both by Hómer, who calls it "great" and "the kingdom of Mínos," and by the later poets. Furthermore, it continued for a long time to win the first honors; then it was humbled and deprived of many of its prerogatives, and its superior rank passed over to Górtyna and Lýctus; but later it again recovered its olden dignity as the metropolis...

In earlier times Cnóssus was called Cærátus, bearing the same name as the river which flows past it. According to history, Mínos was an excellent law-giver, and also the first to gain the mastery of the sea; and he divided the island into three parts and founded a city in each part, Cnóssus in the . . . opposite the Peloponnésus. And it, too, lies to the north. As Éphorus states, Mínos was an emulator of a certain Rhadamánthys of early times, a man most just and bearing the same name as Mínos's brother, who is reputed to have been the first to civilize the island by establishing laws and by uniting cities under one city as metropolis by setting up constitutions, alleging that he brought from Zeus the several decrees which he promulgated. So, in imitation of Rhadamánthys, Mínos would go up every nine years, as it appears, to the cave of Zeus, tarry there, and come back with commandments drawn up in writing, which he alleged were ordinances of Zeus; and it was for this reason that the poet says, "there Mínos reigned as king, who held converse with great Zeus every ninth year." Such is the statement of Éphorus; but again the early writers have given a different account of Mínos, which is contrary to that of Éphorus, saying that he was tyrannical, harsh, and an exactor of tribute, representing in tragedy the story of the Mínotaur and the Lábyrinth, and the adventures of Théseus and Dædalus.

... In regard to Crete, writers agree that in ancient times it had good laws, and rendered the best of the Greeks its emulators, and in particular the Lacedæmónians, as is shown, for instance, by Pláto in his *Laws*, and also by Éphorus, who in his *Éurope* has described its constitution. But later it changed very much for the worse; for after the Tyrrhénians, who more than any other people ravaged Our Sea, the Crétans succeeded to the business of piracy; their piracy was later destroyed by the Cilícians; but all piracy was broken up by the Rómans, who reduced Crete by war and also the piratical strongholds of the Cilícians. And at the present time Cnóssus has even a colony of Rómans.

– Strábo, *Geography*, X.4.7-9 (translated by H. L. Jones)

# CHAPTER VII.

## HÓMER AND THE HOMÉRIC CULTURE

The Homéric Poems, I.—Homéric Industry and Art, II.
Homéric Society and Government, III.—Homéric Religion and Morality, IV.

### I. THE HOMÉRIC POEMS

## Odýsseus Suggests the Trójan Horse

When round the walls of Troy the Dánaän host had borne much travail, and yet the end was not, by Cálchas then assembled were the chiefs; for his heart was instructed by the hests of Phœbus, by the flights of birds, the stars, and all the signs that speak to men the will of Heaven; so he to that assembly cried: "No longer toil in leaguer of yon walls; some other counsel let your hearts devise, some stratagem to help the host and us. For here but yesterday I saw a sign: a falcon chased a dove, and she, hard pressed, entered a cleft of the rock; and chafing he tarried long time hard by that rift, but she abode in covert. Nursing still his wrath, he hid him in a bush. Forth darted she, in folly deeming him afar: he swooped, and to the hapless dove dealt wretched death. Therefore, by force essay we not to smite Troy, but let cunning stratagem avail."

He spake; but no man's wit might find a way to escape their grievous travail, as they sought to find a remedy, till Laértes' son discerned it of his wisdom, and he spake: "Friend, in high honor held of the Heavenly Ones, if doomed it be indeed that Príam's burg by guile must fall before the war-worn Greeks, a great Horse let us fashion, in the which our mightiest shall take ambush. Let the host burn all their tents, and sail from hence away to Ténedos; so the Trójans, from their towers gazing, shall stream forth fearless to the plain. Let some brave man, unknown of any in Troy, with a stout heart abide without the Horse, crouching beneath its shadow, who shall say: "'Achǽa's lords of might, exceeding fain safe to win home, made this their offering for safe return, an image to appease the wrath of Pállas for her image stolen from Troy.' And to this story shall he stand, how long soever they question him, until, though never so relentless, they believe, and drag it, their own doom, within the town. Then shall war's signal unto us be given — to them at sea, by sudden flash of torch, to the ambush, by the cry, 'Come forth the Horse!' when unsuspecting sleep the sons of Troy."

He spake, and all men praised him: most of all extolled him Cálchas, that such marvelous guile he put into the Achǽans' hearts, to be for them assurance of triumph, but for Troy ruin; and to those battle-lords he cried: "Let your hearts seek none other stratagem, friends; to war-strong Odýsseus' rede give ear. His wise thought shall not miss accomplishment. Yea, our desire even now the Gods fulfil. Hark! for new tokens come from the Unseen! Lo, there on high crash through the firmament Zeus' thunder and lightning! See, where birds to right dart past, and scream with long-resounding cry! Go to, no more in endless leaguer of Troy linger we. Hard necessity fills the foe with desperate courage that makes cowards brave; for then are men most dangerous, when they stake their lives in utter recklessness of death, as battle now the aweless sons of Troy all round their burg, mad with the lust of fight."

But cried Achílles' battle-eager son: "Cálchas, brave men meet face to face their foes! Who skulk behind their walls, and fight from towers, are nidderings, hearts palsied with base fear. Hence with all thought of wile and stratagem! The great war-travail of the spear beseems true heroes. Best in battle are the brave."

But answer made to him Laértes' seed: "Bold-hearted child of aweless Æacus' son, this as beseems a hero princely and brave, dauntlessly trusting in thy strength, thou say'st. Yet thine invincible sire's unquailing might availed not to smite Príam's wealthy burg, nor we, for all our travail. Nay, with speed, as counselleth Cálchas, go we to the ships, and fashion we the Horse by Epéus' hands, who in the woodwright's craft is chiefest far of Árgives, for Athéna taught his lore."

Then all their mightiest men gave ear to him save twain, fierce-hearted Neoptólemus and Philoctétes mighty-souled; for these still were insatiate for the bitter fray, still longed for turmoil of the fight. They bade their own folk bear against that giant wall what things soe'er for war's assaults avail, in hope to lay that stately fortress low, seeing Heaven's decrees had brought them both to war. Yea, they had haply accomplished all their will, but from the sky Zeus showed his wrath; he shook the earth beneath their feet, and all the air shuddered, as down before those heroes twain he hurled his thunderbolt: wide echoes crashed through all Dardánia. Unto fear straightway turned were their bold hearts: they forgat their might, and Cálchas' counsels grudgingly obeyed. So with the Árgives came they to the ships in reverence for the seer who spake from Zeus or Phœbus, and they obeyed him utterly.

– Quíntus of Smýrna, *Fall of Troy*, XII.1-105 (translated by A. S. Way)

## The Achæans in the Trójan Horse

Godlike Epéus last of all passed in, the fashioner of the Horse; in his breast lay the secret of the opening of its doors and of their closing: therefore last of all he entered, and he drew the ladders up whereby they climbed: then made he all secure, and set himself beside the bolt. So all in silence sat 'twixt victory and death.

But the rest fired the tents, wherein erewhile they slept, and sailed the wide sea in their ships. Two mighty-hearted captains ordered these, Néstor and Agamémnon lord of spears. Fain had they also entered that great Horse, but all the host withheld them, bidding stay with them a-shipboard, ordering their array: for men far better work the works of war when their kings oversee them; therefore, these abode without, albeit mighty men. So came they swiftly unto Ténedos' shore, and dropped the anchor-stones, then leapt in haste forth of the ships, and silent waited there keen-watching till the signal-torch should flash.

But nigh the foe were they in the Horse, and now looked they for death, and now to smite the town; and on their hopes and fears uprose the dawn.

– Quíntus of Smýrna, *Fall of Troy*, XII.337-377 (translated by A. S. Way)

## The Trójans Debate the Purpose of the Horse

Then marked the Trójans upon Héllespont's strand the smoke upleaping yet through air: no more saw they the ships which brought to them from Greece destruction dire. With joy to the shore they ran, but armed them first, for fear still haunted them then marked they that fair-carven Horse, and stood marvelling round, for a mighty work was there. A hapless-seeming man thereby they spied, Sínon; and this one, that one questioned him touching the Dánaäns, as in a great ring they compassed him, and with unangry words first questioned, then with terrible threatenings. Then tortured they that man of guileful soul long time unceasing. Firm as a rock abode the unquivering limbs, the unconquerable will. His ears, his nose, at last they shore away in every wise tormenting him, until he should declare the truth, whither were gone the ships, what thing the Horse concealed within it. He had armed his mind with resolution, and of outrage foul recked not; his soul endured their cruel stripes, yea, and the bitter torment of the fire; for strong endurance into him Héra breathed; and still he told them the same guileful tale: "The Árgives in their ships flee oversea weary of tribulation of endless war. This horse by Cálchas' counsel fashioned they for wise Athéna, to propitiate her stern wrath for that guardian image stol'n from Troy. And by Odýsseus' prompting I was marked for slaughter, to be sacrificed to the sea-powers, beside the moaning waves, to win them safe return. But their intent I marked; and ere they spilt the drops of wine, and sprinkled hallowed meal upon mine head, swiftly I fled, and, by the help of Heaven, I flung me down, clasping the Horse's feet; and they, sore loth, perforce must leave me there dreading great Zeus's daughter mighty-souled."

In subtlety so he spake, his soul untamed by pain; for a brave man's part is to endure to the uttermost. And of the Trójans some believed him, others for a wily knave held him, of whose mind was Laócoön. wisely he spake: "A deadly fraud is this," He said, "devised by the Achæan chiefs!" And cried to all straightway to burn the Horse and know if aught within its timbers lurked.

– Quíntus of Smýrna, *Fall of Troy*, XII.378-426 (translated by A. S. Way)

## Laócoön and His Sons

Yea, and they had obeyed him, and had escaped destruction; but Athéna, fiercely wroth with him, the Trójans, and their city, shook earth's deep foundations 'neath Laócoön's feet. Straight terror fell on him, and trembling bowed the knees of the presumptuous: round his head horror of darkness poured; a sharp pang thrilled his eyelids; swam his eyes beneath his brows; his eyeballs, stabbed with bitter anguish, throbbed even from the roots, and rolled in frenzy of pain. Clear through his brain the bitter torment pierced even to the filmy inner veil thereof; now bloodshot were his eyes, now ghastly green; anon with rheum they ran, as pours a stream down from a rugged crag, with thawing snow made turbid. As a man distraught he seemed: all things he saw showed double, and he groaned fearfully; yet he ceased not to exhort the men of Troy, and recked not of his pain. Then did the goddess strike him utterly blind. Stared his fixed eyeballs white from pits of blood; and all folk groaned for pity of their friend, and dread of the Prey-Giver, lest he had sinned in folly against her, and his mind was thus warped to destruction yea, lest on themselves like judgment should be visited, to avenge the outrage done to hapless Sínon's flesh, whereby they hoped to wring the truth from him.

So led they him in friendly wise to Troy, pitying him at the last. Then gathered all, and o'er that huge Horse hastily cast a rope, and made it fast above; for under its feet smooth wooden rollers had Epéus laid, that, dragged by Trójan hands, it might glide on into their fortress. One and all they haled with multitudinous tug and strain, as when down to the sea young men sore-laboring drag a ship; hard-crushed the stubborn rollers groan, as, sliding with weird shrieks, the keel descends into the sea-surge; so that host with toil dragged up unto their city their own doom, Epéus' work. With great festoons of flowers they hung it, and their own heads did they wreathe, while answering each other pealed the flutes. Grimly Enýö laughed, seeing the end of that dire war; Héra rejoiced on high; glad was Athéna. When the Trójans came unto their city, brake they down the walls, their city's coronal, that the Horse of Death might be led in. Troy's daughters greeted it with shouts of salutation; marvelling all gazed at the mighty work where lurked their doom.

But still Laócoön ceased not to exhort his countrymen to burn the Horse with fire: they would not hear, for dread of the gods' wrath. But then a yet more hideous punishment Athéna visited on his hapless sons. A cave there was, beneath a rugged cliff exceeding high, unscalable, wherein dwelt fearful monsters of the deadly brood of Týphon, in the rock-clefts of the isle Calýdna that looks Troyward from the sea. Thence stirred she up the strength of serpents twain and summoned them to Troy. By her uproused, they shook the island as with earthquake: roared the sea; the waves disparted as they came. Onward they swept with fearful-flickering tongues: shuddered the very monsters of the deep: Xánthus' and Símoïs' daughters moaned aloud, the River-nymphs: the Cýprian Queen looked down in anguish from Olýmpus. Swiftly they came whither the goddess sped them: with grim jaws whetting their deadly fangs, on his hapless sons sprang they. All Trójans panic-stricken fled, seeing those fearsome dragons in their town. No man, though ne'er so dauntless theretofore, dared tarry; ghastly dread laid hold on all shrinking in horror from the monsters. Screamed the women; yea, the mother forgot her child, fear-frenzied as she fled: all Troy became one shriek of fleers, one huddle of jostling limbs: the streets were choked with cowering fugitives.

Alone was left Laócoön with his sons, for death's doom and the goddess chained their feet. Then, even as from destruction shrank the lads, those deadly fangs had seized and ravined up the twain, outstretching to their sightless sire agonized hands: no power to help had he. Trójans far off looked on from every side weeping, all dazed. And, having now fulfilled upon the Trójans Pállas' awful hest, those monsters vanished beneath the earth; and still stands their memorial, where into the fane they entered of Apóllo in Pérgamus the hallowed. Therebefore the sons of Troy gathered, and reared a cenotaph for those who miserably had perished. Over it their father from his blind eyes rained the tears: over the empty tomb their mother shrieked, boding the while yet worse things, wailing over the ruin wrought by folly of her lord, dreading the anger of the Blessed Ones. As when around her void nest in a brake in sorest anguish moans the nightingale whose fledglings, ere they learned her plaintive song, a hideous serpent's fangs have done to death, and left the mother anguish, endless woe, and bootless crying round her desolate home; so groaned she for her children's wretched death, so moaned she o'er the void tomb; and her pangs were sharpened by her lord's plight stricken blind.

– Quíntus of Smýrna, *Fall of Troy*, XII.427-537 (translated by A. S. Way)

## Cassándra's Prophecy

One heart was steadfast, and one soul clear-eyed, Cassándra. Never her words were unfulfilled; yet was their utter truth, by Fate's decree, ever as idle wind in the hearers' ears, that no bar to Troy's ruin might be set. She saw those evil portents all through Troy conspiring to one end; loud rang her cry, as roars a lioness that mid the brakes a hunter has stabbed or shot, whereat her heart maddens, and down the long hills rolls her roar, and her might waxes tenfold; so with heart aflame with prophecy came she forth her bower. Over her snowy shoulders tossed her hair streaming far down, and wildly blazed her eyes. Her neck writhed, like a sapling in the wind shaken, as moaned and shrieked that noble maid: "O wretches! into the Land of Darkness now we are passing; for all round us full of fire and blood and dismal moan the city is. Everywhere portents of calamity gods show: destruction yawns before your feet. Fools! ye know not your doom: still ye rejoice with one consent in madness, who to Troy have brought the Árgive Horse where ruin lurks! Oh, ye believe not me, though ne'er so loud I cry! The Erínyes and the ruthless Fates, for Hélen's spousals madly wroth, through Troy dart on wild wings. And ye, ye are banqueting there in your last feast, on meats befouled with gore, when now your feet are on the path of ghosts!"

Then cried a scoffing voice an ominous word: "Why doth a raving tongue of evil speech, daughter of Príam, make thy lips to cry words empty as wind? No maiden modesty with purity veils thee: thou art compassed round with ruinous madness; therefore all men scorn thee, babbler! Hence, thine evil bodings speak to the Árgives and thyself! For thee doth wait anguish and shame yet bitterer than befell presumptuous Laócoön. Shame it were in folly to destroy the Immortals' gift."

So scoffed a Trójan: others in like sort cried shame on her, and said she spake but lies, saying that ruin and Fate's heavy stroke were hard at hand. They knew not their own doom, and mocked, and thrust her back from that huge Horse for fain she was to smite its beams apart or burn with ravening fire. She snatched a brand of blazing pinewood from the hearth and ran in fury: in the other hand she bare a two-edged halberd: on that Horse of Doom she rushed, to cause the Trójans to behold with their own eyes the ambush hidden there. But straightway from her hands they plucked and flung afar the fire and steel, and careless turned to the feast; for darkened o'er them their last night. Within the horse the Árgives joyed to hear the uproar of Troy's feasters setting at naught Cassándra, but they marveled that she knew so well the Acháeans' purpose and device.

As mid the hills a furious pantheress, which from the steading hounds and shepherd-folk drive with fierce rush, with savage heart turns back even in departing, galled albeit by darts: so from the great Horse fled she, anguish-racked for Troy, for all the ruin she foreknew.

– Quíntus of Smýrna, Fall of Troy, XII.565-630 (translated by A. S. Way)

## The Sack of Troy

When sleep had locked his fetters everywhere through Troy on folk fulfilled of wine and meat, then Sínon lifted high a blazing torch to show the Árgive men the splendor of fire. But fearfully the while his heart beat, lest the men of Troy might see it, and the plot be suddenly revealed. But on their beds sleeping their last sleep lay they, heavy with wine. The host saw, and from Ténedos set sail.

Then nigh the Horse drew Sínon: softly he called, full softly, that no man of Troy might hear, but only Achǽa's chiefs, far from whose eyes sleep hovered, so athirst were they for fight. They heard, and to Odýsseus all inclined their ears: he bade them urgently go forth softly and fearlessly; and they obeyed that battle-summons, pressing in hot haste to leap to earth: but in his subtlety he stayed them from all thrusting eagerly forth. But first himself with swift unfaltering hands, helped of Epéus, here and there unbarred the ribs of the Horse of beams: above the planks a little he raised his head, and gazed around on all sides, if he haply might descry one Trójan waking yet. As when a wolf, with hunger stung to the heart, comes from the hills, and ravenous for flesh draws nigh the flock penned in the wide fold, slinking past the men and dogs that watch, all keen to ward the sheep, then o'er the fold-wall leaps with soundless feet; so stole Odýsseus down from the Horse: with him followed the war-fain lords of Héllas' League, orderly stepping down the ladders, which Epéus framed for paths of mighty men, for entering and for passing forth the Horse, who down them now on this side, that side, streamed as fearless wasps startled by stroke of axe in angry mood pour all together forth from the tree-bole, at sound of woodman's blow; so battle-kindled forth the Horse they poured into the midst of that strong city of Troy with hearts that leapt expectant. [With swift hands snatched they the brands from dying hearths and fired temple and palace. Onward then to the gates sped they,] and swiftly slew the slumbering guards, [then held the gate-towers till their friends should come.]

Fast rowed the host the while; on swept the ships over the great flood: Thétis made their paths straight, and behind them sent a driving wind speeding them, and the hearts Achǽan glowed. Swiftly to Héllespont's shore they came, and there beached they the keels again, and deftly dealt with whatso tackling appertains to ships. Then leapt they aland, and hasted on to Troy silent as sheep that hurry to the fold from woodland pasture on an autumn eve; so without sound of voices marched they on unto the Trójans' fortress, eager all to help those mighty chiefs with foes begirt. Now these — as famished wolves fierce-glaring round fall on a fold mid the long forest-hills, while sleeps the toil-worn watchman, and they rend the sheep on every hand within the wall in darkness, and all round [are heaped the slain; so these within the city smote and slew, as swarmed the awakened foe around them; yet, fast as they slew, aye faster closed on them those thousands, mad to thrust them from the gates.] Slipping in blood and stumbling o'er the dead [their line reeled,] and destruction loomed o'er them, though Dánaän thousands near and nearer drew.

But when the whole host reached the walls of Troy, into the city of Príam, breathing rage of fight, with reckless battle-lust they poured; and all that fortress found they full of war and slaughter, palaces, temples, horribly blazing on all sides; glowed their hearts with joy. In deadly mood then charged they on the foe. Áres and fell Enýo maddened there: blood ran in torrents, drenched was all the earth, as Trójans and their alien helpers died. Here were men lying quelled by bitter death all up and down the city in their blood; others on them were falling, gasping forth their life's strength; others, clutching in their hands their bowels that looked through hideous gashes forth, wandered in wretched plight around their homes: others, whose feet, while yet asleep they lay, had been hewn off, with groans unutterable crawled mid the corpses. Some, who had rushed to fight, lay now in dust, with hands and heads hewn off. Some were there, through whose backs, even as they fled, the spear had passed, clear through to the breast, and some whose waists the lance had pierced, impaling them where sharpest stings the anguish-laden steel.

And all about the city dolorous howls of dogs uprose, and miserable moans of strong men stricken to death; and every home with awful cries was echoing. Rang the shrieks of women, like to screams of cranes, which see an eagle stooping on them from the sky, which have no courage to resist, but scream long terror-shrieks in dread of Zeus's bird; so here, so there the Trójan women wailed, some starting from their sleep, some to the ground leaping: they thought not in that agony of robe and zone; in naught but tunics clad distraught they wandered: others found nor veil nor cloak to cast about them, but, as came onward their foes, they stood with beating hearts trembling, as lettered by despair, essaying, all-hapless, with their hands alone to hide their nakedness. And some in frenzy of woe: their tresses tore, and beat their breasts, and screamed. Others against that stormy torrent of foes recklessly rushed, insensible of fear, through mad desire to aid the perishing, husbands or children; for despair had given high courage.

Shrieks had startled from their sleep soft little babes whose hearts had never known trouble — and there one with another lay gasping their lives out! Some there were whose dreams changed to a sudden vision of doom. All round the fell Fates gloated horribly o'er the slain. And even as swine be slaughtered in the court of a rich king who makes his folk a feast, so without number were they slain. The wine left in the mixing-bowls was blent with blood gruesomely. No man bare a sword unstained with murder of defenseless folk of Troy, though he were but a weakling in fair fight. And as by wolves or jackals sheep are torn, what time the furnace-breath of midnoon-heat darts down, and all the flock beneath the shade are crowded, and the shepherd is not there, but to the homestead bears afar their milk; and the fierce brutes leap on them, tear their throats, gorge to the full their ravenous maws, and then lap the dark blood, and linger still to slay all in mere lust of slaughter, and provide an evil banquet for that shepherd-lord; so through the city of Príam Dánaäns slew one after other in that last fight of all. No Trójan there was woundless, all men's limbs with blood in torrents spilt were darkly dashed.

– Quíntus of Smýrna, *Fall of Troy*, XIII.21-165 (translated by A. S. Way)

## Æneas Bears His Father and Son out of Troy

Then also princely Anchíses' noble son — hard had he fought through Príam's burg that night with spear and valor, and many had he slain — when now he saw the city set aflame by hands of foes, saw her folk perishing in multitudes, her treasures spoiled, her wives and children dragged to thraldom from their homes, no more he hoped to see the stately walls of his birth-city, but bethought him now how from that mighty ruin to escape. And as the helmsman of a ship, who toils on the deep sea, and matches all his craft against the winds and waves from every side rushing against him in the stormy time, forspent at last, both hand and heart, when now the ship is foundering in the surge, forsakes the helm, to launch forth in a little boat, and heeds no longer ship and lading; so Anchíses' gallant son forsook the town and left her to her foes, a sea of fire. His son and father alone he snatched from death; the old man broken down with years he set on his broad shoulders with his own strong hands, and led the young child by his small soft hand, whose little footsteps lightly touched the ground; and, as he quaked to see that work of deaths his father led him through the roar of fight, and clinging hung on him the tender child, tears down his soft cheeks streaming. But the man o'er many a body sprang with hurrying feet, and in the darkness in his own despite trampled on many.

Cýpris guided them, earnest to save from that wild ruin her son, his father, and his child. As on he pressed, the flames gave back before him everywhere: the blast of the Fire-god's breath to right and left was cloven asunder. Spears and javelins hurled against him by the Acháeans harmless fell. Also, to stay them, Cálchas cried aloud: "Forbear against Ænéas' noble head to hurl the bitter dart, the deadly spear! Fated he is by the high gods' decree to pass from Xánthus, and by Tíber's flood to found a city holy and glorious through all time, and to rule o'er tribes of men far-sundered. Of his seed shall lords of earth rule from the rising to the setting sun. Yea, with the Immortals ever shall he dwell, who is son of Aphrodíte lovely-tressed. From him too is it meet we hold our hands because he hath preferred his father and son to gold, to all things that might profit a man who fleeth exiled to an alien land. This one night hath revealed to us a man faithful to death to his father and his child."

– Quíntus of Smýrna, Fall of Troy, XIII.332-386 (translated by A. S. Way)

## II. HOMÉRIC INDUSTRY AND ART

## Hephǽstus Fashions the Shield of Achílles

Then the famous god of the two strong arms answered her: "Be of good cheer, neither let these things distress thy heart. Would that I might so surely avail to hide him afar from dolorous death, when dread fate cometh upon him, as verily goodly armor shall be his, such that in aftertime many a one among the multitude of men shall marvel, whosoever shall behold it."

So saying he left her there and went unto his bellows, and he turned these toward the fire and bade them work. And the bellows, twenty in all, blew upon the melting-vats, sending forth a ready blast of every force, now to further him as he labored hard, and again in whatsoever way Hephǽstus might wish and his work go on. And on the fire he put stubborn bronze and tin and precious gold and silver; and thereafter he set on the anvil-block a great anvil, and took in one hand a massive hammer, and in the other took he the tongs.

First fashioned he a shield, great and sturdy, adorning it cunningly in every part, and round about it set a bright rim, threefold and glittering, and therefrom made fast a silver baldric. Five were the layers of the shield itself; and on it he wrought many curious devices with cunning skill.

Therein he wrought the earth, therein the heavens therein the sea, and the unwearied sun, and the moon at the full, and therein all the constellations wherewith heaven is crowned—the Pléiades, and the Hýades and the mighty Oríon, and the Bear, that men call also the Wain, that circleth ever in her place, and watcheth Oríon, and alone hath no part in the baths of Ocean.

Therein fashioned he also two cities of mortal men exceeding fair. In the one there were marriages and feastings, and by the light of the blazing torches they were leading the brides from their bowers through the city, and loud rose the bridal song. And young men were whirling in the dance, and in their midst flutes and lyres sounded continually; and there the women stood each before her door and marveled. But the folk were gathered in the place of assembly; for there a strife had arisen, and two men were striving about the blood-price of a man slain; the one avowed that he had paid all, declaring his cause to the people, but the other refused to accept aught; and each was fain to win the issue on the word of a daysman. Moreover, the folk were cheering both, shewing favor to this side and to that. And heralds held back the folk, and the elders were sitting upon polished stones in the sacred circle, holding in their hands the staves of the loud-voiced heralds. Therewith then would they spring up and give judgment, each in turn. And in the midst lay two talents of gold, to be given to him whoso among them should utter the most righteous judgment.

But around the other city lay in leaguer two hosts of warriors gleaming in armor. And twofold plans found favor with them, either to lay waste the town or to divide in portions twain all the substance that the lovely city contained within. Howbeit the besieged would nowise hearken thereto but were arming to meet the foe in an ambush. The wall were their dear wives and little children guarding, as they stood thereon, and therewithal the men that were holden of old age; but the rest were faring forth, led of Áres and Pállas Athéna, both fashioned in gold, and of gold was the raiment wherewith they were clad. Goodly were they and tall in their harness, as beseemeth gods, clear to view amid the rest, and the folk at their feet were smaller. But when they were come to the place where it seemed good unto them to set their ambush, in a riverbed where was a watering-place for all herds alike, there they sat them down, clothed about with flaming bronze. Thereafter were two scouts set by them apart from the host, waiting till they should have sight of the sheep and sleek cattle. And these came presently, and two herdsmen followed with them playing upon pipes; and of the guile wist they not at all.

But the liers-in-wait, when they saw these coming on, rushed forth against them and speedily cut off the herds of cattle and fair flocks of white-fleeced sheep, and slew the herdsmen withal. But the besiegers, as they sat before the places of gathering and heard much tumult among the kine, mounted forthwith behind their high-stepping horses, and set out thitherward, and speedily came upon them. Then set they their battle in array and fought beside the riverbanks, and were ever smiting one another with bronze-tipped spears. And amid them Strife and Tumult joined in the fray, and deadly Fate, grasping one man alive, fresh-wounded, another without a wound, and another she dragged dead through the mellay by the feet; and the raiment that she had about her shoulders was red with the blood of men. Even as living mortals joined they in the fray and fought; and they were haling away each the bodies of the others' slain.

Therein he set also soft fallow-land, rich tilth and wide, that was three times ploughed; and ploughers full many therein were wheeling their yokes and driving them this way and that. And whensoever after turning they came to the headland of the field, then would a man come forth to each and give into his hands a cup of honey-sweet wine; and the ploughmen would turn them in the furrows, eager to reach the headland of the deep tilth. And the field grew black behind and seemed verily as it had been ploughed, for all that it was of gold; herein was the great marvel of the work.

Therein he set also a king's demesne-land, wherein laborers were reaping, bearing sharp sickles in their hands. Some handfuls were falling in rows to the ground along the swathe, while others the binders of sheaves were binding with twisted ropes of straw. Three binders stood hard by them, while behind them boys would gather the handfuls, and bearing them in their arms would busily give them to the binders; and among them the king, staff in hand, was standing in silence at the swathe, joying in his heart. And heralds apart beneath an oak were making ready a feast and were dressing a great ox they had slain for sacrifice; and the women sprinkled the flesh with white barley in abundance, for the workers' mid-day meal.

Therein he set also a vineyard heavily laden with clusters, a vineyard fair and wrought of gold; black were the grapes, and the vines were set up throughout on silver poles. And around it he drave a trench of cyanus, and about that a fence of tin; and one single path led thereto, whereby the vintagers went and came, whensoever they gathered the vintage. And maidens and youths in childish glee were bearing the honey-sweet fruit in wicker baskets. And in their midst a boy made pleasant music with a clear-toned lyre, and thereto sang sweetly the Línos-song with his delicate voice; and his fellows beating the earth in unison therewith followed on with bounding feet mid dance and shoutings.

And therein he wrought a herd of straight-horned kine: the kine were fashioned of gold and tin, and with lowing hasted they forth from byre to pasture beside the sounding river, beside the waving reed. And golden were the herdsmen that walked beside the kine, four in number, and nine dogs swift of foot followed after them. But two dread lions amid the foremost kine were holding a loud-lowing bull, and he, bellowing mightily, was haled of them, while after him pursued the dogs and young men. The lions twain had rent the hide of the great bull, and were devouring the inward parts and the black blood, while the herdsmen vainly sought to fright them, tarring on the swift hounds. Howbeit, these shrank from fastening on the lions but stood hard by and barked and sprang aside.

Therein also the famed god of the two strong arms wrought a pasture in a fair dell, a great pasture of white-fleeced sheep, and folds, and roofed huts, and pens.

Therein furthermore the famed god of the two strong arms cunningly wrought a dancing-floor like unto that which in wide Cnóssus Dǽdalus fashioned of old for fair-tressed Ariádne. There were youths dancing and maidens of the price of many cattle, holding their hands upon the wrists one of the other. Of these the maidens were clad in fine linen, while the youths wore well-woven tunics faintly glistening with oil; and the maidens had fair chaplets, and the youths had daggers of gold hanging from silver baldrics. Now would they run round with cunning feet exceeding lightly, as when a potter sitteth by his wheel that is fitted between his hands and maketh trial of it whether it will run; and now again would they run in rows toward each other. And a great company stood around the lovely dance, taking joy therein; and two tumblers whirled up and down through the midst of them as leaders in the dance.

Therein he set also the great might of the river Océanus, around the uttermost rim of the strongly wrought shield. But when he had wrought the shield, great and sturdy, then wrought he for him a corselet brighter than the blaze of fire, and he wrought for him a heavy helmet, fitted to his temples, a fair helm, richly-dight, and set thereon a crest of gold; and he wrought him greaves of pliant tin. But when the glorious god of the two strong arms had fashioned all the armor, he took and laid it before the mother of Achílles. And like a falcon she sprang down from snowy Olýmpus, bearing the flashing armor from Hephǽstus.

— Hómer, *Iliad*, XVIII.452-608 (translated by Augustus Taber Murray)


### III. HOMÉRIC SOCIETY AND GOVERNMENT


## The Oracle of Dodóna

The following tale is commonly told in Égypt concerning the oracle of Dodóna in Greece, and that of Ámmon in Líbya. My informants on the point were the priests of Júpiter at Thebes. They said that "two of the sacred women were once carried off from Thebes by the Phœnícians, and that the story went that one of them was sold into Líbya, and the other into Greece, and these women were the first founders of the oracles in the two countries." On my inquiring how they came to know so exactly what became of the women, they answered, "that diligent search had been made after them at the time, but that it had not been found possible to discover where they were; afterwards, however, they received the information which they had given me."

This was what I heard from the priests at Thebes; at Dodóna, however, the women who deliver the oracles relate the matter as follows: "Two black doves flew away from Egýptian Thebes, and while one directed its flight to Líbya, the other came to them. She alighted on an oak and sitting there began to speak with a human voice and told them that on the spot where she was, there should henceforth be an oracle of Jove. They understood the announcement to be from heaven, so they set to work at once and erected the shrine. The dove which flew to Líbya bade the Líbyans to establish there the oracle of Ámmon." This likewise is an oracle of Júpiter...

My own opinion of these matters is as follows: I think that, if it be true that the Phœnícians carried off the holy women, and sold them for slaves, the one into Líbya and the other into Greece, or Pelásgia (as it was then called), this last must have been sold to the Thesprótians. Afterwards, while undergoing servitude in those parts, she built under a real oak a temple to Júpiter, her thoughts in her new abode reverting—as it was likely they would do, if she had been an attendant in a temple of Júpiter at Thebes—to that particular god. Then, having acquired a knowledge of the Greek tongue, she set up an oracle. She also mentioned that her sister had been sold for a slave into Líbya by the same persons as herself.

The Dodonǽans called the women doves because they were foreigners and seemed to them to make a noise like birds. After a while the dove spoke with a human voice, because the woman, whose foreign talk had previously sounded to them like the chattering of a bird, acquired the power of speaking what they could understand. For how can it be conceived possible that a dove should really speak with the voice of a man? Lastly, by calling the dove black the Dodonǽans indicated that the woman was an Egýptian. And certainly the character of the oracles at Thebes and Dodóna is very similar. Besides this form of divination, the Greeks learnt also divination by means of victims from the Egýptians.

— Heródotus, *History*, II.54-57 (translated by George Rawlinson)


## IV. HOMÉRIC RELIGION AND MORALITY

# On Greek Religion

Gladly would I have avoided an investigation of the institutions of other nations for Greeks. It is our traditional custom to observe our own laws and to refrain from criticism of those of aliens. Our legislator has expressly forbidden us to deride or blaspheme the gods recognized by others, out of respect for the very word "God." But since our accusers expect to confute us by a comparison of the rival religions, it is impossible to remain silent. I speak with the more assurance because the statement which I am about to make is no invention of my own for the occasion but has been made by many writers of the highest reputation. Who, in fact, is there among the admired sages who in their gross of Greece has not censured their most famous poets and their most trusted legislators for sowing in the minds of the masses the first seeds of such notions about the gods? They represent them to be as numerous as they choose, born of one another and engendered in all manner of ways. They assign them different localities and habits, like animal species, some living under ground, others in the sea, the oldest of all being chained in Tártarus. Those to whom they have allotted heaven have set over them one who is nominally father, but in reality a tyrant and despot; with the result that his wife and brother and the daughter, whom he begot from his own head, conspire against him, to arrest and imprison him, just as he himself had treated his own father.

Justly do these tales merit the severe censure which they receive from their intellectual leaders. Moreover, they ridicule the belief that some gods are beardless striplings, others old and bearded; that some are appointed to trades, this one being a smith, that goddess a weaver, a third a warrior who fights along with men, others lute-players or devoted to archery; and again that they are divided into factions and quarrel about men, in so much that they not only come to blows with each other, but actually lament over and suffer from wounds inflicted by mortals...

Then there are the gods in bondage to men, hired now as builders, now as shepherds; and others chained, like criminals, in a prison of brass. What man in his senses would not be stirred to reprimand the inventors of such fables and to condemn the consummate folly of those who believed them? They have even deified Terror and Fear, nay, Frenzy and Deceit—which of the worst passions have they not transfigured into the nature and form of a god?—and have induced cities to offer sacrifices to the more respectable members of this pantheon. Thus they have been absolutely compelled to regard some of the gods as givers of blessings and to call others "to be averted." They then rid themselves of the latter, as they would of the worst scoundrels of humanity, by means of favors and presents, expecting to be visited by some serious mischief if they fail to pay them their price.

Now, what is the cause of such irregular and erroneous conceptions of the deity? For my part, I trace it to the ignorance of the true nature of God, to the neglect with which their legislators entered on their task, and to their failure to formulate even such correct knowledge of it as they were able to attain and to make the rest of their constitution conform to it. Instead, as if this were the most trifling of details, they allowed the poets to introduce what gods they chose, subject to all the passions, and the orators to pass decrees for entering the name of any suitable foreign god into the pantheon.

Painters also and sculptors were given great license in this matter by the Greeks, each designing a figure of his own imagination, one molding it of clay, another using paints. The artists who are the most admired of all use ivory and gold as the material for the novelties which they are constantly producing. And now the gods who once flourished with honors are grown old, that is the kinder way of putting it; and others, newly introduced, are the objects of worship. Some temples are left to desolation, others are but now being erected, according to individual caprice; whereas they ought, on the contrary, to have preserved immutably their belief in God and the honor which they rendered to Him.

– Joséphus, *Against Ápion*, II.33-35 (translated by H. St. J. Thackeray)

# CHAPTER VIII.

## THE CHARACTER OF THE GREEK CITY STATE

The Elements of the City State, I.—The Organization of the City State, II.—Political Development in Greece, III.

### I. THE ELEMENTS OF THE CITY STATE

## The Origin of the City State

Now of these two societies the domestic is the first, and Hésiod is right when he says, "First a house, then a wife, then an ox for the plough," for the poor man has always an ox before a household slave. That society then which nature has established for daily support is the domestic, ... but the society of many families, which was first instituted for their lasting, mutual advantage, is called a village, and a village is most naturally composed of the descendants of one family, ... the children and the children's children thereof: for which reason cities were originally governed by kings, as the barbarian states now are, which are composed of those who had before submitted to kingly government; for every family is governed by the elder, as are the branches thereof, on account of their relationship thereunto, which is what Hómer says, "Each one ruled his wife and child;" and in this scattered manner they formerly lived. And the opinion which universally prevails, that the gods themselves are subject to kingly government, arises from hence, that all men formerly were, and many are so now; and as they imagined themselves to be made in the likeness of the gods, so they supposed their manner of life must needs be the same.

And when many villages so entirely join themselves together as in every respect to form but one society, that society is a city, and contains in itself, if I may so speak, the end and perfection of government: first founded that we might live, but continued that we may live happily. For which reason every city must be allowed to be the work of nature, if we admit that the original society between male and female is; for to this as their end all subordinate societies tend, and the end of everything is the nature of it. For what every being is in its most perfect state, that certainly is the nature of that being, whether it be a man, a horse, or a house: besides, whatsoever produces the final cause and the end which we desire, must be best; but a government complete in itself is that final cause and what is best. Hence it is evident that a city is a natural production, and that man is naturally a political animal, and that whosoever is naturally and not accidentally unfit for society, must be either inferior or superior to man: thus the man in Hómer, who is reviled for being "without society, without law, without family." Such a one must naturally be of a quarrelsome disposition, and as solitary as the birds.

The gift of speech also evidently proves that man is a more social animal than the bees, or any of the herding cattle: for nature, as we say, does nothing in vain, and man is the only animal who enjoys it. Voice indeed, as being the token of pleasure and pain, is imparted to others also, and thus much their nature is capable of, to perceive pleasure and pain, and to impart these sensations to others; but it is by speech that we are enabled to express what is useful for us, and what is hurtful, and of course what is just and what is unjust: for in this particular man differs from other animals, that he alone has a perception of good and evil, of just and unjust, and it is a participation of these common sentiments which forms a family and a city.

Besides, the notion of a city naturally precedes that of a family or an individual, for the whole must necessarily be prior to the parts, for if you take away the whole man, you cannot say a foot or a hand remains, unless by equivocation, as supposing a hand of stone to be made, but that would only be a dead one; but everything is understood to be this or that by its energic qualities and powers, so that when these no longer remain, neither can that be said to be the same, but something of the same name. That a city then precedes an individual is plain, for if an individual is not in himself sufficient to compose a perfect government, he is to a city as other parts are to a whole; but he that is incapable of society, or so complete in himself as not to want it, makes no part of a city, as a beast or a god. There is then in all persons a natural impetus to associate with each other in this manner, and he who first founded civil society was the cause of the greatest good; for as by the completion of it man is the most excellent of all living beings, so without law and justice he would be the worst of all, for nothing is so difficult to subdue as injustice in arms...

— Áristotle, *Politics*, I.1-2 (translated by William Ellis)

## II. THE ORGANIZATION OF THE CITY-STATE

## Types of Government

Having established these points, we proceed next to consider whether one form of government only should be established, or more than one; and if more, how many, and of what sort, and what are the differences between them. The form of government is the ordering and regulating of the city, and all the offices in it, particularly those wherein the supreme power is lodged; and this power is always possessed by the administration; but the administration itself is that particular form of government which is established in any state: thus in a democracy the supreme power is lodged in the whole people; on the contrary, in an oligarchy it is in the hands of a few. We say then, that the form of government in these states is different, and we shall find the same thing hold good in others. Let us first determine for whose sake a city is established; and point out the different species of rule which man may submit to in social life.

— Áristotle, *Politics*, III.6 (translated by William Ellis)

## On Democratic Government

Now the foundation of a democratical state is liberty, and people have been accustomed to say this as if here only liberty was to be found; for they affirm that this is the end proposed by every democracy. But one part of liberty is to govern and be governed alternately; for, according to democratical justice, equality is measured by numbers, and not by worth: and this being just, it is necessary that the supreme power should be vested in the people at large; and that what the majority determine should be final: so that in a democracy the poor ought to have more power than the rich, as being the greater number; for this is one mark of liberty which all framers of a democracy lay down as a criterion of that state; another is, to live as every one likes; for this, they say, is a right which liberty gives, since he is a slave who must live as he likes not. This, then, is another criterion of a democracy. Hence arises the claim to be under no command whatsoever to anyone, upon any account, any otherwise than by rotation, and that just as far only as that person is, in his turn, under his also. This also is conducive to that equality which liberty demands.

These things being premised, and such being the government, it follows that such rules as the following should be observed in it, that all the magistrates should be chosen out of all the people, and all to command each, and each in his turn all: that all the magistrates should be chosen by lot, except to those offices only which required some particular knowledge and skill: that no census, or a very small one, should be required to qualify a man for any office: that none should be in the same employment twice, or very few, and very seldom, except in the army: that all their appointments should be limited to a very short time, or at least as many as possible: that the whole community should be qualified to judge in all causes whatsoever, let the object be ever so extensive, ever so interesting, or of ever so high a nature; as at Áthens, where the people at large judge the magistrates when they come out of office, and decide concerning public affairs as well as private contracts: that the supreme power should be in the public assembly; and that no magistrate should be allowed any discretionary power but in a few instances, and of no consequence to public business.

Of all magistrates a senate is best suited to a democracy, where the whole community is not paid for giving their attendance; for in that case it loses its power; for then the people will bring all causes before them, by appeal, as we have already mentioned in a former book. In the next place, there should, if possible, be a fund to pay all the citizens—who have any share in the management of public affairs, either as members of the assembly, judges, and magistrates; but if this cannot be done, at least the magistrates, the judges the senators, and members of the supreme assembly, and also those officers who are obliged to eat at a common table ought to be paid. Moreover, as an oligarchy is said to be a government of men of family, fortune, and education; so, on the contrary, a democracy is a government in the hands of men of no birth, indigent circumstances, and mechanical employments. In this state also no office should be for life; and, if any such should remain after the government has been long changed into a democracy, they should endeavor by degrees to diminish the power; and also elect by lot instead of vote. These things, then, appertain to all democracies; namely, to be established on that principle of justice which is homogeneous to those governments; that is, that all the members of the state, by number, should enjoy an equality, which seems chiefly to constitute a democracy, or government of the people: for it seems perfectly equal that the rich should have no more share in the government than the poor, nor be alone in power; but that all should be equal, according to number; for thus, they think, the equality and liberty of the state best preserved.

— Áristotle, *Politics*, VI.2 (translated by William Ellis)

## III. POLITICAL DEVELOPMENT IN GREECE

# The Corruption of Governments

It is evident that every form of government or administration, for the words are of the same import, must contain a supreme power over the whole state, and this supreme power must necessarily be in the hands of one person, or a few, or many; and when either of these apply their power for the common good, such states are well governed; but when the interest of the one, the few, or the many who enjoy this power is alone consulted, then ill; for you must either affirm that those who make up the community are not citizens, or else let these share in the advantages of government. We usually call a state which is governed by one person for the common good, a kingdom; one that is governed by more than one, but by a few only, an aristocracy; either because the government is in the hands of the most worthy citizens, or because it is the best form for the city and its inhabitants. When the citizens at large govern for the public good, it is called a state; which is also a common name for all other governments, and these distinctions are consonant to reason; for it will not be difficult to find one person, or a very few, of very distinguished abilities, but almost impossible to meet with the majority of a people eminent for every virtue; but if there is one common to a whole nation it is valor; for this is created and supported by numbers: for which reason in such a state the profession of arms will always have the greatest share in the government. Now the corruptions attending each of these governments are these; a kingdom may degenerate into a tyranny, an aristocracy into an oligarchy, and a state into a democracy. Now a tyranny is a monarchy where the good of one man only is the object of government, an oligarchy considers only the rich, and a democracy only the poor; but neither of them have a common good in view.

— Áristotle, *Politics*, III.7 (translated by William Ellis)

# CHAPTER IX.

## THE DÓRIAN CITY STATE —SPÁRTA

Political Growth of Spárta, I.—The Spártan Discipline and Education, II.
Supremacy of Spárta in the Peloponnésus, III.

## I. POLITICAL GROWTH OF SPÁRTA

### The Voluntarily Exile of Lycúrgus

He, too, dying soon after, the right of succession (as every one thought) rested in Lycúrgus; and reign he did, until it was found that the queen, his sister-in-law, was with child; upon which he immediately declared that the kingdom belonged to her issue, provided it were male, and that he himself exercised the regal jurisdiction only as his guardian; the Spártan name for which office is pródicus. Soon after, an overture was made to him by the queen, that she would herself in some way destroy the infant, upon condition that he would marry her when he came to the crown. Abhorring the woman's wickedness, he nevertheless did not reject her proposal, but, making show of closing with her, dispatched the messenger with thanks and expressions of joy, but dissuaded her earnestly from procuring herself to miscarry, which would impair her health, if not endanger her life; he himself, he said, would see to it, that the child, as soon as born, should be taken out of the way. By such artifices having drawn on the woman to the time of her lying-in, as soon as he heard that she was in labor, he sent persons to be by and observe all that passed, with orders that if it were a girl they should deliver it to the women, but if a boy, should bring it to him wheresoever he were, and whatsoever doing.

It so fell out that when he was at supper with the principal magistrates the queen was brought to bed of a boy, who was soon after presented to him as he was at the table; he, taking him into his arms, said to those about him, "Men of Spárta, here is a king born unto us;" this said, he laid him down in the king's place, and named him Chariláüs, that is, the joy of the people; because that all were transported with joy and with wonder at his noble and just spirit. His reign had lasted only eight months, but he was honored on other accounts by the citizens, and there were more who obeyed him because of his eminent virtues than because he was regent to the king and had the royal power in his hands. Some, however, envied and sought to impede his growing influence while he was still young; chiefly the kindred and friends of the queen mother, who pretended to have been dealt with injuriously. Her brother Leónidas, in a warm debate which fell out betwixt him and Lycúrgus, went so far as to tell him to his face that he was well assured that ere long he should see him king; suggesting suspicions and preparing the way for an accusation of him, as though he had made away with his nephew, if the child should chance to fail though by a natural death. Words of the like import were designedly cast abroad by the queen-mother and her adherents.

Troubled at this, and not knowing what it might come to, he thought it his wisest course to avoid their envy by a voluntary exile, and to travel from place to place until his nephew came to marriageable years, and, by having a son, had secured the succession; setting sail, therefore, with this resolution, he first arrived at Crete, where, having considered their several forms of government, and having got an acquaintance with the principal men amongst them, some of their laws he very much approved of, and resolved to make use of them in his own country; a good part he rejected as useless. Amongst the persons there the most renowned for learning all their wisdom in state matters was one Tháles, whom Lycúrgus, by importunities and assurances of friendship, persuaded to go over to Lacedǽmon; where, though by his outward appearance and his own profession he seemed to be no other than a lyric poet, in reality he performed the part of one of the ablest lawgivers in the world. The very songs which he composed were exhortations to obedience and concord, and the very measure and cadence of the verse, conveying impressions of order and tranquility, had so great an influence on the minds of the listeners, that they were insensibly softened and civilized, insomuch that they renounced their private feuds and animosities, and were reunited in a common admiration of virtue. So that it may truly be said that Tháles prepared the way for the discipline introduced by Lycúrgus.

– Plútarch, Life of Lycúrgus (translated by John Dryden)

## Lycúrgus Gives New Laws to the Spártans

Lycúrgus was much missed at Spárta, and often sent for, "for kings indeed we have," they said, "who wear the marks and assume the titles of royalty, but as for the qualities of their minds, they have nothing by which they are to be distinguished from their subjects;" adding, that in him alone was the true foundation of sovereignty to be seen, a nature made to rule, and a genius to gain obedience. Nor were the kings themselves averse to see him back, for they looked upon his presence as a bulwark against the insolence of the people.

Things being in this posture at his return, he applied himself, without loss of time, to a thorough reformation and resolved to change the whole face of the commonwealth; for what could a few particular laws and a partial alteration avail? He must act as wise physicians do, in the case of one who labors under a complication of diseases, by force of medicines reduce and exhaust him, change his whole temperament, and then set him upon a totally new regimen of diet. Having thus projected things, away he goes to Délphi to consult Apóllo there; which having done, and offered his sacrifice, he returned with that renowned oracle, in which he is called beloved of the god, and rather a god than man; that his prayers were heard, that his laws should be the best, and the commonwealth which observed them the most famous in the world. Encouraged by these things, he set himself to bring over to his side the leading men of Spárta, exhorting them to give him a helping hand in his great undertaking; he broke it first to his particular friends, and then by degrees gained others, and animated them all to put his design in execution. When things were ripe for action, he gave order to thirty of the principal men of Spárta to be ready armed at the market-place by break of day, to the end that he might strike a terror into the opposite party... Things growing to a tumult, king Chariláüs, apprehending that it was a conspiracy against his person, took sanctuary in the temple of Minérva of the Brazen House; but, being soon after undeceived, and having taken an oath of them that they had no designs against him, he quitted his refuge, and himself also entered into confederacy with them; of so gentle and flexible a disposition he was...

– Plútarch, Life of Lycúrgus (translated by John Dryden)

## Lycúrgus Creates a Spártan Senate

Amongst the many changes and alterations which Lycúrgus made, the first and of greatest importance was the establishment of the senate, which, having a power equal to the kings' in matters of great consequence, and, as Pláto expresses it, allaying and qualifying the fiery genius of the royal office, gave steadiness and safety to the commonwealth. For the state, which before had no firm basis to stand upon, but leaned one way while towards an absolute monarchy, when the kings had the upper hand, and another while towards a pure democracy, when the people had the better, found in this establishment of the senate a central weight, like ballast in a ship, which always kept things in a just equilibrium; the twenty-eight always adhering to the kings so far as to resist democracy, and, on the other hand, supporting the people against the establishment of absolute monarchy

– Plútarch, Life of Lycúrgus (translated by John Dryden)

## The Creation of the Éphors

Although Lycúrgus had, in this manner, used all the qualifications possible in the constitution of his commonwealth, yet those who succeeded him found the oligarchical element still too strong and dominant, and, to check its high temper and its violence, put, as Pláto says, a bit in its mouth, which was the power of the Éphors, established one hundred and thirty years after the death of Lycúrgus. Elátus and his colleagues were the first who had this dignity conferred upon them, in the reign of king Theopómpus, who, when his queen upbraided him one day that he would leave the regal power to his children less than he had received it from his ancestors, said, in answer, "No, greater; for it will last longer." For, indeed, their prerogative being thus reduced within reasonable bounds, the Spártan kings were at once freed from all further jealousies and consequent danger, and never experienced the calamities of their neighbors at Messéne and Árgos, who, by maintaining their prerogative too strictly, for want of yielding a little to the populace, lost it all.

Indeed, whosoever shall look at the sedition and misgovernment which befell these bordering nations to whom they were as near related in blood as situation, will find in them the best reason to admire the wisdom and foresight of Lycúrgus. For these three states, in their first rise, were equal, or, if there were any odds, they lay on the side of the Messénians and Árgives, who, in the first allotment, were thought to have been luckier than the Spártans; yet their happiness was but of small continuance, partly the tyrannical temper of their kings and partly the ungovernableness of the people quickly bringing upon them such disorders and so complete an overthrow of all existing institutions as clearly to show how truly divine a blessing the Spártans had had in that wise lawgiver, who gave their government its happy balance and temper.

– Plútarch, *Life of Lycúrgus* (translated by John Dryden)

## Prerogatives of the Spártan Kings

The prerogatives which the Spártans have allowed their kings are the following. In the first place, two priesthoods, those (namely) of Lacedæmónian and of Celestial Zeus; also the right of making war on what country soever they please, without hindrance from any of the other Spártans, under pain of outlawry; on service the privilege of marching first in the advance and last in the retreat, and of having a hundred picked men for their body guard while with the army; likewise the liberty of sacrificing as many cattle in their expeditions as it seems them good, and the right of having the skins and the chines of the slaughtered animals for their own use.

Such are their privileges in war; in peace their rights are as follows. When a citizen makes a public sacrifice the kings are given the first seats at the banquet; they are served before any of the other guests, and have a double portion of everything; they take the lead in the libations; and the hides of the sacrificed beasts belong to them. Every month, on the first day, and again on the seventh of the first decade, each king receives a beast without blemish at the public cost, which he offers up to Apóllo; likewise a medímnus of meal, and of wine a Lacónian quart. In the contests of the Games they have always the seat of honor; they appoint the citizens who have to entertain foreigners; they also nominate, each of them, two of the Pýthians, officers whose business it is to consult the oracle at Délphi, who eat with the kings, and, like them, live at the public charge. If the kings do not come to the public supper, each of them must have two rations of meal and a half pint of wine sent home to him at his house; if they come, they are given a double quantity of each, and the same when any private man invites them to his table. They have the custody of all the oracles which are pronounced; but the Pýthians must likewise have knowledge of them. They have the whole decision of certain causes, which are these, and these only: When a maiden is left the heiress of her father's estate, and has not been betrothed by him to any one, they decide who is to marry her; in all matters concerning the public highways they judge; and if a person wants to adopt a child, he must do it before the kings. They likewise have the right of sitting in council with the eight-and-twenty senators; and if they are not present, then the senators nearest of kin to them have their privileges, and give two votes as the royal proxies, besides a third vote, which is their own.

Such are the honors which the Spártan people have allowed their kings during their lifetime; after they are dead other honors await them. Horsemen carry the news of their death through all Lacónia, while in the city the women go hither and thither drumming upon a kettle. At this signal, in every house two free persons, a man and a woman, must put on mourning, or else be subject to a heavy fine. The Lacedæmónians have likewise a custom at the demise of their kings which is common to them with the barbarians of Ásia—indeed with the greater number of the barbarians everywhere—namely, that when one of their kings dies, not only the Spártans, but a certain number of the country people from every part of Lacónia are forced, whether they will or no, to attend the funeral. So these persons and the Hélots, and likewise the Spártans themselves, flock together to the number of several thousands, men and women intermingled; and all of them smite their foreheads violently, and weep and wail without stint, saying always that their last king was the best. If a king dies in battle, then they make a statue of him, and placing it upon a couch right bravely decked, so carry it to the grave. After the burial, by the space of ten days there is no assembly, nor do they elect magistrates, but continue mourning the whole time.

They hold with the Pérsians also in another custom. When a king dies, and another comes to the throne, the newly made monarch forgives all the Spártans the debts which they owe either to the king or to the public treasury. And in like manner among the Pérsians each king when he begins to reign remits the tribute due from the provinces.

— Heródotus, *History*, VI.56-59 (translated by George Rawlinson)


## II. THE SPÁRTAN DISCIPLINE AND EDUCATION

## Spártan Property Laws

After the creation of the thirty senators, his next task, and, indeed, the most hazardous he ever undertook, was the making a new division of their lands. For there was an extreme inequality amongst them, and their state was overloaded with a multitude of indigent and necessitous persons, while its whole wealth had centered upon a very few. To the end, therefore, that he might expel from the state arrogance and envy, luxury and crime, and those yet more inveterate diseases of want and superfluity, he obtained of them to renounce their properties, and to consent to a new division of the land, and that they should live all together on an equal footing; merit to be their only road to eminence, and the disgrace of evil, and credit of worthy acts, their one measure of difference between man and man.

Upon their consent to these proposals, proceeding at once to put them into execution, he divided the country of Lacónia in general into thirty thousand equal shares, and the part attached to the city of Spárta into nine thousand; these he distributed among the Spártans, as he did the others to the country citizens... A lot was so much as to yield, one year with another, about seventy bushels of grain for the master of the family, and twelve for his wife, with a suitable proportion of oil and wine. And this he thought sufficient to keep their bodies in good health and strength; superfluities they were better without. It is reported, that, as he returned from a journey shortly after the division of the lands, in harvest time, the ground being newly reaped, seeing the stacks all standing equal and alike, he smiled, and said to those about him, "Methinks all Lacónia looks like one family estate just divided among a number of brothers."

Not contented with this, he resolved to make a division of their movables too, that there might be no odious distinction or inequality left amongst them; but finding that it would be very dangerous to go about it openly, he took another course, and defeated their avarice by the following stratagem: he commanded that all gold and silver coin should be called in, and that only a sort of money made of iron should be current, a great weight and quantity of which was but very little worth; so that to lay up twenty or thirty pounds there was required a pretty large closet, and, to remove it, nothing less than a yoke of oxen. With the diffusion of this money, at once a number of vices were banished from Lacedæmon; for who would rob another of such a coin? Who would unjustly detain or take by force, or accept as a bribe, a thing which it was not easy to hide, nor a credit to have, nor indeed of any use to cut in pieces? For when it was just red hot, they quenched it in vinegar, and by that means spoilt it, and made it almost incapable of being worked.

In the next place, he declared an outlawry of all needless and superfluous arts; but here he might almost have spared his proclamation; for they of themselves would have gone after the gold and silver, the money which remained being not so proper payment for curious work; for, being of iron, it was scarcely portable, neither, if they should take the pains to export it, would it pass amongst the other Greeks, who ridiculed it. So there was now no more means of purchasing foreign goods and small wares; merchants sent no shiploads into Lacónian ports; no rhetoric-master, no itinerant fortune-teller, no harlot-monger or gold or silversmith, engraver, or jeweler, set foot in a country which had no money; so that luxury, deprived little by little of that which fed and fomented it, wasted to nothing, and died away of itself. For the rich had no advantage here over the poor, as their wealth and abundance had no road to come abroad by, but were shut up at home doing nothing.

And in this way they became excellent artists in common, necessary things; bedsteads, chairs, and tables, and such like staple utensils in a family, were admirably well made there; their cup, particularly, was very much in fashion, and eagerly bought up by soldiers, as Crítias reports; for its color was such as to prevent water, drunk upon necessity and disagreeable to look at, from being noticed; and the shape of it was such that the mud stuck to the sides, so that only the purer part came to the drinker's mouth. For this, also, they had to thank their lawgiver, who, by relieving the artisans of the trouble of making useless things, set them to show their skill in giving beauty to those of daily and indispensable use.

– Plútarch, *Life of Lycúrgus* (translated by John Dryden)

## Common Meals

The third and most masterly stroke of this great lawgiver, by which he struck a yet more effectual blow against luxury and the desire of riches, was the ordinance he made, that they should all eat in common, of the same bread and same meat, and of kinds that were specified, and should not spend their lives at home, laid on costly couches at splendid tables, delivering themselves up into the hands of their tradesmen and cooks, to fatten them in corners, like greedy brutes, and to ruin not their minds only but their very bodies, which, enfeebled by indulgence and excess, would stand in need of long sleep, warm bathing, freedom from work, and, in a word, of as much care and attendance as if they were continually sick. It was certainly an extraordinary thing to have brought about such a result as this, but a greater yet to have taken away from wealth, as Theophrastus observes, not merely the property of being coveted, but its very nature of being wealth. For the rich, being obliged to go to the same table with the poor, could not make use of or enjoy their abundance, nor so much as please their vanity by looking at or displaying it. So that the common proverb, that Plútus, the god of riches, is blind, was nowhere in all the world literally verified but in Spárta. There, indeed, he was not only blind, but like a picture, without either life or motion. Nor were they allowed to take food at home first, and then attend the public tables, for every one had an eye upon those who did not eat and drink like the rest, and reproached them with being dainty and effeminate.

This last ordinance in particular exasperated the wealthier men. They collected in a body against Lycúrgus, and from ill words came to throwing stones, so that at length he was forced to run out of the marketplace, and make to sanctuary to save his life; by good-hap he outran all excepting one Alcánder, a young man otherwise not ill accomplished, but hasty and violent, who came up so close to him, that, when he turned to see who was near him, he struck him upon the face with his stick, and put out one of his eyes. Lycúrgus, so far from being daunted and discouraged by this accident, stopped short, and showed his disfigured face and eye beat out to his countrymen; they, dismayed and ashamed at the sight, delivered Alcánder into his hands to be punished, and escorted him home, with expressions of great concern for his ill usage.

Lycúrgus, having thanked them for their care of his person, dismissed them all, excepting only Alcánder; and, taking him with him into his house, neither did nor said anything severely to him, but, dismissing those whose place it was bade Alcánder to wait upon him at table. The young man who was of an ingenuous temper, without murmuring did as he was commanded; and, being thus admitted to live with Lycúrgus, he had an opportunity to observe in him, besides his gentleness and calmness of temper, an extraordinary sobriety and an indefatigable industry, and so, from an enemy, became one of his most zealous admirers, and told his friends and relations that Lycúrgus was not that morose and ill-natured man they had formerly taken him for, but the one mild and gentle character of the world. And thus did Lycúrgus, for chastisement of his fault, make of a wild and passionate young man one of the discreetest citizens of Spárta...

But to return to their public repasts... they met by companies of fifteen, more or less, and each of them stood bound to bring in monthly a bushel of meal, eight gallons of wine, five pounds of cheese, two pounds and a half of figs, and some very small sum of money to buy flesh or fish with. Besides this, when any of them made sacrifice to the gods, they always sent a dole to the common hall; and, likewise, when any of them had been a hunting, he sent thither a part of the venison he had killed; for these two occasions were the only excuses allowed for supping at home. The custom of eating together was observed strictly for a great while afterwards; insomuch that king Ágis himself, after having vanquished the Athénians, sending for his commons at his return home, because he desired to eat privately with his queen, was refused them by the Pólemarchs; which refusal when he resented so much as to omit next day the sacrifice due for a war happily ended, they made him pay a fine.

They used to send their children to these tables as to schools of temperance; here they were instructed in state affairs by listening to experienced statesmen; here they learnt to converse with pleasantry, to make jests without scurrility, and take them without ill humor. In this point of good breeding, the Lacedæmónians excelled particularly, but if any man were uneasy under it, upon the least hint given, there was no more to be said to him. It was customary also for the eldest man in the company to say to each of them, as they came in, "Through this" (pointing to the door), "no words go out." When any one had a desire to be admitted into any of these little societies; he was to go through the following probation, each man in the company took a little ball of soft bread, which they were to throw into a deep basin, which a waiter carried round upon his head; those that liked the person to be chosen dropped their ball into the basin without altering its figure, and those who disliked him pressed it between their fingers, and made it flat; and this signified as much as a negative voice. And if there were but one of these pieces in the basin, the suitor was rejected, so desirous were they that all the members of the company should be agreeable to each other. The basin was called cáddichus, and the rejected candidate had a name thence derived. Their most famous dish was the black broth, which was so much valued that the elderly men fed only upon that, leaving what flesh there was to the younger.

They say that a certain king of Póntus, having heard much of this black broth of theirs, sent for a Lacedæmónian cook on purpose to make him some, but had no sooner tasted it than he found it extremely bad, which the cook observing, told him, "Sir, to make this broth relish, you should have bathed yourself first in the river Eurótas."

After drinking moderately, every man went to his home without lights, for the use of them was, on all occasions, forbid, to the end that they might accustom themselves to march boldly in the dark. Such was the common fashion of their meals.

– Plútarch, *Life of Lycúrgus* (translated by John Dryden)

## Spártan Rhétras

Lycúrgus would never reduce his laws into writing; nay, there is a Rhétra expressly to forbid it. For he thought that the most material points, and such as most directly tended to the public welfare, being imprinted on the hearts of their youth by a good discipline, would be sure to remain, and would find a stronger security than any compulsion would be, in the principles of action formed in them by their best lawgiver, education. And as for things of lesser importance, as pecuniary contracts, and such like, the forms of which have to be changed as occasion requires, he thought it the best way to prescribe no positive rule or inviolable usage in such cases, willing that their manner and form should be altered according to the circumstances of time, and determinations of men of sound judgment. Every end and object of law and enactment it was his design education should effect.

One, then, of the Rhétras was, that their laws should not be written; another is particularly leveled against luxury and expensiveness, for by it was it ordained that the ceilings of their houses should only be wrought by the axe, and their gates and doors smoothed only by the saw. Epaminóndas's famous dictum about his own table, that "Treason and a dinner like this do not keep company together," may be said to have been anticipated by Lycúrgus... It is reported that king Leotýchides, the first of that name, was so little used to the sight of any other kind of work, that, being entertained at Córinth in a stately room, he was much surprised to see the timber and ceiling so finely carved and paneled, and asked his host whether the trees grew so in his country.

A third ordinance or Rhétra was, that they should not make war often, or long, with the same enemy, lest that they should train and instruct them in war, by habituating them to defend themselves. And this is what Agesiláüs was much blamed for, a long time after; it being thought, that, by his continual incursions into Bœótia, he made the Thébans a match for the Lacedæmónians; and therefore Antálcidas, seeing him wounded one day, said to him, that he was very well paid for taking such pains to make the Thébans good soldiers, whether they would or no. These laws were called the Rhétras, to intimate that they were divine sanctions and revelations.

– Plútarch, *Life of Lycúrgus* (translated by John Dryden)

## The Education of Spártan Children

Nor was it in the power of the father to dispose of the child as he thought fit; he was obliged to carry it before certain triers at a place called Lésche; these were some of the elders of the tribe to which the child belonged; their business it was carefully to view the infant, and, if they found it stout and well made, they gave order for its rearing, and allotted to it one of the nine thousand shares of land above mentioned for its maintenance, but, if they found it puny and ill-shaped, ordered it to be taken to what was called the Apóthetæ, a sort of chasm under Taýgetus; as thinking it neither for the good of the child itself, nor for the public interest, that it should be brought up, if it did not, from the very outset, appear made to be healthy and vigorous. Upon the same account, the women did not bathe the new-born children with water, as is the custom in all other countries, but with wine, to prove the temper and complexion of their bodies; from a notion they had that epileptic and weakly children faint and waste away upon their being thus bathed, while, on the contrary, those of a strong and vigorous habit acquire firmness and get a temper by it, like steel. There was much care and art, too, used by the nurses; they had no swaddling bands; the children grew up free and unconstrained in limb and form, and not dainty and fanciful about their food; not afraid in the dark, or of being left alone; without any peevishness or ill humor or crying. Upon this account, Spártan nurses were often bought up, or hired by people of other countries; and it is recorded that she who suckled Alcibíades was a Spártan; who, however, if fortunate in his nurse, was not so in his preceptor; his guardian, Péricles, as Pláto tells us, chose a servant for that office ... no better than any common slave.

Lycúrgus was of another mind; he would not have masters bought out of the market for his young Spártans, nor such as should sell their pains; nor was it lawful, indeed, for the father himself to breed up the children after his own fancy; but as soon as they were seven years old they were to be enrolled in certain companies and classes, where they all lived under the same order and discipline, doing their exercises and taking their play together. Of these, he who showed the most conduct and courage was made captain; they had their eyes always upon him, obeyed his orders, and underwent patiently whatsoever punishment he inflicted; so that the whole course of their education was one continued exercise of a ready and perfect obedience. The old men, too, were spectators of their performances, and often raised quarrels and disputes among them, to have a good opportunity of finding out their different characters, and of seeing which would be valiant, which a coward, when they should come to more dangerous encounters. Reading and writing they gave them, just enough to serve their turn; their chief care was to make them good subjects, and to teach them to endure pain and conquer in battle. To this end, as they grew in years, their discipline was proportionally increased; their heads were close-clipped, they were accustomed to go bare-foot, and for the most part to play naked.

– Plútarch, *Life of Lycúrgus* (translated by John Dryden)

## Learning to Steal

Besides all this, there was always one of the best and honestest men in the city appointed to undertake the charge and governance of them; he again arranged them into their several bands, and set over each of them for their captain the most temperate and boldest of those they called Írens, who were usually twenty years old, two years out of the boys; and the eldest of the boys, again, were Mell-Írens, as much as to say, who would shortly be men. This young man, therefore, was their captain when they fought, and their master at home, using them for the offices of his house; sending the oldest of them to fetch wood, and the weaker and less able, to gather salads and herbs, and these they must either go without or steal; which they did by creeping into the gardens, or conveying themselves cunningly and closely into the eating-houses; if they were taken in the fact, they were whipped without mercy, for thieving so ill and awkwardly. They stole, too, all other food they could lay their hands on, looking out and watching all opportunities, when people were asleep or more careless than usual. If they were caught, they were not only punished with whipping, but hunger, too, being reduced to their ordinary allowance, which was but very slender, and so contrived on purpose, that they might set about to help themselves, and be forced to exercise their energy and address...

– Plútarch, *Life of Lycúrgus* (translated by John Dryden)

## Lacónic Speech

They taught them, also, to speak with a natural and graceful raillery, and to comprehend much matter of thought in few words. For Lycúrgus, who ordered, as we saw, that a great piece of money should be but of an inconsiderable value, on the contrary would allow no discourse to be current which did not contain in few words a great deal of useful and curious sense; children in Spárta, by a habit of long silence, came to give just and sententious answers; for, indeed, as loose and incontinent livers are seldom fathers of many children, so loose and incontinent talkers seldom originate many sensible words. King Ágis, when some Athénian laughed at their short swords, and said that the jugglers on the stage swallowed them with ease, answered him, "We find them long enough to reach our enemies;" and as their swords were short and sharp, so, it seems to me, were their sayings. They reach the point and arrest the attention of the hearers better than any.

Lycúrgus himself seems to have been short and sententious, if we may trust the anecdotes of him; as appears by his answer to one who by all means would set up democracy in Lacedǽmon. "Begin, friend," said he, "and set it up in your family." Another asked him why he allowed of such mean and trivial sacrifices to the gods. He replied, "That we may always have something to offer to them." Being asked what sort of martial exercises or combats he approved of, he answered, "All sorts, except that in which you stretch out your hands." Similar answers, addressed to his countrymen by letter, are ascribed to him; as, being consulted how they might best oppose an invasion of their enemies, he returned this answer, "By continuing poor, and not coveting each man to be greater than his fellow." Being consulted again whether it were requisite to enclose the city with a wall, he sent them word, "The city is well fortified which hath a wall of men instead of brick." But whether these letters are counterfeit or not is not easy to determine.

Of their dislike to talkativeness, the following apothegms are evidence. King Leónidas said to one who held him in discourse upon some useful matter, but not in due time and place, "Much to the purpose, Sir, elsewhere." King Chariláüs, the nephew of Lycúrgus, being asked why his uncle had made so few laws, answered, "Men of few words require but few laws." When one blamed Hecatǽus the sóphist because that, being invited to the public table, he had not spoken one word all supper-time, Archidámidas answered in his vindication, "He who knows how to speak, knows also when."

The sharp and yet not ungraceful retorts which I mentioned may be instanced as follows. Demarátus, being asked in a troublesome manner by an importunate fellow, "Who was the best man in Lacedǽmon?" answered at last, "He that is the least like you." Some, in company where Ágis was, much extolled the Éleans for their just and honorable management of the Olýmpic games; "Indeed," said Ágis, "they are highly to be commended if they can do justice one day in five years." Theopómpus answered a stranger who talked much of his affection to the Lacedæmónians and said that his countrymen called him Philólacon (a lover of the Lacedæmónians), that it had been more for his honor if they had called him Philopólites (a lover of his own countrymen). And Plistóanax, the son of Pausánias, when an orator of Áthens said the Lacedæmónians had no learning, told him, "You say true; we alone of all the Greeks have learned none of your bad qualities." One asked Archidámidas what number there might, be of the Spártans; he answered, "Enough to keep out wicked men."

– Plútarch, *Life of Lycúrgus* (translated by John Dryden)

## The Spártans in Battle

For, indeed, before they engaged in battle, the king first did sacrifice to the Múses, in all likelihood to put them in mind of the manner of their education, and of the judgment that would be passed upon their actions, and thereby to animate them to the performance of exploits that should deserve a record...

When they were in the field, their exercises were generally more moderate, their fare not so hard, nor so strict a hand held over them by their officers, so that they were the only people in the world to whom war gave repose. When their army was drawn up in battle array and the enemy near, the king sacrificed a goat, commanded the soldiers to set their garlands upon their heads, and the pipers to play the tune of the hymn to Cástor, and himself began the pæan of advance. It was at once a magnificent and a terrible sight to see them march on to the tune of their flutes, without any disorder in their ranks, any discomposure in their minds or change in their countenance, calmly and cheerfully moving with the music to the deadly fight. Men, in this temper, were not likely to be possessed with fear or any transport of fury, but with the deliberate valor of hope and assurance, as if some divinity were attending and conducting them. The king had always about his person someone who had been crowned in the Olýmpic games; and upon this account a Lacedæmónian is said to have refused a considerable present, which was offered to him upon condition that he would not come into the lists; and when he had with much to-do thrown his antagonist, some of the spectators saying to him, "And now, Lacedæmónian, what are you the better for your victory?" he answered smiling, "I shall fight next the king." After they had routed an enemy, they pursued him till they were well assured of the victory, and then they sounded a retreat, thinking it base and unworthy of a Grécian people to cut men in pieces, who had given up and abandoned all resistance. This manner of dealing with their enemies did not only show magnanimity, but was politic too; for, knowing that they killed only those who made resistance, and gave quarter to the rest, men generally thought it their best way to consult their safety by flight.

– Plútarch, *Life of Lycúrgus* (translated by John Dryden)

## Spártan Laws on Burial and Travel

Touching burials, Lycúrgus made very wise regulations; for, first of all, to cut of all superstition, he allowed them to bury their dead within the city, and even round about their temples, to the end that their youth might be accustomed to such spectacles, and not be afraid to see a dead body, or imagine that to touch a corpse or to tread upon a grave would defile a man. In the next place, he commanded them to put nothing into the ground with them, except, if they pleased, a few olive leaves, and the scarlet cloth that they were wrapped in. He would not suffer the names to be inscribed, except only of men who fell in the wars, or women who died in a sacred office. The time, too, appointed for mourning, was very short, eleven days; on the twelfth, they were to do sacrifice to Céres, and leave it off; so that we may see, that as he cut off all superfluity, so in things necessary there was nothing so small and trivial which did not express some homage of virtue or scorn of vice. He filled Lacedæmon all through with proofs and examples of good conduct; with the constant sight of which from their youth up, the people would hardly fail to be gradually formed and advanced in virtue.

And this was the reason why he forbade them to travel abroad and go about acquainting themselves with foreign rules of morality, the habits of ill-educated people, and different views of government. Withal he banished from Lacedæmon all strangers who could not give a very good reason for their coming thither; not because he was afraid lest they should inform themselves of and imitate his manner of government—as Thucýdides says—or learn any thing to their good; but rather lest they should introduce something contrary to good manners. With strange people, strange words must be admitted; these novelties produce novelties in thought; and on these follow views and feelings whose discordant character destroys the harmony of the state. He was as careful to save his city from the infection of foreign bad habits, as men usually are to prevent the introduction of a pestilence.

– Plútarch, *Life of Lycúrgus* (translated by John Dryden)

## Genuine Valor

Cáto the Elder, hearing some commend one that was rash, and inconsiderately daring in a battle, said, "There is a difference between a man's prizing valor at a great rate, and valuing life at little"—a very just remark. Antígonus, we know, at least, had a soldier, a venturous fellow, but of wretched health and constitution; the reason of whose ill looks he took the trouble to inquire into; and, on understanding from him that it was a disease, commanded his physicians to employ their utmost skill, and if possible recover him; which brave hero, when once cured, never afterwards sought danger or showed himself venturous in battle; and, when Antígonus wondered and upbraided him with his change, made no secret of the reason, and said, "Sir, you are the cause of my cowardice, by freeing me from those miseries which made me care little for life." With the same feeling, the Sýbarite seems to have said of the Spártans, that it was no commendable thing in them to be so ready to die in the wars, since by that they were freed from such hard labor, and miserable living. In truth, the Sýbarites, a soft and dissolute people, might very well imagine they hated life, because in their eager pursuit of virtue and glory, they were not afraid to die: but, in fact, the Lacedæmónians found their virtue secured them happiness alike in living or in dying; as we see in the epitaph that says:

> They died, but not as lavish of their blood,
> Or thinking death itself was simply good;
> Their wishes neither were to live nor die,
> But to do both alike commendably.

An endeavor to avoid death is not blamable, if we do not basely desire to live; nor a willingness to die good and virtuous, if it proceeds from a contempt of life. And therefore Hómer always takes care to bring his bravest and most daring heroes well armed into battle; and the Greek lawgivers punished those that threw away their shields, but not him that lost his sword or spear; intimating that self-defense is more a man's business than offense. This is especially true of a governor of a city, or a general; for if, as Iphícrates divides it out, the light-armed are the hands; the horse the feet; the infantry the breast; and the general the head; he, when he puts himself upon danger, not only ventures his own person, but all those whose safety depends on his; and so on the contrary.

– Plútarch, *Life of Pelópidas* (translated by John Dryden)


## III. SUPREMACY OF SPÁRTA IN THE PELOPONNÉSUS

## The Outcome of the First Messénian War

Even then the Messénians were not inferior in courage and brave deeds, but all their generals were killed and their most notable men. After this they held out for some five months, but as the year was coming to an end deserted Ithóme, the war having lasted twenty years in all, as is stated in the poems of Tyrtæus... All the Messénians who had ties with Sícyon and Árgos and among any of the Arcádians retired to these states, but those who belonged to the family of the Priests and performed the mysteries of the Great Goddesses, to Eléusis. The majority of the common people were scattered in their native towns, as before.

The Lacedæmónians first razed Ithóme to the ground, then attacked and captured the remaining towns. Of the spoils they dedicated bronze tripods to the god of Amýclæ. A statue of Aphrodíte stands under the first tripod, of Ártemis under the second, of Kóre or Deméter under the third. Dedicating these offerings at Amýclæ, they gave to the people of Ásine, who had been driven out by the Árgives, that part of Messénia on the coast which they still occupy; to the descendants of Ándrocles (he had a daughter, who with her children had fled at his death and come to Spárta) they assigned the part called Hyámia.

The Messénians themselves were treated in this way: First they exacted an oath that they would never rebel or attempt any kind of revolution. Secondly, though no fixed tribute was imposed on them, they used to bring the half of all the produce of their fields to Spárta. It was also ordained that for the funerals of the kings and other magistrates men should come from Messéne with their wives in black garments, and a penalty was laid on those who disobeyed...

— Pausánias, *Description of Greece*, 4.13.6-4.14.6 (translated by W. H. S. Jones)

# CHAPTER X.

## THE IÓNIAN CITY STATE —ÁTHENS

The Athénian Monarchy and its Decline, I.—Sólon and the Athénian Aristocracy, II. Pisístratus and the Athénian Tyranny, III.—Clísthenes and the Athénian Democracy, IV.

## I. THE ATHÉNIAN MONARCHY AND ITS DECLINE

### Théseus and the Athénian State

Now, after the death of his father Ægéus, forming in his mind a great and wonderful design, he gathered together all the inhabitants of Áttica into one town, and made them one people of one city, whereas before they lived dispersed, and were not easy to assemble upon any affair for the common interest. Nay, differences and even wars often occurred between them, which he by his persuasions appeased, going from township to township, and from tribe to tribe. And those of a more private and mean condition readily embracing such good advice, to those of greater power he promised a commonwealth without monarchy, a democracy, or people's government in which he should only be continued as their commander in war and the protector of their laws, all things else being equally distributed among them; and by this means brought a part of them over to his proposal. The rest, fearing his power, which was already grown very formidable, and knowing his courage and resolution, chose rather to be persuaded than forced into a compliance. He then dissolved all the distinct state-houses, council halls, and magistracies, and built one common state-house and council hall on the site of the present upper town, and gave the name of Áthens to the whole state, ordaining a common feast and sacrifice, which he called Panathenǽa, or the sacrifice of all the united Athénians...

Farther yet designing to enlarge his city, he invited all strangers to come and enjoy equal privileges with the natives, and it is said that the common form, Come hither, all ye people, was the words that Théseus proclaimed when he thus set up a commonwealth, in a manner, for all nations. Yet he did not suffer his state, by the promiscuous multitude that flowed in, to be turned into confusion and be left without any order or degree, but was the first that divided the Commonwealth into three distinct ranks: the noblemen, the husbandmen, and artificers. To the nobility he committed the care of religion, the choice of magistrates, the teaching and dispensing of the laws, and interpretation and direction in all sacred matters; the whole city being, as it were, reduced to an exact equality, the nobles excelling the rest in honor, the husbandmen in profit, and the artificers in number...

He also coined money, and stamped it with the image of an ox, either in memory of the Marathónian bull, or of Táurus, whom he vanquished, or else to put his people in mind to follow husbandry; and from this coin came the expression so frequent among the Greeks, of a thing being worth ten or a hundred oxen. After this he joined Mégara to Áttica, and erected that famous pillar on the Ísthmus, which bears an inscription of two lines, showing the bounds of the two countries that meet there. On the east side the inscription is, "Peloponnésus there, Iónia here," and on the west side, "Peloponnésus here, Iónia there."

He also instituted the games, in emulation of Hércules, being ambitious that as the Greeks, by that hero's appointment, celebrated the Olýmpian games to the honor of Júpiter, so, by his institution, they should celebrate the Ísthmian to the honor of Néptune.

– Plútarch, *Life of Théseus* (translated by John Dryden)

## Théseus Unites Twelve Cities

It suffices, then, to add thus much: According to Philóchorus, when the country was being devastated, both from the sea by the Cárians, and from the land by the Bœótians, who were called Aónians, Cécrops first settled the multitude in twelve cities, the names of which were Cecrópia, Tetrápolis, Epácria, Decélea, Eléusis, Aphídna (also called Aphídnæ, in the plural), Thóricus, Bráuron, Cythérus, Sphéttus, and Cephísia. At a later time Théseus is said to have united the twelve into one city, that of today. Now in earlier times the Athénians were ruled by kings; and then they changed to a democracy; but tyrants assailed them, Pisístratus and his sons; and later an oligarchy arose, not only that of the four hundred, but also that of the thirty tyrants, who were set over them by the Lacedæmónians; of these they easily rid themselves, and preserved the democracy until the Róman conquest. For even though they were molested for a short time by the Macedónian kings, and were even forced to obey them, they at least kept the general type of their government...

— Strábo, *Geography*, X.1.20 (translated by H. L. Jones)

## The Athénian Constitution Before Dráco

Now the ancient constitution, as it existed before the time of Dráco, was organized as follows. The magistrates were elected according to qualifications of birth and wealth. At first they governed for life, but subsequently for terms of ten years. The first magistrates, both in date and in importance, were the King, the Pólemarch, and the Árchon. The earliest of these offices was that of the King, which existed from ancestral antiquity. To this was added, secondly, the office of Pólemarch, on account of some of the kings proving feeble in war; for it was on this account that Íon was invited to accept the post on an occasion of pressing need. The last of the three offices was that of the Árchon... The Thesmóthetæ were appointed many years afterwards, when these offices had already become annual, with the object that they might publicly record all legal decisions, and act as guardians of them with a view to determining the issues between litigants. Accordingly their office, alone of those which have been mentioned, was never of more than annual duration.

Such, then, is the relative chronological precedence of these offices. At that time the nine Árchons did not all live together. The King occupied the building now known as the Bucólium, near the Prytanéum, as may be seen from the fact that even to the present day the marriage of the King's wife to Dionýsus takes place there. The Árchon lived in the Prytanéum, the Pólemarch in the Epilycéum. The latter building was formerly called the Polemarchéum, but after Epílycus, during his term of office as Pólemarch, had rebuilt it and fitted it up, it was called the Epilycéum. The Thesmóthetæ occupied the Thesmothetéum. In the time of Sólon, however, they all came together into the Thesmothetéum. They had power to decide cases finally on their own authority, not, as now, merely to hold a preliminary hearing. Such then was the arrangement of the magistracies. The Council of Areópagus had as its constitutionally assigned duty the protection of the laws; but in point of fact it administered the greater and most important part of the government of the state and inflicted personal punishments and fines summarily upon all who misbehaved themselves. This was the natural consequence of the facts that the Árchons were elected under qualifications of birth and wealth, and that the Areópagus was composed of those who had served as Árchons; for which latter reason the membership of the Areópagus is the only office which has continued to be a life-magistracy to the present day.

— School of Áristotle, *Athénian Constitution*, 3 (translated by Frederic G. Kenyon)

## The Constitution of Dráco

Such was, in outline, the first constitution, but not very long after the events above recorded ... Dráco enacted his ordinances. Now his constitution had the following form. The franchise was given to all who could furnish themselves with a military equipment. The nine Árchons and the Treasurers were elected by this body from persons possessing an unencumbered property of not less than ten mínas, the less important officials from those who could furnish themselves with a military equipment, and the generals [Stratégi] and commanders of the cavalry [Hippárchi] from those who could show an unencumbered property of not less than a hundred mínas, and had children born in lawful wedlock over ten years of age. These officers were required to hold to bail the Prýtanes, the Stratégi, and the Hippárchi of the preceding year until their accounts had been audited, taking four securities of the same class as that to which the Stratégi and the Hippárchi belonged. There was also to be a Council, consisting of four hundred and one members, elected by lot from among those who possessed the franchise. Both for this and for the other magistracies the lot was cast among those who were over thirty years of age; and no one might hold office twice until everyone else had had his turn, after which they were to cast the lot afresh. If any member of the Council failed to attend when there was a sitting of the Council or of the Assembly, he paid a fine... The Council of Areópagus was guardian of the laws and kept watch over the magistrates to see that they executed their offices in accordance with the laws. Any person who felt himself wronged might lay an information before the Council of Areópagus, on declaring what law was broken by the wrong done to him. But, as has been said before, loans were secured upon the persons of the debtors, and the land was in the hands of a few.

— School of Áristotle, *Athénian Constitution*, 3 (translated by Frederic G. Kenyon)


## II. SÓLON AND THE ATHÉNIAN ARISTOCRACY


### Sólon and Tháles

Sólon went, they say, to Tháles at Milétus, and wondered that Tháles took no care to get himself a wife and children. To this, Tháles made no answer for the present; but, a few days after, procured a stranger to pretend that he had left Áthens ten days ago; and Sólon inquiring what news there, the man, according to his instructions, replied, "None but a young man's funeral, which the whole city attended; for he was the son, they said, of an honorable man, the most virtuous of the citizens, who was not then at home, but had been traveling a long time." Sólon replied, "What a miserable man is he! But what was his name?" "I have heard it," says the man, "but have now forgotten it—only there was great talk of his wisdom and his justice." Thus Sólon was drawn on by every answer, and his fears heightened, till at last, being extremely concerned, he mentioned his own name, and asked the stranger if that young man was called Sólon's son; and the stranger assenting, he began to beat his head, and to do and say all that is usual with men in transports of grief. But Tháles took his hand, and, with a smile, said, "These things, Sólon, keep me from marriage and rearing children, which are too great for even your constancy to support; however, be not concerned at the report, for it is a fiction."

– Plútarch, *Life of Sólon* (translated by John Dryden)


### Sólon and the Cylónian Pollution

Now the Cylónian pollution had a long while disturbed the commonwealth, ever since the time when Megácles the Árchon persuaded the conspirators with Cýlon that took sanctuary in Minérva's temple to come down and stand to a fair trial. And they, tying a thread to the image, and holding one end of it, went down to the tribunal; but when they came to the temple of the Fúries, the thread broke of its own accord, upon which, as if the goddess had refused them protection, they were seized by Megácles and the other magistrates; as many as were without the temples were stoned, those that fled for sanctuary were butchered at the altar, and only those escaped who made supplication to the wives of the magistrates. But they from that time were considered under pollution and regarded with hatred. The remainder of the faction of Cýlon grew strong again, and had continual quarrels with the family of Megácles; and now the quarrel being at its height, and the people divided, Sólon, being in reputation, interposed with the chiefest of the Athénians, and by entreaty and admonition persuaded the polluted to submit to a trial and the decision of three hundred noble citizens. And Mýron of Phlýa being their accuser, they were found guilty, and as many as were then alive were banished, and the bodies of the dead were dug up, and scattered beyond the confines of the country. In the midst of these distractions, the Megárians fell upon them and they lost Nisǽa and Sálamis again; besides, the city was disturbed with superstitious fears and strange appearances, and the priests declared that the sacrifices intimated some villainies and pollutions that were to be expiated. Upon this, they sent for Epiménides the Phǽstian from Crete, who is counted the seventh wise man by those that will not admit Periánder into the number. He seems to have been thought a favorite of heaven, possessed of knowledge in all the supernatural and ritual parts of religion; and, therefore, the men of his age called him a new Cúres, and son of a nymph named Bálte. When he came to Áthens, and grew acquainted with Sólon, he served him in many instances, and prepared the way for his legislation. He made them moderate in their forms of worship, and abated their mourning by ordering some sacrifices presently after the funeral, and taking off those severe and barbarous ceremonies which the women usually practiced; but the greatest benefit was his purifying and sanctifying the city by certain propitiatory and expiatory lustrations, and founding sacred buildings—by that means making them more submissive to justice, and more inclined to harmony.

– Plútarch, Life of Sólon (translated by John Dryden)

## The Debt Burden

The Athénians, now that the Cylónian sedition was over and the polluted gone into banishment, fell into their old quarrels about the government, there being as many different parties as there were diversities in the country. The Hill quarter favored democracy, the Plain, oligarchy, and those that lived by the Seaside stood for a mixed sort of government, and so hindered either of the other parties from prevailing. And the disparity of fortune between the rich and the poor, at that time, also reached its height; so that the city seemed to be in a truly dangerous condition, and no other means for freeing it from disturbances and settling it to be possible but a despotic power. All the people were indebted to the rich; and either they tilled their land for their creditors, paying them a sixth part of the increase, and were, therefore, called Hectemórii and Thétes, or else they engaged their body for the debt, and might be seized, and either sent into slavery at home, or sold to strangers; some (for no law forbade it) were forced to sell their children, or fly their country to avoid the cruelty of their creditors; but the most part and the bravest of them began to combine together and encourage one another to stand up to it and choose a leader, to liberate the condemned debtors, divide the land, and change the government.

– Plútarch, Life of Sólon (translated by John Dryden)

## The Reforms of Sólon

First, then, he repealed all Dráco's laws, except those concerning homicide, because they were too severe, and the punishments too great; for death was appointed for almost all offenses, insomuch that those that were convicted of idleness were to die, and those that stole a cabbage or an apple to suffer even as villains that committed sacrilege or murder. So that Démades, in after time, was thought to have said very happily, that Dráco's laws were written not with ink, but blood; and he himself, being once asked why he made death the punishment of most offenses, replied, "Small ones deserve that, and I have no higher for the greater crimes."

Next, Sólon, being willing to continue the magistracies in the hands of the rich men, and yet receive the people into the other part of the government, took an account of the citizens' estates, and those that were worth five hundred measures of fruits, dry and liquid, he placed in the first rank, calling them Pentacósio-medímni; those that could keep an horse, or were worth three hundred measures, were named Híppeis, and made the second class; the Zéugitæ, that had two hundred measures, were in the third; and all the others were called Thétes, who were not admitted to any office, but could come to the assembly, and act as jurors; which at first seemed nothing, but afterwards was found an enormous privilege, as almost every matter of dispute came before them in this latter capacity. Even in the cases which he assigned to the Árchons' cognizance, he allowed an appeal to the courts. Besides, it is said that he was obscure and ambiguous in the wording of his laws, on purpose to increase the honor of his courts; for since their differences could not be adjusted by the letter, they would have to bring all their causes to the judges, who thus were in a manner masters of the laws...

And for the greater security of the weak commons, he gave general liberty of indicting for an act of injury; if any one was beaten, maimed, or suffered any violence, any man that would and was able, might prosecute the wrongdoer; intending by this to accustom the citizens, like members of the same body, to resent and be sensible of one another's injuries. And there is a saying of his agreeable to this law, for, being asked what city was best modeled, "That," said he, "where those that are not injured try and punish the unjust as much as those that are."

When he had constituted the Areópagus of those who had been yearly Árchons, of which he himself was a member therefore, observing that the people, now free from their debts, were unsettled and imperious, he formed another council of four hundred, a hundred out of each of the four tribes, which was to inspect all matters before they were propounded to the people, and to take care that nothing but what had been first examined should be brought before the general assembly. The upper council, or Areópagus, he made inspectors and keepers of the laws, conceiving that the commonwealth, held by these two councils, like anchors, would be less liable to be tossed by tumults, and the people be more at quiet.

– Plútarch, *Life of Sólon* (translated by John Dryden)

## The Constitution of Sólon

As soon as he was at the head of affairs, Sólon liberated the people once and for all, by prohibiting all loans on the security of the debtor's person: and in addition he made laws by which he cancelled all debts, public and private. This measure is commonly called the "removal of burdens," since thereby the people had their loads removed from them... Next Sólon drew up a constitution and enacted new laws; and the ordinances of Dráco ceased to be used, with the exception of those relating to murder. The laws were inscribed on the wooden stands, and set up in the King's Porch, and all swore to obey them; and the nine Árchons made oath upon the stone, declaring that they would dedicate a golden statue if they should transgress any of them. This is the origin of the oath to that effect which they take to the present day. Sólon ratified his laws for a hundred years...

– Plútarch, *Life of Sólon* (translated by John Dryden)

### III. PISÍSTRATUS AND THE ATHÉNIAN TYRANNY

## The Rise of Pisístratus

This Pisístratus, at a time when there was civil contention in Áttica between the party of the Seacoast headed by Megácles the son of Alcmǽon, and that of the Plain headed by Lycúrgus, one of the Aristoláïds, formed the project of making himself tyrant, and with this view created a third party. Gathering together a band of partisans and giving himself out for the protector of the Highlanders, he contrived the following stratagem. He wounded himself and his mules, and then drove his chariot into the marketplace, professing to have just escaped an attack of his enemies, who had attempted his life as he was on his way into the country. He besought the people to assign him a guard to protect his person, reminding them of the glory which he had gained when he led the attack upon the Megárians, and took the town of Nisæa, at the same time performing many other exploits. The Athénians, deceived by his story, appointed him a band of citizens to serve as a guard, who were to carry clubs instead of spears, and to accompany him wherever he went. Thus strengthened, Pisístratus broke into revolt and seized the citadel. In this way he acquired the sovereignty of Áthens, which he continued to hold without disturbing the previously existing offices or altering any of the laws. He administered the state according to the established usages, and his arrangements were wise and salutary.

However, after a little time, the partisans of Megácles and those of Lycúrgus agreed to forget their differences, and united to drive him out. So Pisístratus, having by the means described first made himself master of Áthens, lost his power again before it had time to take root. No sooner, however, was he departed than the factions which had driven him out quarreled anew, and at last Megácles, wearied with the struggle, sent a herald to Pisístratus, with an offer to reestablish him on the throne if he would marry his daughter. Pisístratus consented, and on these terms an agreement was concluded between the two, after which they proceeded to devise the mode of his restoration. And here the device on which they hit was the silliest that I find on record, more especially considering that the Greeks have been from very ancient times distinguished from the barbarians by superior sagacity and freedom from foolish simpleness, and remembering that the persons on whom this trick was played were not only Greeks but Athénians, who have the credit of surpassing all other Greeks in cleverness. There was in the Pæánian district a woman named Phýa, whose height only fell short of four cúbits by three fingers' breadth, and who was altogether comely to look upon. This woman they clothed in complete armor, and, instructing her as to the carriage which she was to maintain in order to beseem her part, they placed her in a chariot and drove to the city. Heralds had been sent forward to precede her, and to make proclamation to this effect: "Citizens of Áthens, receive again Pisístratus with friendly minds. Minérva, who of all men honors him the most, herself conducts him back to her own citadel." This they proclaimed in all directions, and immediately the rumor spread throughout the country districts that Minérva was bringing back her favorite. They of the city also, fully persuaded that the woman was the veritable goddess, prostrated themselves before her, and received Pisístratus back.

Pisístratus, having thus recovered the sovereignty, married, according to agreement, the daughter of Megácles. As, however, he had already a family of grown up sons, and the Alcmæónidæ were supposed to be under a curse, he determined that there should be no issue of the marriage. His wife at first kept this matter to herself, but after a time, either her mother questioned her, or it may be that she told it of her own accord. At any rate, she informed her mother, and so it reached her father's ears. Megácles, indignant at receiving an affront from such a quarter, in his anger instantly made up his differences with the opposite faction, on which Pisístratus, aware of what was planning against him, took himself out of the country. Arrived at Erétria, he held a council with his children to decide what was to be done. The opinion of Híppias prevailed, and it was agreed to aim at regaining the sovereignty. The first step was to obtain advances of money from such states as were under obligations to them. By these means they collected large sums from several countries, especially from the Thébans, who gave them far more than any of the rest. To be brief, time passed, and all was at length got ready for their return. A band of Árgos mercenaries arrived from the Peloponnésus, and a certain Náxian named Lýgdamis, who volunteered his services, was particularly zealous in the cause, supplying both men and money.

In the eleventh year of their exile the family of Pisístratus set sail from Erétria on their return home. They made the coast of Áttica, near Márathon, where they encamped, and were joined by their partisans from the capital and by numbers from the country districts, who loved tyranny better than freedom. At Áthens, while Pisístratus was obtaining funds, and even after he landed at Márathon, no one paid any attention to his proceedings. When, however, it became known that he had left Márathon, and was marching upon the city, preparations were made for resistance, the whole force of the state was levied, and led against the returning exiles. Meantime the army of Pisístratus, which had broken up from Márathon, meeting their adversaries near the temple of the Pallénian Minérva, pitched their camp opposite them.

... The Athénians from the city had just finished their midday meal, after which they had betaken themselves, some to dice, others to sleep, when Pisístratus with his troops fell upon them and put them to the rout. As soon as the flight began, Pisístratus bethought himself of a most wise contrivance, whereby they might be induced to disperse and not unite in a body anymore. He mounted his sons on horseback and sent them on in front to overtake the fugitives, and exhort them to be of good cheer, and return each man to his home. The Athénians took the advice, and Pisístratus became for the third time master of Áthens.

Upon this he set himself to root his power more firmly, by the aid of a numerous body of mercenaries, and by keeping up a full exchequer, partly supplied from native sources, partly from the countries about the river Strýmon. He also demanded hostages from many of the Athénians who had remained at home and had not left Áthens at his approach; and these he sent to Náxos, which he had conquered by force of arms, and given over into the charge of Lýgdamis.

— Heródotus, *History*, I.59-64 (translated by George Rawlinson)

## The Banishment of the Pisístradæ

Upon the death of Hippárchus, Híppias, who was king, grew harsh towards the Athénians; and the Alcmæónidæ, an Athénian family which had been banished by the Pisistrátidæ, joined the other exiles, and endeavored to procure their own return and to free Áthens by force... They therefore resolved to shrink from no contrivance that might bring them success; and accordingly they contracted with the Amphíctyons to build the temple which now stands at Délphi, but which in those days did not exist. Having done this, they proceeded, being men of great wealth and members of an ancient and distinguished family, to build the temple much more magnificently than the plan obliged them. Besides other improvements, instead of the coarse stone whereof by the contract the temple was to have been constructed, they made the facings of Párian marble.

These same men, if we may believe the Athénians, during their stay at Délphi persuaded the Pýthoness by a bribe to tell the Spártans, whenever any of them came to consult the oracle, either on their own private affairs or on the business of the state, that they must free Áthens...

Afterwards, the Lacedæmónians dispatched a larger force against Áthens, which they put under the command of Cleómenes, son of Anaxándridas, one of their kings. These troops were not sent by sea, but marched by the mainland. When they were come into Áttica, their first encounter was with the Thessálian horse, which they shortly put to flight, killing above forty men; the remainder made good their escape, and fled straight to Théssaly. Cleómenes proceeded to the city, and, with the aid of such of the Athénians as wished for freedom, besieged the tyrants, who had shut themselves up in the Pelásgic fortress.

And now there had been small chance of the Pisistrátidæ falling into the hands of the Spártans, who did not even design to sit down before the place, which had moreover been well provisioned beforehand with stores both of meat and drink—nay, it is likely that after a few days' blockade the Lacedæmónians would have quitted Áttica altogether, and gone back to Spárta—had not an event occurred most unlucky for the besieged and most advantageous for the besiegers. The children of the Pisistrátidæ were made prisoners, as they were being removed out of the country. By this calamity all their plans were deranged, and—as the ransom of their children—they consented to the demands of the Athénians and agreed within five days' time to quit Áttica. Accordingly, they soon afterwards left the country, and withdrew to Sigéum on the Scamánder, after reigning thirty-six years over the Athénians...

— Heródotus, *History*, V.62-65 (translated by George Rawlinson)


## IV. CLÍSTHENES AND THE ATHÉNIAN DEMOCRACY

### Clísthenes Returns from Exile

The Athénian Clísthenes, who was grandson by the mother's side of the other, and had been named after him, resolved, from contempt (as I believe) of the Iónians, that his tribes should not be the same as theirs; and so followed the pattern set him by his namesake of Sícyon. Having brought entirely over to his own side the common people of Áthens, whom he had before disdained, he gave all the tribes new names, and made the number greater than formerly; instead of the four phýlarchs he established ten; he likewise placed ten demes in each of the tribes; and he was, now that the common people took his part, very much more powerful than his adversaries. Iságoras in his turn lost ground; and therefore, to counterplot his enemy, he called in Cleómenes the Lacedæmónian, who had already, at the time when he was besieging the Pisistrátidæ, made a contract of friendship with him... At this time the first thing that he did was to send a herald and require that Clísthenes, and a large number of Athénians besides, whom he called "The Accursed," should leave Áthens. This message he sent at the suggestion of Iságoras: for in the affair referred to, the blood-guiltiness lay on the Alcmæónidæ and their partisans, while he and his friends were quite clear of it....

When the message of Cleómenes arrived, requiring Clísthenes and "The Accursed" to quit the city, Clísthenes departed of his own accord. Cleómenes, however, notwithstanding his departure, came to Áthens, with a small band of followers; and on his arrival sent into banishment seven hundred Athénian families, which were pointed out to him by Iságoras. Succeeding here, he next endeavored to dissolve the council, and to put the government into the hands of three hundred of the partisans of that leader. But the council resisted, and refused to obey his orders; whereupon Cleómenes, Iságoras, and their followers took possession of the citadel. Here they were attacked by the rest of the Athénians, who took the side of the council, and were besieged for the space of two days: on the third day they accepted terms, being allowed—at least such of them as were Lacedæmónians—to quit the country. And so the word which came to Cleómenes received its fulfillment. For when he first went up into the citadel, meaning to seize it, just as he was entering the sanctuary of the goddess, in order to question her, the priestess arose from her throne, before he had passed the doors, and said, "Stranger from Lacedǣmon, depart hence, and presume not to enter the holy place; it is not lawful for a Dórian to set foot there." But he answered, "Oh! woman, I am not a Dórian, but an Achǣan." Slighting this warning, Cleómenes made his attempt, and so he was forced to retire, together with his Lacedæmónians. The rest were cast into prison by the Athénians, and condemned to die...

So these men died in prison. The Athénians directly afterwards recalled Clísthenes, and the seven hundred families which Cleómenes had driven out; and, further, they sent envoys to Sárdis, to make an alliance with the Pérsians, for they knew that war would follow with Cleómenes and the Lacedæmónians.

— Heródotus, *History*, V.69-73 (translated by George Rawlinson)

## The Situation of Politicians

The fable of Ixíon, who, embracing a cloud instead of Júno, begot the Céntaurs, has been ingeniously enough supposed to have been invented to represent to us ambitious men, whose minds, doting on glory, which is a mere image of virtue, produce nothing that is genuine or uniform, but only, as might be expected of such a conjunction, misshapen and unnatural actions. Running after their emulations and passions, and carried away by the impulses of the moment, they may say with the herdsmen, in the tragedy of Sóphocles,

We follow these, though born their rightful lords,
And they command us, though they speak no words.

For this is indeed the true condition of men in public life, who, to gain the vain title of being the people's leaders and governors, are content to make themselves the slaves and followers of all the people's humors and caprices. For as the lookout men at the ship's prow, though they see what is ahead before the men at the helm, yet constantly look back to the pilots there, and obey the orders they give; so these men steered, as I may say, by popular applause, though they bear the name of governors, are in reality the mere underlings of the multitude. The man who is completely wise and virtuous has no need at all of glory, except so far as it disposes and eases his way to action by the greater trust that it procures him ...

When this passion [for glory] is exorbitant, it is dangerous in all men, and in those who govern a commonwealth, utterly destructive. For in the possession of large power and authority, it transports men to a degree of madness; so that now they no more think what is good to be glorious, but will have only those actions esteemed good that are glorious. As Phócion, therefore, answered king Antípater, who sought his approbation of some unworthy action, "I cannot be your flatterer, and your friend," so these men should answer the people, "I cannot govern, and obey you." For it may happen to the commonwealth, as to the serpent in the fable, whose tail, rising in rebellion against the head, complained, as of a great grievance, that it was always forced to follow, and required that it should be permitted by turns to lead the way. And taking the command accordingly, it soon indicted by its senseless courses mischiefs in abundance upon itself, while the head was torn and lacerated with following, contrary to nature, a guide that was deaf and blind. And such we see to have been the lot of many, who, submitting to be guided by the inclinations of an uninformed and unreasoning multitude, could neither stop nor recover themselves out of the confusion.

– Plútarch, *Life of Ágis* (translated by John Dryden)

## On Governing the People

So it happens in political affairs; if the motions of rulers be constantly opposite and cross to the tempers and inclination of the people, they will be resented as arbitrary and harsh; as, on the other side, too much deference, or encouragement, as too often it has been, to popular faults and errors, is full of danger and ruinous consequences. But where concession is the response to willing obedience, and a statesman gratifies his people, that he may the more imperatively recall them to a sense of the common interest, then, indeed, human beings, who are ready enough to serve well and submit to much, if they are not always ordered about and roughly handled, like slaves, may be said to be guided and governed upon the method that leads to safety. Though it must be confessed, it is a nice point and extremely difficult, so to temper this lenity as to preserve the authority of the government. But if such a blessed mixture and temperament may be obtained, it seems to be of all concords and harmonies the most concordant and most harmonious. For thus we are taught even God governs the world, not by irresistible force, but persuasive argument and reason, controlling it into compliance with his eternal purposes.

– Plútarch, *Life of Phócion* (translated by John Dryden)

# CHAPTER XI.

## THE EXPANSION OF GREECE — THE COLONIES

The Extension of Héllas, I.—The Eastern Colonies of Héllas, II.—The Western Colonies of Héllas, III.

## I. THE EXTENSION OF HÉLLAS

### The Rise of Greek Sea Power

But as the power of Héllas grew, and the acquisition of wealth became more an object, the revenues of the states increasing, tyrannies were by their means established almost everywhere—the old form of government being hereditary monarchy with definite prerogatives—and Héllas began to fit out fleets and apply herself more closely to the sea. It is said that the Corínthians were the first to approach the modern style of naval architecture, and that Córinth was the first place in Héllas where galleys were built... Again, the earliest sea-fight in history was between the Corínthians and Corcýræans; this was about two hundred and sixty years ago, dating from the same time. Planted on an isthmus, Córinth had from time out of mind been a commercial emporium; as formerly almost all communication between the Héllenes within and without Peloponnésus was carried on overland, and the Corínthian territory was the highway through which it travelled. She had consequently great money resources, as is shown by the epithet "wealthy" bestowed by the old poets on the place, and this enabled her, when traffic by sea became more common, to procure her navy and put down piracy; and as she could offer a mart for both branches of the trade, she acquired for herself all the power which a large revenue affords.

Subsequently the Iónians attained to great naval strength in the reign of Cýrus, the first king of the Pérsians, and of his son Cambýses, and while they were at war with the former commanded for a while the Iónian sea. Polýcrates also, the tyrant of Sámos, had a powerful navy in the reign of Cambýses, with which he reduced many of the islands, and among them Rhenéa, which he consecrated to the Délian Apóllo. About this time also the Phocǽans, while they were founding Massília [Marseilles], defeated the Carthagínians in a sea-fight. These were the most powerful navies. And even these, although so many generations had elapsed since the Trójan war, seem to have been principally composed of the old fifty-oars and long-boats, and to have counted few galleys among their ranks. Indeed, it was only shortly the Pérsian war, and the death of Daríus the successor of Cambýses, that the Sicílian tyrants and the Corcýræans acquired any large number of galleys. For after these there were no navies of any account in Héllas till the expedition of Xérxes; Ægína, Áthens, and others may have possessed a few vessels, but they were principally fifty-oars. It was quite at the end of this period that the war with Ægína and the prospect of the barbarian invasion enabled Themístocles to persuade the Athénians to build the fleet with which they fought at Sálamis; and even these vessels had not complete decks.

... All their insignificance did not prevent their being an element of the greatest power to those who cultivated them, alike in revenue and in dominion. They were the means by which the islands were reached and reduced, those of the smallest area falling the easiest prey. Wars by land there were none, none at least by which power was acquired; we have the usual border contests, but of distant expeditions with conquest for object we hear nothing among the Héllenes. There was no union of subject cities round a great state, no spontaneous combination of equals for confederate expeditions; what fighting there was consisted merely of local warfare between rival neighbors.

– Thucýdides, *Peloponnésian War*, I.13-15 (translated by Richard Crawley)

## The Foundation of Byzántium

The Horn, which is close to the wall of the Býzantines, is a gulf that extends approximately towards the west for a distance of sixty stádia; it resembles a stag's horn, for it is split into numerous gulfs—branches, as it were. The fish rush into these gulfs and are easily caught—because of their numbers, the force of the current that drives them together, and the narrowness of the gulfs; in fact, because of the narrowness of the area, they are even caught by hand. Now these fish are hatched in the marshes of Lake Mæótis, and when they have gained a little strength they rush out through the mouth of the lake in schools and move along the Ásian shore as far as Trapézus and Pharnácia. It is here that the catching of the fish first takes place, though the catch is not considerable, for the fish have not yet grown to their normal size. But when they reach Sinópe, they are mature enough for catching and salting. Yet ... the creatures take such fright at a certain white rock which projects from the Chalcedónian shore that they forthwith turn to the opposite shore. There they are caught by the current, and since at the same time the region is so formed by nature as to turn the current of the sea there to Byzántium and the Horn at Byzántium, they naturally are driven together thither and thus afford the Býzantines and the Róman people considerable revenue. But the Chalcedónians, though situated nearby, on the opposite shore, have no share in this abundance, because the fish do not approach their harbors; hence the saying that Apóllo, when the men who founded Byzántium at a time subsequent to the founding of Chalcédon by the Megárians consulted the oracle, ordered them to "make their settlement opposite the blind," thus calling the Chalcedónians "blind", because, although they sailed the regions in question at an earlier time, they failed to take possession of the country on the far side, with all its wealth, and chose the poorer country.

– Strábo, *Geography*, VII.6.2 (translated by H. L. Jones)

## Náucratis in Égypt

It is said that the reign of Amásis was the most prosperous time that Égypt ever saw; the river was more liberal to the land, and the land brought forth more abundantly for the service of man than had ever been known before; while the number of inhabited cities was not less than twenty thousand. It was this king Amásis who established the law that every Egýptian should appear once a year before the governor of his canton, and show his means of living; or, failing to do so, and to prove that he got an honest livelihood, should be put to death. Sólon the Athénian borrowed this law from the Egýptians, and imposed it on his countrymen, who have observed it ever since. It is indeed an excellent custom.

Amásis was partial to the Greeks, and among other favors which he granted them, gave to such as liked to settle in Égypt the city of Náucratis for their residence. To those who only wished to trade upon the coast, and did not want to fix their abode in the country, he granted certain lands where they might set up altars and erect temples to the gods. Of these temples the grandest and most famous, which is also the most frequented, is that called "the Hellénium." It was built conjointly by the Iónians, Dórians, and Æólians, the following cities taking part in the work: the Iónian states of Chíos, Téos, Phocǽa, and Clazómenæ; Rhodes, Cnídus, Halicarnássus, and Phasélis of the Dórians; and Mytiléne of the Æólians. These are the states to whom the temple belongs, and they have the right of appointing the governors of the factory; the other cities which claim a share in the building, claim what in no sense belongs to them. Three nations, however, consecrated for themselves separate temples: the Ægínetans one to Júpiter, the Sámians to Júno, and the Milésians to Apóllo.

In ancient times there was no factory but Náucratis in the whole of Égypt; and if a person entered one of the other mouths of the Nile, he was obliged to swear that he had not come there of his own free will. Having so done, he was bound to sail in his ship to the Canópic mouth, or were that impossible owing to contrary winds, he must take his wares by boat all round the Delta, and so bring them to Náucratis, which had an exclusive privilege.

— Heródotus, History, II.177-179 (translated by George Rawlinson)

## III. THE WESTERN COLONIES OF HÉLLAS

## The Origin of Náples

After Dicæárchia comes Neápolis [Náples], a city of the Cumæans. At a later time, it was re-colonized by Chalcídians, and also by some Pithecúsæans and Athénians, and hence, for this reason, was called Neápolis. A monument of Parthénope, one of the Sírens, is pointed out in Neápolis, and in accordance with an oracle a gymnastic contest is celebrated there. But at a still later time, as the result of a dissension, they admitted some of the Campáni as fellow-inhabitants, and thus they were forced to treat their worst enemies as their best friends, now that they had alienated their proper friends. This is disclosed by the names of their démarchs, for the earliest names are Greek only, whereas the later are Greek mixed with Campánian.

– Strábo, Geography, V.4.7 (translated by H. L. Jones)

## Cities of Mágna Grǽcia

After the mouth of the Sílaris one comes to Lucánia, and to the temple of the Árgoan Héra, built by Jason, and near by, within fifty stádia, to Posidónia. Thence, sailing out past the gulf, one comes to Leucósia, an island, from which it is only a short voyage across to the continent. The island is named after one of the Sírens, who was cast ashore here after the Sírens had flung themselves, as the myth has it, into the depths of the sea. In front of the island lies that promontory which is opposite the Sirenúsæ and with them forms the Posidónian Gulf. On doubling this promontory one comes immediately to another gulf, in which there is a city ... called by the men of today "Élea." This is the native city of Parménides and Zéno, the Pythagoréan philosophers.

It is my opinion that not only through the influence of these men but also in still earlier times the city was well governed; and it was because of this good government that the people not only held their own against the Lucáni and the Posidónians, but even returned victorious, although they were inferior to them both in extent of territory and in population. At any rate, they are compelled, on account of the poverty of their soil, to busy themselves mostly with the sea and to establish factories for the salting of fish, and other such industries. According to Antíochus, after the capture of Phocǽa by Hárpagus, the general of Cýrus, all the Phocǽans who could do so embarked with their entire families on their light boats and, under the leadership of Creontíades, sailed first to Cýrnus and Massília [Marseilles], but when they were beaten off from those places founded Élea. It is about two hundred stádia distant from Posidónia...

Rhégium was founded by the Chalcídians who, it is said, in accordance with an oracle, were dedicated, one man out of every ten Chalcídians, to Apóllo, because of a dearth of crops, but later on emigrated hither from Délphi, taking with them still others from their home. But according to Antíochus, the Zanclǽans sent for the Chalcídians and appointed Antimnéstus their founder-in-chief. To this colony also belonged the refugees of the Peloponnésian Messénians who had been defeated by the men of the opposing faction. These men were unwilling to be punished by the Lacedæmónians for the violation of the maidens which took place at Límnæ, though they were themselves guilty of the outrage done to the maidens, who had been sent there for a religious rite, and had also killed those who came to their aid. So the refugees, after withdrawing to Macístus, sent a deputation to the oracle of the god to find fault with Apóllo and Ártemis if such was to be their fate in return for their trying to avenge those gods, and also to enquire how they, now utterly ruined, might be saved. Apóllo bade them go forth with the Chalcídians to Rhégium, and to be grateful to his sister; for, he added, they were not ruined, but saved, inasmuch as they were surely not to perish along with their native land, which would be captured a little later by the Spártans...

Sýracuse was founded by Árchias, who sailed from Córinth about the same time that Náxos and Mégara were colonized. It is said that Árchias went to Délphi at the same time as Myscéllus, and when they were consulting the oracle, the god asked them whether they chose wealth or health; now Árchias chose wealth, and Myscéllus health; accordingly, the god granted to the former to found Sýracuse, and to the latter Cróton. And it actually came to pass that the Crotóniates took up their abode in a city that was exceedingly healthful, as I have related, and that Sýracuse fell into such exceptional wealth that the name of the Syracúsans was spread abroad in a proverb applied to the excessively extravagant—"the tithe of the Syracúsans would not be sufficient for them."

– Strábo, *Geography*, VI.1.1,1.6,2.4 (translated by H. L. Jones)

# CHAPTER XII.

## THE CULTURE OF THE EARLY GREEK STATES

The Religious Culture of the Greeks, I.—The Beginnings of Greek Art, II.
The Greek Language and Early Literature, III.—Early Greek Philosophy, IV.

## I. THE RELIGIOUS CULTURE OF THE GREEKS

### The Olýmpic Games

It remains for me to tell about Olýmpia, and how everything fell into the hands of the people of Élis. The temple is ... less than three hundred stádia distant from Élis. In front of the temple is situated a grove of wild olive-trees, and the stádium is in this grove. Past the temple flows the Álpheus, which, rising in Arcádia, flows between the west and the south into the Triphýlian Sea. At the outset the temple got fame on account of the oracle of the Olýmpian Zeus; and yet, after the oracle failed to respond, the glory of the temple persisted none the less, and it received all that increase of fame of which we know, on account both of the festal assembly and of the Olýmpian Games, in which the prize was a crown and which were regarded as sacred, the greatest games in the world. The temple was adorned by its numerous offerings, which were dedicated there from all parts of Greece. Among these was the Zeus of beaten gold dedicated by ... the tyrant of Córinth... The Éleans above all others are to be credited both with the magnificence of the temple at Olýmpia and with the honor in which it was held... What is more, the Olýmpian Games are an invention of theirs; and it was they who celebrated the first Olýmpiads, for one should disregard the ancient stories both of the founding of the temple and of the establishment of the games—some alleging that it was Héracles ... who was the originator of both... It is nearer the truth to say that from the first Olýmpiad ... until the twenty-sixth Olýmpiad, the Éleans had charge both of the temple and of the games.

– Strábo, *Geography*, VIII.3.30 (translated by H. L. Jones)

## II. THE BEGINNINGS OF GREEK ART

### Principles of Architecture

1. Architecture depends on Order (in Greek τάξις), Arrangement (in Greek διάθεσις), Eurythmy, Symmetry, Propriety, and Economy (in Greek οἰκονομία).

2. Order gives due measure to the members of a work considered separately, and symmetrical agreement to the proportions of the whole. It is an adjustment according to quantity (in Greek ποσότης). By this I mean the selection of modules from the members of the work itself and, starting from these individual parts of members, constructing the whole work to correspond. Arrangement includes the putting of things in their proper places and the elegance of effect which is due to adjustments appropriate to the character of the work. Its forms of expression (in Greek ἰδέαι) are these: ground plan, elevation, and perspective. A ground plan is made by the proper successive use of compasses and rule, through which we get outlines for the plane surfaces of buildings. An elevation is a picture of the front of a building, set upright and properly drawn in the proportions of the contemplated work. Perspective is the method of sketching a front with the sides withdrawing into the background, the lines all meeting in the center of a circle. All three come of reflection and invention. Reflection is careful and laborious thought, and watchful

attention directed to the agreeable effect of one's plan. Invention, on the other hand, is the solving of intricate problems and the discovery of new principles by means of brilliancy and versatility. These are the departments belonging under Arrangement.

3. Eurythmy is beauty and fitness in the adjustments of the members. This is found when the members of a work are of a height suited to their breadth, of a breadth suited to their length, and, in a word, when they all correspond symmetrically.

4. Symmetry is a proper agreement between the members of the work itself, and relation between the different parts and the whole general scheme, in accordance with a certain part selected as standard. Thus in the human body there is a kind of symmetrical harmony between forearm, foot, palm, finger, and other small parts; and so it is with perfect buildings. In the case of temples, symmetry may be calculated from the thickness of a column, from a triglyph, or even from a module; in the ballista, from the hole or from what the Greeks call the περίτρητος; in a ship, from the space between the tholepins (διάπηγμα); and in other things, from various members.

5. Propriety is that perfection of style which comes when a work is authoritatively constructed on approved principles. It arises from prescription (Greek θεματισμῷ), from usage, or from nature. From prescription, in the case of hypæthral edifices, open to the sky, in honor of Júpiter Lightning, the Heaven, the Sun, or the Moon: for these are gods whose semblances and manifestations we behold before our very eyes in the sky when it is cloudless and bright. The temples of Minérva, Mars, and Hércules, will be Dóric, since the virile strength of these gods makes daintiness entirely inappropriate to their houses. In temples to Vénus, Flóra, Prosérpina, Spring-Water, and the Nymphs, the Corínthian order will be found to have peculiar significance, because these are delicate divinities and so its rather slender outlines, its flowers, leaves, and ornamental volutes will lend propriety where it is due. The construction of temples of the Iónic order to Júno, Diána, Father Bácchus, and the other gods of that kind, will be in keeping with the middle position which they hold; for the building of such will be an appropriate combination of the severity of the Dóric and the delicacy of the Corínthian.

6. Propriety arises from usage when buildings having magnificent interiors are provided with elegant entrance-courts to correspond; for there will be no propriety in the spectacle of an elegant interior approached by a low, mean entrance. Or, if déntils be carved in the córnice of the Dóric entáblature or tríglyphs represented in the Iónic entáblature over the cushion-shaped cápitals of the columns, the effect will be spoilt by the transfer of the peculiarities of the one order of building to the other, the usage in each class having been fixed long ago.

7. Finally, propriety will be due to natural causes if, for example, in the case of all sacred precincts we select very healthy neighborhoods with suitable springs of water in the places where the fanes are to be built, particularly in the case of those to Æsculápius and to Health, gods by whose healing powers great numbers of the sick are apparently cured. For when their diseased bodies are transferred from an unhealthy to a healthy spot, and treated with waters from health-giving springs, they will the more speedily grow well. The result will be that the divinity will stand in higher esteem and find his dignity increased, all owing to the nature of his site. There will also be natural propriety in using an eastern light for bedrooms and libraries, a western light in winter for baths and winter apartments, and a northern light for picture galleries and other places in which a steady light is needed; for that quarter of the sky grows neither light nor dark with the course of the sun, but remains steady and unshifting all day long.

8. Economy denotes the proper management of materials and of site, as well as a thrifty balancing of cost and common sense in the construction of works. This will be observed if, in the first place, the architect does not demand things which cannot be found or made ready without great expense. For example: it is not everywhere that there is plenty of pit sand, rubble, fir, clear fir, and marble, since they are produced in different places and to assemble them is difficult and

costly. Where there is no pit sand, we must use the kinds washed up by rivers or by the sea; the lack of fir and clear fir may be evaded by using cypress, poplar, elm, or pine; and other problems we must solve in similar ways.

9. A second stage in Economy is reached when we have to plan the different kinds of dwellings suitable for ordinary householders, for great wealth, or for the high position of the statesman. A house in town obviously calls for one form of construction; that into which stream the products of country estates requires another; this will not be the same in the case of money-lenders and still different for the opulent and luxurious; for the powers under whose deliberations the commonwealth is guided dwellings are to be provided according to their special needs: and, in a word, the proper form of economy must be observed in building houses for each and every class.

— Vitrúvius, *The Ten Books on Architecture*, 1.2 (translated by Morris Hicky Morgan)

## Symmetry in Temple Design

1. The design of a temple depends on symmetry, the principles of which must be most carefully observed by the architect. They are due to proportion, in Greek ἀναλογία. Proportion is a correspondence among the measures of the members of an entire work, and of the whole to a certain part selected as standard. From this result the principles of symmetry. Without symmetry and proportion there can be no principles in the design of any temple; that is, if there is no precise relation between its members, as in the case of those of a well shaped man.

2. For the human body is so designed by nature that the face, from the chin to the top of the forehead and the lowest roots of the hair, is a tenth part of the whole height; the open hand from the wrist to the tip of the middle finger is just the same; the head from the chin to the crown is an eighth, and with the neck and shoulder from the top of the breast to the lowest roots of the hair is a sixth; from the middle of the breast to the summit of the crown is a fourth. If we take the height of the face itself, the distance from the bottom of the chin to the under side of the nostrils is one third of it; the nose from the under side of the nostrils to a line between the eyebrows is the same; from there to the lowest roots of the hair is also a third, comprising the forehead. The length of the foot is one sixth of the height of the body; of the forearm, one fourth; and the breadth of the breast is also one fourth. The other members, too, have their own symmetrical proportions, and it was by employing them that the famous painters and sculptors of antiquity attained to great and endless renown.

3. Similarly, in the members of a temple there ought to be the greatest harmony in the symmetrical relations of the different parts to the general magnitude of the whole. Then again, in the human body the central point is naturally the navel. For if a man be placed flat on his back, with his hands and feet extended, and a pair of compasses centered at his navel, the fingers and toes of his two hands and feet will touch the circumference of a circle described therefrom. And just as the human body yields a circular outline, so too a square figure may be found from it. For if we measure the distance from the soles of the feet to the top of the head, and then apply that measure to the outstretched arms, the breadth will be found to be the same as the height, as in the case of plane surfaces which are perfectly square.

4. Therefore, since nature has designed the human body so that its members are duly proportioned to the frame as a whole, it appears that the ancients had good reason for their rule, that in perfect buildings the different members must be in exact symmetrical relations to the whole general scheme. Hence, while transmitting to us the proper arrangements for buildings of all kinds, they were particularly careful to do so in the case of temples of the gods, buildings in which merits and faults usually last forever.

5. Further, it was from the members of the body that they derived the fundamental ideas of the measures which are obviously necessary in all works, as the finger, palm, foot, and cúbit. These

they apportioned so as to form the "perfect number," called in Greek τέλειον, and as the perfect number the ancients fixed upon ten. For it is from the number of the fingers of the hand that the palm is found, and the foot from the palm. Again, while ten is naturally perfect, as being made up by the fingers of the two palms, Pláto also held that this number was perfect because ten is composed of the individual units, called by the Greeks μονάδες. But as soon as eleven or twelve is reached, the numbers, being excessive, cannot be perfect until they come to ten for the second time; for the component parts of that number are the individual units.

6. The mathematicians, however, maintaining a different view, have said that the perfect number is six, because this number is composed of integral parts which are suited numerically to their method of reckoning: thus, one is one sixth; two is one third; three is one half; four is two thirds, or δίμοιρος as they call it; five is five sixths, called πεντάμοιρος; and six is the perfect number. As the number goes on growing larger, the addition of a unit above six is the ἔφεκτος; eight, formed by the addition of a third part of six, is the integer and a third, called ἐπίτριτος; the addition of one half makes nine, the integer and a half, termed the addition of two thirds, making the number ten, is the integer and two thirds, which they call ἐπιδίμοιρος; in the number eleven, where five are added, we have the five sixths, called ἐπίπεμπτος; finally, twelve, being composed of the two simple integers, is called διπλάσιος.

7. And further, as the foot is one sixth of a man's height, the height of the body as expressed in number of feet being limited to six, they held that this was the perfect number, and observed that the cúbit consisted of six palms or of twenty-four fingers. This principle seems to have been followed by the states of Greece. As the cúbit consisted of six palms, they made the dráchma, which they used as their unit, consist in the same way of six bronze coins, like our which they call óbols; and, to correspond to the fingers, divided the dráchma into twenty-four quarter-óbols, which some call dichalca others trichalca.

8. But our countrymen at first fixed upon the ancient number and made ten bronze pieces go to the denárius, and this is the origin of the name which is applied to the denárius to this day. And the fourth part of it, consisting of two asses and half of a third, they called "sesterce." But later, observing that six and ten were both of them perfect numbers, they combined the two, and thus made the most perfect number, sixteen. They found their authority for this in the foot. For if we take two palms from the cúbit, there remains the foot of four palms; but the palm contains four fingers. Hence the foot contains sixteen fingers, and asses.

9. Therefore, if it is agreed that number was found out from the human fingers, and that there is a symmetrical correspondence between the members separately and the entire form of the body, in accordance with a certain part selected as standard, we can have nothing but respect for those who, in constructing temples of the immortal gods, have so arranged the members of the works that both the separate parts and the whole design may harmonize in their proportions and symmetry.

— Vitrúvius, *The Ten Books on Architecture*, 3.1 (translated by Morris Hicky Morgan)

## III. THE GREEK LANGUAGE AND EARLY LITERATURE

## Praise of the Múses

Come thou, let us begin with the Múses who gladden the great spirit of their father Zeus in Olýmpus with their songs, telling of things that are and that shall be and that were aforetime with consenting voice. Unwearying flows the sweet sound from their lips, and the house of their father Zeus the loud-thunderer is glad at the lily-like voice of the goddesses as it spread abroad, and the peaks of snowy Olýmpus resound, and the homes of the immortals. And they uttering their immortal voice, celebrate in song first of all the reverend race of the gods from the beginning, those whom Earth and wide Heaven begot, and the gods sprung of these, givers of good things. Then, next, the goddesses sing of Zeus, the father of gods and men, as they begin and end their strain, how much he is the most excellent among the gods and supreme in power. And again, they chant the race of men and strong giants, and gladden the heart of Zeus within Olýmpus, the Olýmpian Múses, daughters of Zeus the ægis-holder.

Them ... did Mnemósyne (Memory) ... bear of union with the father, the son of Crónos, a forgetting of ills and a rest from sorrow... And when a year was passed and the seasons came round as the months waned, and many days were accomplished, she bare nine daughters, all of one mind, whose hearts are set upon song and their spirit free from care, a little way from the topmost peak of snowy Olýmpus. There are their bright dancing-places and beautiful homes, and beside them the Graces and Desire live in delight. And they, uttering through their lips a lovely voice, sing the laws of all and the goodly ways of the immortals, uttering their lovely voice. Then went they to Olýmpus, delighting in their sweet voice, with heavenly song, and the dark earth resounded about them as they chanted, and a lovely sound rose up beneath their feet as they went to their father. And he was reigning in heaven, himself holding the lightning and glowing thunderbolt, when he had overcome by might his father Crónos; and he distributed fairly to the immortals their portions and declared their privileges.

These things, then, the Múses sang who dwell on Olýmpus, nine daughters begotten by great Zeus: Clío [history] and Eutérpe [lyric poetry], Thalía [comedy and pastoral poetry], Melpómene [tragedy] and Terpsíchore [dance], and Érato [love poetry] and Polyhýmnia [sacred poetry] and Uránia [astronomy] and Callíope [epic poetry], who is the chiefest of them all, for she attends on worshipful princes. Whomsoever of heaven-nourished princes the daughters of great Zeus honor, and behold him at his birth, they pour sweet dew upon his tongue, and from his lips flow gracious words. All the people look towards him while he settles causes with true judgements: and he, speaking surely, would soon make wise end even of a great quarrel; for therefore are there princes wise in heart, because when the people are being misguided in their assembly, they set right the matter again with ease, persuading them with gentle words. And when he passes through a gathering, they greet him as a god with gentle reverence, and he is conspicuous amongst the assembled: such is the holy gift of the Múses to men. For it is through the Múses and far-shooting Apóllo that there are singers and harpers upon the earth; but princes are of Zeus, and happy is he whom the Múses love: sweet flows speech from his mouth. For though a man have sorrow and grief in his newly-troubled soul and live in dread because his heart is distressed, yet, when a singer, the servant of the Múses, chants the glorious deeds of men of old and the blessed gods who inhabit Olýmpus, at once he forgets his heaviness and remembers not his sorrows at all; but the gifts of the goddesses soon turn him away from these.

– Hesíod, *Theógony*, 36-103 (translated by Hugh G. Evelyn-White)

## The Origin of Aphrodíte

And so soon as he had cut off the members with flint and cast them from the land into the surging sea, they were swept away over the main a long time: and a white foam spread around them from the immortal flesh, and in it there grew a maiden. First she drew near holy Cythéra, and from there, afterwards, she came to sea-girt Cýprus, and came forth an awful and lovely goddess, and grass grew up about her beneath her shapely feet. Her gods and men call Aphrodíte, and the foam-born goddess and rich-crowned Cytheréa, because she grew amid the foam, and Cythéra because she reached Cythéra, and Cyprógenes because she was born in billowy Cýprus, and Philomédes because sprang from the members. And with her went Éros, and comely Desire followed her at her birth at the first and as she went into the assembly of the gods. This honor she has from the beginning, and this is the portion allotted to her amongst men and undying gods, — the whisperings of maidens and smiles and deceits with sweet delight and love and graciousness.

– Hésiod, *Theógony*, 176-206 (translated by Hugh G. Evelyn-White)

## The Birth of Zeus

But Rhéa was subject in love to Crónos and bare splendid children, Héstia, Deméter, and gold-shod Héra and strong Hádes, pitiless in heart, who dwells under the earth, and the loud-crashing Earth-Shaker, and wise Zeus, father of gods and men, by whose thunder the wide earth is shaken. These great Crónos swallowed as each came forth from the womb to his mother's knees with this intent, that no other of the proud sons of Heaven should hold the kingly office amongst the deathless gods. For he learned from Earth and starry Heaven that he was destined to be overcome by his own son, strong though he was, through the contriving of great Zeus. Therefore, he kept no blind outlook, but watched and swallowed down his children: and unceasing grief seized Rhéa. But when she was about to bear Zeus, the father of gods and men, then she besought her own dear parents, Earth and starry Heaven, to devise some plan with her that the birth of her dear child might be concealed, and that retribution might overtake great, crafty Crónos for his own father and also for the children whom he had swallowed down. And they readily heard and obeyed their dear daughter and told her all that was destined to happen touching Crónos the king and his stout-hearted son. So they sent her to Lyétus, to the rich land of Crete, when she was ready to bear great Zeus, the youngest of her children. Him did vast Earth receive from Rhéa in wide Crete to nourish and to bring up. Thither came Earth carrying him swiftly through the black night to Lýctus first, and took him in her arms and hid him in a remote cave beneath the secret places of the holy earth on thick-wooded Mount Ægéum; but to the mightily ruling son of Heaven, the earlier king of the gods, she gave a great stone wrapped in swaddling clothes. Then he took it in his hands and thrust it down into his belly: wretch! he knew not in his heart that in place of the stone his son was left behind, unconquered and untroubled, and that he was soon to overcome him by force and might and drive him from his honors, himself to reign over the deathless gods.

After that, the strength and glorious limbs of the prince increased quickly, and as the years rolled on, great Crónos the wily was beguiled by the deep suggestions of Earth, and brought up again his offspring, vanquished by the arts and might of his own son, and he vomited up first the stone which he had swallowed last. And Zeus set it fast in the wide-pathed earth at goodly Pýtho under the glens of Parnássus, to be a sign thenceforth and a marvel to mortal men. And he set free from their deadly bonds the brothers of his father, sons of Heaven whom his father in his foolishness had bound. And they remembered to be grateful to him for his kindness and gave him thunder and the glowing thunderbolt and lightening: for before that, huge Earth had hidden these. In them he trusts and rules over mortals and immortals.

– Hésiod, *Theógony*, 453-506 (translated by Hugh G. Evelyn-White)

## Prométheus

Now Iápetus took to wife the neat-ankled mad Clýmene, daughter of Océanus... and she bare him a stout-hearted son, Atlas: also she bare very glorious Menœtius and clever Prométheus, full of various wiles, and scatter-brained Epimétheus who from the first was a mischief to men who eat bread; for it was he who first took of Zeus the woman, the maiden whom he had formed. But Menœtius was outrageous, and far-seeing Zeus struck him with a lurid thunderbolt and sent him down to Érebus because of his mad presumption and exceeding pride. And Átlas through hard constraint upholds the wide heaven with unwearying head and arms, standing at the borders of the earth before the clear-voiced Hespérides; for this lot wise Zeus assigned to him. And ready-witted Prométheus he bound with inextricable bonds, cruel chains, and drove a shaft through his middle, and set on him a long-winged eagle, which used to eat his immortal liver; but by night the liver grew as much again everyway as the long-winged bird devoured in the whole day. That bird Héracles, the valiant son of shapely-ankled Alcméne, slew; and delivered the son of Iápetus from the cruel plague, and released him from his affliction—not without the will of Olýmpian Zeus who reigns on high, that the glory of Héracles the Théban-born might be yet greater than it was before over the plenteous earth. This, then, he regarded, and honored his famous son; though he was angry, he ceased from the wrath which he had before because Prométheus matched himself in wit with the almighty son of Crónos.

For when the gods and mortal men had a dispute at Mécone, even then Prométheus was forward to cut up a great ox and set portions before them, trying to befool the mind of Zeus. Before the rest he set flesh and inner parts thick with fat upon the hide, covering them with an ox paunch; but for Zeus he put the white bones dressed up with cunning art and covered with shining fat. Then the father of men and of gods said to him: "Son of Iápetus, most glorious of all lords, good sir, how unfairly you have divided the portions!"

So said Zeus whose wisdom is everlasting, rebuking him. But wily Prométheus answered him, smiling softly and not forgetting his cunning trick: "Zeus, most glorious and greatest of the eternal gods, take which ever of these portions your heart within you bids." So he said, thinking trickery. But Zeus, whose wisdom is everlasting, saw and failed not to perceive the trick, and in his heart he thought mischief against mortal men which also was to be fulfilled. With both hands he took up the white fat and was angry at heart, and wrath came to his spirit when he saw the white ox-bones craftily tricked out: and because of this the tribes of men upon earth burn white bones to the deathless gods upon fragrant altars.

But Zeus who drives the clouds was greatly vexed and said to him: "Son of Iápetus, clever above all! So, sir, you have not yet forgotten your cunning arts!"

So spake Zeus in anger, whose wisdom is everlasting; and from that time he was always mindful of the trick, and would not give the power of unwearying fire to the Mélian race of mortal men who live on the earth. But the noble son of Iápetus outwitted him and stole the far-seen gleam of unwearying fire in a hollow fennel stalk. And Zeus who thunders on high was stung in spirit, and his dear heart was angered when he saw amongst men the far-seen ray of fire.

– Hésiod, Theógony, 507-565 (translated by Hugh G. Evelyn-White)

## War of the Gods and Títans

But when first their father was vexed in his heart with Obriáreus and Cóttus and Gýes, he bound them in cruel bonds, because he was jealous of their exceeding manhood and comeliness and great size: and he made them live beneath the wide-pathed earth, where they were afflicted, being set to dwell under the ground, at the end of the earth, at its great borders, in bitter anguish for a long time and with great grief at heart. But the son of Crónos and the other deathless gods whom rich-haired Rhéa bare from union with Crónos, brought them up again to the light at Earth's advising. For she herself recounted all things to the gods fully, how that with these they would gain victory and a glorious cause to vaunt themselves. For the Títan gods and as many as sprang from Crónos had long been fighting together in stubborn war with heart-grieving toil, the lordly Títans from high Óthrys, but the gods, givers of good, whom rich-haired Rhéa bare in union with Crónos, from Olýmpus. So they, with bitter wrath, were fighting continually with one another at that time for ten full years, and the hard strife had no close or end for either side, and the issue of the war hung evenly balanced. But when he had provided those three with all things fitting, nectar and ambrósia which the gods themselves eat, and when their proud spirit revived within them all after they had fed on nectar and delicious ambrósia, then it was that the father of men and gods spoke amongst them: "Hear me, bright children of Earth and Heaven, that I may say what my heart within me bids. A long while now have we, who are sprung from Crónos and the Títan gods, fought with each other every day to get victory and to prevail. But do you show your great might and unconquerable strength and face the Títans in bitter strife; for remember our friendly kindness, and from what sufferings you are come back to the light from your cruel bondage under misty gloom through our counsels."

So he said. And blameless Cóttus answered him again: "Divine one, you speak that which we know well: nay, even of ourselves we know that your wisdom and understanding is exceeding, and that you became a defender of the deathless ones from chill doom. And through your devising we are come back again from the murky gloom and from our merciless bonds, enjoying what we looked not for, O lord, son of Crónos. And so now with fixed purpose and deliberate counsel we will aid your power in dreadful strife and will fight against the Títans in hard battle."

So he said: and the gods, givers of good things, applauded when they heard his word, and their spirit longed for war even more than before, and they all, both male and female, stirred up hated battle that day, the Títan gods, and all that were born of Crónos together with those dread, mighty ones of overwhelming strength whom Zeus brought up to the light from Erebus beneath the earth. A hundred arms sprang from the shoulders of all alike, and each had fifty heads growing upon his shoulders upon stout limbs. These, then, stood against the Títans in grim strife, holding huge rocks in their strong hands. And on the other part the Títans eagerly strengthened their ranks, and both sides at one time showed the work of their hands and their might. The boundless sea rang terribly around, and the earth crashed loudly: wide Heaven was shaken and groaned, and high Olýmpus reeled from its foundation under the charge of the undying gods, and a heavy quaking reached dim Tártarus and the deep sound of their feet in the fearful onset and of their hard missiles. So, then, they launched their grievous shafts upon one another, and the cry of both armies as they shouted reached to starry heaven; and they met together with a great battle-cry.

Then Zeus no longer held back his might; but straight his heart was filled with fury and he showed forth all his strength. From Heaven and from Olýmpus he came forthwith, hurling his lightning: the bold flew thick and fast from his strong hand together with thunder and lightning, whirling an awesome flame. The life-giving earth crashed around in burning, and the vast wood crackled loud with fire all about. All the land seethed, and Ocean's streams and the unfruitful sea. The hot vapor lapped round the earthborn Títans: flame unspeakable rose to the bright upper air: the flashing glare of the thunder-stone and lightning blinded their eyes for all that there were strong. Astounding heat seized Cháos: and to see with eyes and to hear the sound with ears it seemed even as if Earth and wide Heaven above came together; for such a mighty crash would have arisen if Earth were being hurled to ruin, and Heaven from on high were hurling her down; so great a crash was there while the gods were meeting together in strife. Also the winds brought rumbling earthquake and dust storm, thunder and lightning and the lurid thunderbolt, which are the shafts of great Zeus, and carried the clangor and the war cry into the midst of the two hosts. A horrible uproar of terrible strife arose: mighty deeds were shown and the battle inclined. But until then, they kept at one another and fought continually in cruel war.

And amongst the foremost Cóttus and Briáreos and Gýes insatiate for war raised fierce fighting: three hundred rocks, one upon another, they launched from their strong hands and overshadowed the Títans with their missiles, and buried them beneath the wide-pathed earth, and bound them in bitter chains when they had conquered them by their strength for all their great spirit, as far beneath the earth to Tártarus. For a brazen anvil falling down from heaven nine nights and days would reach the earth upon the tenth: and again, a brazen anvil falling from earth nine nights and days would reach Tártarus upon the tenth. Round it runs a fence of bronze, and night spreads in triple line all about it like a neck-circlet, while above grow the roots of the earth and unfruitful sea. There by the counsel of Zeus who drives the clouds the Títan gods are hidden under misty gloom, in a dank place where are the ends of the huge earth. And they may not go out; for

Poséidon fixed gates of bronze upon it, and a wall runs all round it on every side. There Gýes and Cóttus and great-souled Obriáreus live, trusty warders of Zeus who holds the ægis.

– Hésiod, Theógony, 617-735 (translated by Hugh G. Evelyn-White)

## The Underworld

There, in front, stand the echoing halls of the god of the lower-world, strong Hádes, and of awful Perséphone. A fearful hound guards the house in front, pitiless, and he has a cruel trick. On those who go in he fawns with his tail and both is ears, but suffers them not to go out back again, but keeps watch and devours whomsoever he catches going out of the gates of strong Hádes and awful Perséphone.

– Hésiod, Theógony, 767-774 (translated by Hugh G. Evelyn-White)

## Pandóra's Jar

For the gods keep hidden from men the means of life. Else you would easily do work enough in a day to supply you for a full year even without working; soon would you put away your rudder over the smoke, and the fields worked by ox and sturdy mule would run to waste. But Zeus in the anger of his heart hid it, because Prométheus the crafty deceived him; therefore he planned sorrow and mischief against men. He hid fire; but that the noble son of Iápetus stole again for men from Zeus the counsellor in a hollow fennel-stalk, so that Zeus who delights in thunder did not see it. But afterwards Zeus who gathers the clouds said to him in anger:

'Son of Iápetus, surpassing all in cunning, you are glad that you have outwitted me and stolen fire—a great plague to you yourself and to men that shall be. But I will give men as the price for fire an evil thing in which they may all be glad of heart while they embrace their own destruction.'

So said the father of men and gods and laughed aloud. And he bade famous Hephæstus make haste and mix earth with water and to put in it the voice and strength of human kind, and fashion a sweet, lovely maiden-shape, like to the immortal goddesses in face; and Athéna to teach her needlework and the weaving of the varied web; and golden Aphrodíte to shed grace upon her head and cruel longing and cares that weary the limbs. And he charged Hérmes the guide, the Slayer of Árgus, to put in her a shameless mind and a deceitful nature.

So he ordered. And they obeyed the lord Zeus the son of Crónos. Forthwith the famous Lame God molded clay in the likeness of a modest maid, as the son of Crónos purposed. And the goddess bright-eyed Athéna girded and clothed her, and the divine Graces and queenly Persuasion put necklaces of gold upon her, and the rich-haired Hours crowned her head with spring flowers. And Pállas Athéna bedecked her form with all manners of finery. Also the Guide, the Slayer of Árgus, contrived within her lies and crafty words and a deceitful nature at the will of loud thundering Zeus, and the Herald of the gods put speech in her. And he called this woman Pandóra (All Endowed), because all they who dwelt on Olýmpus gave each a gift, a plague to men who eat bread.

But when he had finished the sheer, hopeless snare, the Father sent glorious Árgus-Slayer, the swift messenger of the gods, to take it to Epimétheus as a gift. And Epimétheus did not think on what Prométheus had said to him, bidding him never take a gift of Olýmpian Zeus, but to send it back for fear it might prove to be something harmful to men. But he took the gift, and afterwards, when the evil thing was already his, he understood.

For ere this the tribes of men lived on earth remote and free from ills and hard toil and heavy sickness which bring the Fates upon men; for in misery men grow old quickly. But the woman took off the great lid of the jar with her hands and scattered all these and her thought caused sorrow and mischief to men. Only Hope remained there in an unbreakable home within under the rim of the great jar and did not fly out at the door; for ere that, the lid of the jar stopped her, by the will of Ægis-holding Zeus who gathers the clouds. But the rest, countless plagues, wander amongst men; for earth is full of evils and the sea is full. Of themselves diseases come upon men continually by day and by night, bringing mischief to mortals silently; for wise Zeus took away speech from them. So is there no way to escape the will of Zeus.

— Hésiod, *Works and Days*, 42-105 (translated by Hugh G. Evelyn-White)

## The Ages of Man

Or if you will, I will sum you up another tale well and skillfully — and do you lay it up in your heart, — how the gods and mortal men sprang from one source.

First of all, the deathless gods who dwell on Olýmpus made a golden race of mortal men who lived in the time of Crónos when he was reigning in heaven. And they lived like gods without sorrow of heart, remote and free from toil and grief: miserable age rested not on them; but with legs and arms never failing they made merry with feasting beyond the reach of all evils. When they died, it was as though they were overcome with sleep, and they had all good things; for the fruitful earth unforced bare them fruit abundantly and without stint. They dwelt in ease and peace upon their lands with many good things, rich in flocks and loved by the blessed gods.

But after earth had covered this generation—they are called pure spirits dwelling on the earth, and are kindly, delivering from harm, and guardians of mortal men; for they roam everywhere over the earth, clothed in mist and keep watch on judgements and cruel deeds, givers of wealth; for this royal right also they received; then they who dwell on Olýmpus made a second generation which was of silver and less noble by far. It was like the golden race neither in body nor in spirit. A child was brought up at his good mother's side a hundred years, an utter simpleton, playing childishly in his own home. But when they were full grown and were come to the full measure of their prime, they lived only a little time in sorrow because of their foolishness, for they could not keep from sinning and from wronging one another, nor would they serve the immortals, nor sacrifice on the holy altars of the blessed ones as it is right for men to do wherever they dwell. Then Zeus the son of Crónos was angry and put them away, because they would not give honor to the blessed gods who live on Olýmpus.

But when earth had covered this generation also—they are called blessed spirits of the underworld by men, and, though they are of second order, yet honor attends them also—Zeus the Father made a third generation of mortal men, a brazen race, sprung from ash-trees; and it was in no way equal to the silver age, but was terrible and strong. They loved the lamentable works of Áres and deeds of violence; they ate no bread, but were hard of heart like adamant, fearful men. Great was their strength and unconquerable the arms which grew from their shoulders on their strong limbs. Their armor was of bronze, and their houses of bronze, and of bronze were their implements: there was no black iron. These were destroyed by their own hands and passed to the dank house of chill Hádes, and left no name: terrible though they were, black Death seized them, and they left the bright light of the sun.

But when earth had covered this generation also, Zeus the son of Crónos made yet another, the fourth, upon the fruitful earth, which was nobler and more righteous, a god-like race of hero-men who are called demi-gods, the race before our own, throughout the boundless earth. Grim war and dread battle destroyed a part of them, some in the land of Cádmus at seven-gated Thebes when they fought for the flocks of Œdipus, and some, when it had brought them in ships over the great sea gulf to Troy for rich-haired Hélen's sake: there death's end enshrouded a part of them. But to the others father Zeus the son of Crónos gave a living and an abode apart from men, and made them dwell at the ends of earth. And they live untouched by sorrow in the islands of the blessed along the shore of deep swirling Ocean, happy heroes for whom the grain-giving earth bears honey-sweet fruit flourishing thrice a year, far from the deathless gods, and Crónos rules over them; for the father of men and gods released him from his bonds. And these last equally have honor and glory.

And again far-seeing Zeus made yet another generation, the fifth, of men who are upon the bounteous earth.

Thereafter, would that I were not among the men of the fifth generation, but either had died before or been born afterwards. For now truly is a race of iron, and men never rest from labor and sorrow by day, and from perishing by night; and the gods shall lay sore trouble upon them. But, notwithstanding, even these shall have some good mingled with their evils. And Zeus will destroy this race of mortal men also when they come to have grey hair on the temples at their birth. The father will not agree with his children, nor the children with their father, nor guest with his host, nor comrade with comrade; nor will brother be dear to brother as aforetime. Men will dishonor their parents as they grow quickly old, and will carp at them, chiding them with bitter words, hard-hearted they, not knowing the fear of the gods. They will not repay their aged parents the cost their nurture, for might shall be their right: and one man will sack another's city. There will be no favor for the man who keeps his oath or for the just or for the good; but rather men will praise the evildoer and his violent dealing. Strength will be right and reverence will cease to be; and the wicked will hurt the worthy man, speaking false words against him, and will swear an oath upon them. Envy, foul-mouthed, delighting in evil, with scowling face, will go along with wretched men one and all. And then Áidos and Némesis [shame of wrongdoing and indignation against the wrongdoer], with their sweet forms wrapped in white robes, will go from the wide-pathed earth and forsake mankind to join the company of the deathless gods: and bitter sorrows will be left for mortal men, and there will be no help against evil.

> – Hésiod, *Theógony*, 106-201 (translated by Hugh G. Evelyn-White)

## An Exhortation to Battle

How long will ye slumber? when will ye take heart
And fear the reproach of your neighbors at hand?
Fie! comrades, to think ye have peace for your part,
Whilst the sword and the arrow are wasting our land!
Shame! grasp the shield close! cover well the bold breast!
Aloft raise the spear as ye march on your foe!
With no thought of retreat, with no terror confessed,
Hurl your last dart in dying, or strike your last blow.
Oh, 'tis noble and glorious to fight for our all,—
For our country, our children, the wife of our love!
Death comes not the sooner; no soldier shall fall,
Ere his thread is spun out by the sisters above.
Once to die is man's doom; rush, rush to the fight!
He cannot escape, though his blood were Jove's own.
For a while let him cheat the shrill arrow by flight;
Fate will catch him at last in his chamber alone.
Unlamented he dies; — unregretted. Not so,
When, the tower of his country, in death falls the brave;
Thrice hallowed his name amongst all, high or low,
As with blessings alive, so with tears in the grave.

> — Callínus, *Exhortation to Battle* (translated by Henry Nelson Coleridge)

## A Martial Elegy

How glorious fall the valiant, sword in hand,
In front of battle for their native land!
But oh! what ills await the wretch that yields.
A recreant outcast from his country's fields!
The mother whom he loves shall quit her home,
An aged father at his side shall roam;
His little ones shall weeping with him go,
And a young wife participate his woe;
While scorned and scowled upon by every face,
They pine for food, and beg from place to place.

Stain of his breed! dishonoring manhood's form,
All ills shall cleave to him: affliction's storm
Shall blind him wandering in the vale of years,
Till, lost to all but ignominious fears,
He shall not blush to leave a recreant's name,
And children, like himself, inured to shame.
But we will combat for our father's land,
And we will drain the life-blood where we stand,
To save our children,—Fight ye side by side,
and serried close, ye men of youthful pride,
Disdaining fear, and deeming light the cost
Of life itself in glorious battle lost.

Leave not our sires to stem the unequal fight,
Whose limbs are nerved no more with buoyant might;
Nor, lagging backward, let the younger breast
Permit the man of age (a sight unblest)
To welter in the combat's foremost thrust,
His hoary head disheveled in the dust,
And venerable bosom bleeding bare.
But youth's fair form, though fallen, is ever fair,
And beautiful in death the boy appears,
The hero boy, that dies in blooming years:
In man's regret he lives, and woman's tears;
More sacred than in life, and lovelier far,
For having perished in the front of war.

— Tyrtæus, *Martial Elegy* (translated by Thomas Campbell)

## To His Soul

Tossed on a sea of troubles, Soul, my Soul,
        Thyself do thou control;
And to the weapons of advancing foes
        A stubborn breast oppose;
Undaunted 'mid the hostile might
Of squadrons burning for the fight.

Thine be no boasting when the victor's crown
      Wins thee deserved renown;
Thine no dejected sorrow, when defeat
      Would urge a base retreat;
Rejoice in joyous things—nor overmuch
      Let grief thy bosom touch
Midst evil, and still bear in mind
How changeful are the ways of humankind.

      — Archílochus, *To His Soul* (translated by William Hay)

## Winter

The rain of Zeus descends, and from high heaven
      A storm is driven:
And on the running water-brooks the cold
      Lays icy hold:
Then up! beat down the winter; make the fire
      Blaze high and higher;
Mix wine as sweet as honey of the bee
      Abundantly;
Then drink with comfortable wool around
      Your temples bound.
We must not yield our hearts to woe, or wear
      With wasting care;
For grief will profit us no whit, my friend,
      Nor nothing mend;
But this is our best medicine, with wine fraught
      To cast out thought.

      — Alcæus, *Winter* (translated by John Addington Symonds)

## A Hymn to Vénus

Vénus, beauty of the skies,
To whom a thousand temples rise,
Gayly false in gentle smiles,
Full of love-perplexing wiles,
O goddess! from my heart remove
The wasting cares and pains of love.

If ever thou hast kindly heard
A song in soft distress preferred,
Propitious to my tuneful vow,
O gentle goddess! hear me now.
Descend thou bright, immortal, guest,
In all thy radiant charms confessed.

Thou once didst leave almighty Jove,
And all the golden roofs above:
The car thy wanton sparrows drew;
Hovering in air they lightly flew;

As to my bower they winged their way,
I saw their quivering pinions play.

The birds dismissed (while you remain)
Bore back their empty car again;
Then you, with looks divinely mild,
In every heavenly feature smiled,
and asked, what mew complaints I made,
And why I called you to my aid?

What frenzy in my bosom raged,
And by what care to be assuaged?
What gentle youth I would allure,
Whom in my artful toils secure?
Who does thy tender heart subdue,
Tell me, my Sáppho, tell me who?

Though now he shuns thy longing arms,
He soon shall court thy slighted charms;
Though now thy offerings he despise,
He soon to thee shall sacrifice;
Though now he freeze, he soon shall burn,
And be thy victim in his turn.

Celestial visitant, once more
Thy needful presence I implore!
In pity come and ease my grief,
Bring my distempered soul relief:
Favor thy suppliant's hidden fires,
And give me all my heart desires.

— Sáppho, *Hymn to Vénus* (translated by Ambrose Philips)

## A Poetic Fragment

Blest as the immortal gods is he,
The youth who fondly sits by thee,
And hears and sees thee all the while
Softly speak and sweetly smile.

'Twas this deprived my soul of rest,
And raised such tumults in my breast;
For while I gazed, in transport tossed,
My breath was gone, my voice was lost.

My bosom glowed; the subtle flame
Ran quick through all my vital frame;
O'er my dim eyes a darkness hung,
My ears with hollow murmurs rung.

In dewy damps my limbs were chilled,
My blood with gentle horrors thrilled;
My feeble pulse forgot to play,
I fainted, sunk, and died away.

— Sáppho, *Fragment* (translated by Ambrose Philips)

# Love's Assault

I will, I will, the conflict's past,
And I'll consent to love at last.
Cúpid has long, with smiling art,
Invited me to yield my heart,
And I have thought that peace of mind
Should not be for a smile resigned;
And so repelled the tender lure,
And hoped my heart would sleep secure.

But, slighted in his boasted charms,
The angry infant flew to arms;
He slung his quiver's golden frame,
He took his bow, his shafts of flame,
And proudly summoned me to yield,
Or meat him on the martial field.
And what did I unthinking do?
I took to arms, undaunted too;
Assumed the corslet, shield, and spear,
And, like Pelídes, smiled at fear.
Then (hear it, all ye powers above)
I fought with Love! I fought with Love!

And now his arrows all were shed,
And I had just in terror fled—
When, hearing an indignant sigh,
To see me thus unwounded fly,
And having now no other dart,
He shot himself into my heart!
My heart—alas the luckless day!
Received the god, and died away.
Farewell, farewell, my faithless shield!
Thy lord at length is forced to yield.
Vain, vain, is every outward care,
The foe's within, and triumphs there.

— Anácreon, *Odes*, XIII. (translated by Thomas Moore)

# A Recantation for Hélen

False is that word of mine—
The truth is that thou didst not embark in ships
Nor ever go to the walls of Troy...

— Stesíchorus, *Palinode*, quoted in Pláto's *Phædrus* (translated by Benjamin Jowett)

## A Legend of the Poet Aríon

In his time a very wonderful thing is said to have happened. The Corínthians and the Lésbians agree in their account of the matter. They relate that Aríon of Methýmna, who as a player on the harp, was second to no man living at that time, and who was, so far as we know, the first to invent the dithyrambic measure, to give it its name, and to recite in it at Córinth, was carried to Tǽnarum on the back of a dolphin.

He had lived for many years at the court of Periánder, when a longing came upon him to sail across to Ítaly and Sícily. Having made rich profits in those parts, he wanted to recross the seas to Córinth. He therefore hired a vessel, the crew of which were Corínthians, thinking that there was no people in whom he could more safely confide; and, going on board, he set sail from Taréntum. The sailors, however, when they reached the open sea, formed a plot to throw him overboard and seize upon his riches. Discovering their design, he fell on his knees, beseeching them to spare his life, and making them welcome to his money. But they refused; and required him either to kill himself outright, if he wished for a grave on the dry land, or without loss of time to leap overboard into the sea. In this strait Aríon begged them, since such was their pleasure, to allow him to mount upon the quarter-deck, dressed in his full costume, and there to play and sing, and promising that, as soon as his song was ended, he would destroy himself. Delighted at the prospect of hearing the very best harper in the world, they consented, and withdrew from the stern to the middle of the vessel: while Aríon dressed himself in the full costume of his calling, took his harp, and standing on the quarter-deck, chanted the Órthian.

His strain ended, he flung himself, fully attired as he was, headlong into the sea. The Corínthians then sailed on to Córinth. As for Aríon, a dolphin, they say, took him upon his back and carried him to Tǽnarum, where he went ashore, and thence proceeded to Córinth in his musician's dress, and told all that had happened to him. Periánder, however, disbelieved the story, and put Aríon in ward, to prevent his leaving Córinth, while he watched anxiously for the return of the mariners. On their arrival he summoned them before him and asked them if they could give him any tiding of Aríon. They returned for answer that he was alive and in good health in Ítaly, and that they had left him at Taréntum, where he was doing well. Thereupon Aríon appeared before them, just as he was when he jumped from the vessel: the men, astonished and detected in falsehood, could no longer deny their guilt. Such is the account which the Corínthians and Lésbians give; and there is to this day at Tǽnarum an offering of Aríon's at the shrine, which is a small figure in bronze, representing a man seated upon a dolphin.

— Heródotus, *History*, I.23-24 (translated by Benjamin Jowett)


## IV. EARLY GREEK PHILOSOPHY


## The Philosophical Schools

The men who were commonly regarded as sages were the following: Tháles, Sólon, Periánder, Cleobúlus, Chílon, Bías, Píttacus... So much for the sages or wise men.

But philosophy, the pursuit of wisdom, has had a twofold origin; it started with Anaximánder on the one hand, with Pythágoras on the other. The former was a pupil of Tháles; Pythágoras was taught by Pherecýdes. The one school was called Iónian, because Tháles, a Milesian and therefore an Iónian, instructed Anaximánder; the other school was called Italian from Pythágoras, who worked for the most part in Ítaly. And the one school, that of Iónia, terminates with Clitómachus and Chrysíppus and Theophrástus, that of Ítaly with Epicúrus. The succession passes from Tháles through Anaximánder, Anaxímenes, Anaxágoras, Archeláüs, to Sócrates, who introduced ethics or moral philosophy; from Sócrates to his pupils the Socrátics, and especially to Pláto, the founder of the Old Academy; from Pláto, through Speusíppus and Xenócrates, the succession passes to Pólemo, Crántor, and Crátes, Arcesiláüs, founder of the Middle Academy, Lacýdes, founder of the New Academy, Carnéades, and Clitómachus. This line brings us to Clitómachus.

There is another which ends with Chrysíppus, that is to say by passing from Sócrates to Antísthenes, then to Diógenes the Cýnic, Crátes of Thebes, Zéno of Cítium, Cleánthes, Chrysíppus. And yet again another ends with Theophrástus; thus from Pláto it passes to Áristotle, and from Áristotle to Theophrástus. In this manner the school of Iónia comes to an end.

In the Italian school the order of succession is as follows: first Pherecýdes, next Pythágoras, next his son Teláuges, then Xenóphanes, Parménides, Zéno of Élea, Leucíppus, Demócritus, who had many pupils, in particular Nausíphanes [and Naucýdes], who were teachers of Epicúrus.

— Diógenes Laértius, *Lives of the Eminent Philosophers*, I.13-15 (translated by R. D. Hicks)

## Sayings of Tháles of Milétus

Of all things that are, the most ancient is God, for He is uncreated.
The most beautiful is the universe, for it is God's workmanship.
The greatest is space, for it holds all things.
The swiftest is mind, for it speeds everywhere.
The strongest, necessity, for it masters all.
The wisest, time, for it brings everything to light.

— Diógenes Laértius, *Lives of the Eminent Philosophers*, I.35 (translated by R. D. Hicks)

## Anaximánder

Anaximánder, the son of Praxíades, was a native of Milétus. He laid down as his principle and element that which is unlimited without defining it as air or water or anything else. He held that the parts undergo change, but the whole is unchangeable; that the earth, which is of spherical shape, lies in the midst, occupying the place of a center; that the moon, shining with borrowed light, derives its illumination from the sun; further, that the sun is as large as the earth and consists of the purest fire.

He was the first inventor of the gnomon and set it up for a sundial in Lacedǽmon, as is stated by Favorínus in his *Miscellaneous History*, in order to mark the solstices and the equinoxes; he also constructed clocks to tell the time. He was the first to draw on a map the outline of land and sea, and he constructed a globe as well.

His exposition of his doctrines took the form of a summary which no doubt came into the hands, among others, of Apollodórus of Áthens. He says in his *Chronology* that in the second year of the 58th Olýmpiad Anaximánder was sixty-four, and that he died not long afterwards. Thus he flourished almost at the same time as Polýcrates the tyrant of Sámos. There is a story that the boys laughed at his singing, and that, when he heard of it, he rejoined, "Then to please the boys I must improve my singing."

— Diógenes Laértius, *Lives of the Eminent Philosophers*, II.1 (translated by R. D. Hicks)

## On the Origin of "Philosophy"

Pythágoras called the principles he taught philosophía or love of wisdom, but not sophía or wisdom. For he criticized the Seven Wise Men, as they were called, who lived before his time, saying that no man is wise, being human, and many a time, by reason of the weakness of his nature, has not the strength to bring all matters to a successful issue, but that he who emulates both the ways and the manner of life of a wise man may more fittingly be called a "lover of wisdom."

– Diodórus Sículus, *Library of History*, X.10.1 (translated by C. H. Oldfather)

## Doctrines of the Pythagoréans

Alexánder in his *Successions of Philosophers* says that he found in the Pythagoréan memoirs the following tenets as well. The principle of all things is the monad or unit; arising from this monad the indeterminate dyad or two serves as material substratum to the monad, which is cause; from the monad and the undefined dyad spring numbers; from numbers, points; from points, lines; from lines, plane figures; from plane figures, solid figures; from solid figures, sensible bodies, the elements of which are four, fire, water, earth and air; these elements interchange and turn into one another completely, and combine to produce a universe animate, intelligent, spherical, with the earth at its center, the earth itself too being spherical and inhabited round about. There are also antipodes, and our "down" is their "up." Light and darkness have equal part in the universe, so have hot and cold, and dry and moist; and of these, if hot preponderates, we have summer; if cold, winter; if dry, spring; if moist, late autumn. If all are in equilibrium, we have the best periods of the year, of which the freshness of spring constitutes the healthy season, and the decay of late autumn the unhealthy. So too, in the day, freshness belongs to the morning, and decay to the evening, which is therefore more unhealthy. The air about the earth is stagnant and unwholesome, and all within it is mortal; but the uppermost air is ever moved and pure and healthy, and all within it is immortal and consequently divine.

The sun, the moon, and the other stars are gods; for, in them, there is a preponderance of heat, and heat is the cause of life. The moon is illumined by the sun. Gods and men are akin, inasmuch as man partakes of heat; therefore God takes thought for man. Fate is the cause of things being thus ordered both as a whole and separately. The sun's ray penetrates through the æther, whether cold or dense – the air they call cold æther, and the sea and moisture dense æther – and this ray descends even to the depths and for this reason quickens all things. All things live which partake of heat – this is why plants are living things – but all have not soul, which is a detached part of æther, partly the hot and partly the cold, for it partakes of cold æther too. Soul is distinct from life; it is immortal, since that from which it is detached is immortal. Living creatures are reproduced from one another by germination; there is no such thing as spontaneous generation from earth. The germ is a clot of brain containing hot vapor within it; and this, when brought to the womb, throws out, from the brain, ichor, fluid and blood, whence are formed flesh, sinews, bones, hairs, and the whole of the body, while soul and sense come from the vapor within. First congealing in about forty days, it receives form and, according to the ratios of "harmony," in seven, nine, or at the most ten, months, the mature child is brought forth. It has in it all the relations constituting life, and these, forming a continuous series, keep it together according to the ratios of harmony, each appearing at regulated intervals. Sense generally, and sight in particular, is a certain unusually hot vapor. This is why it is said to see through air and water, because the hot æther is resisted by the cold; for, if the vapor in the eyes had been cold, it would have been dissipated on meeting the air, its like. As it is, in certain [lines] he calls the eyes the portals of the sun. His conclusion is the same with regard to hearing and the other senses.

The soul of man, he says, is divided into three parts, understanding, reason, and passion. Understanding and passion are possessed by other animals as well, but reason by man alone. The seat of the soul extends from the heart to the brain; the part of it which is in the heart is passion, while the parts located in the brain are reason and understanding. The senses are distillations from these. Reason is immortal, all else mortal. The soul draws nourishment from the blood; the faculties of the soul are winds, for they as well as the soul are invisible, just as the æther is invisible. But when it is strong and settled down into itself, reasonings and deeds become its bonds. When cast out upon the earth, it wanders in the air like the body. Hérmes is the steward of souls, and for that reason is called Hérmes the Escorter, Hérmes the Keeper of the Gate, and Hérmes of the Underworld, since it is he who brings in the souls from their bodies both by land and sea; and the pure are taken into the uppermost region, but the impure are not permitted to approach the pure or each other, but are bound by the Fúries in bonds unbreakable. The whole air is full of souls which are called genii or heroes; these are they who send men dreams and signs of future disease and health, and not to men alone, but to sheep also and cattle as well; and it is to them that purifications and lustrations, all divination, omens and the like, have reference. The most momentous thing in human life is the art of winning the soul to good or to evil...

— Diógenes Laértius, *Lives of the Eminent Philosophers*, VIII.24-32 (translated by R. D. Hicks)

## The Doctrine of Pythágoras

As the geometers cannot express incorporeal forms in words, and have recourse to the descriptions of figures, as that is a triangle, and yet do not mean that the actually seen lines are the triangle, but only what they represent, the knowledge in the mind, so the Pythagoréans used the same objective method in respect to first reasons and forms. As these incorporeal forms and first principles could not be expressed in words, they had recourse to demonstration by numbers. Number one denoted to them the reason of Unity, Identity, Equality, the purpose of friendship, sympathy, and conservation of the Universe, which results from persistence in Sameness. For unity in the details harmonizes all the parts of a whole, as by the participation of the First Cause.

Number two, or Dýad, signifies the two-fold reason of diversity and inequality, of everything that is divisible, or mutable, existing at one time in one way, and at another time in another way. After all these methods were not confined to the Pythagoréans, being used by other philosophers to denote unitive powers, which contain all things in the universe, among which are certain reasons of equality, dissimilitude and diversity. These reasons are what they meant by the terms Mónad and Dýad, or by the words uniform, biform, or diversiform.

The same reasons apply to their use of other numbers, which were ranked according to certain powers. Things that had a beginning, middle and end, they denoted by the number Three, saying that anything that has a middle is triform, which was applied to every perfect thing. They said that if anything was perfect it would make use of this principle and be adorned, according to it; and as they had no other name for it, they invented the form Tríad; and whenever they tried to bring us to the knowledge of what is perfect they led us to that by the form of this Tríad. So also with the other numbers, which were ranked according to the same reasons.

All other things were comprehended under a single form and power which they called Décad, explaining it by a pun as décad, meaning comprehension. That is why they called Ten a perfect number, the most perfect of all as comprehending all difference of numbers, reasons, species and proportions. For if the nature of the universe be defined according to the reasons and proportions of members, and if that which is produced, increased and perfected, proceed according to the reason of numbers; and since the Décad comprehends every reason of numbers, every proportion, and every species, why should Nature herself not be denoted by the most perfect number, Ten? Such was the use of numbers among the Pythagoréans.

— Pórphyry, *Life of Pythágoras*, 49-52 (translated by K. S. Guthrie)

# Pythágoras and the Ratios of Musical Harmony

[Editor's note: The following account is surely apocryphal, for the ratios obtained by weights, as opposed to string lengths, would not be such as are described. Nevertheless, Pythágoras is credited with the discovery of the ratios of harmony, as there seem to be no prior claims.]

Once as he was intently considering music, and reasoning with himself whether it would be possible to devise some instrumental assistance to the sense of hearing, so as to systematize it—as sight is made precise by the compass rule, and glass, or touch is made reckonable by balance and measures—so thinking of these things Pythágoras happened to pass by a brazier's shop, where providentially he heard the hammers beating out a piece of iron on the anvil, producing sounds that harmonized, except one. But he recognized in these sounds, the concord of the octave, the fifth, and the fourth. He saw that the sound between the fourth and the fifth, taken by itself, was a dissonance, and yet completed the greater sound among them. Delighted, therefore, to find that the thing he was anxious to discover had by divine assistance succeeded, he went into the smithy, and by various experiments discovered that the difference of sound arose from the magnitude of the hammers, but not from the force of the strokes, nor from the shape of the hammers, nor from the change of position of the beaten iron. Having then accurately examined the weights and the swing of the hammers, he returned home, and fixed one stake diagonally to the walls, lest some difference should arise from there being several of them, or from some difference in the material of the stakes. From this stake he then suspended four gut-strings, of similar materials, size, thickness and twist. A weight was suspended from the bottom of each. When the strings were equal in length, he struck two of them simultaneously, he reproduced the former intervals, forming different pairs.

He discovered that the string stretched by the greatest weight, when compared with that stretched by the smallest weight, the interval of an octave. The weight of the first was twelve pounds, and that of the latter six. Being therefore in a double ratio, it formed the octave, which was made plain by the weights themselves. Then he found that the string from which the greater weight was suspended compared with that from which was suspended the weight next to the smallest, and which weight was eight pounds, produced the interval known as the fifth. Hence he discovered that this interval is in a ratio of one and a half to one, or three to two, in which ratio the weights also were to each other. Then he found that the string stretched by the greatest weight produced, when compared with that which was next to it, in weight, namely, nine pounds, the interval called the fourth, analogous to the weights. This ratio, therefore, he discovered to be in the ratio of one and a third to one, or four to three; while that of the from string from which a weight of nine pounds was suspended to the string which had the smallest weight, again in a ratio of three to two, which is 9 to 6.

In like manner, the string next to that from which the small weight was suspended, was to that which had the smallest weight, in the ratio of 4 to 3 (being 8 to 6) but to the string which had the greatest weight, in a ratio of 3 to 2, being 12 to 8. Hence that which is between the fifth and fourth, and by which the fifth exceeds the fourth is proved to be as nine is to eight. But either way it may be proved that the octave is a system consisting of the fifth in conjunction with fourth, just as the double ratio consists of three to two, and four to three; as for instance 12, 8 and 6; or, conversely of the fourth and the fifth, as in the double ratio of four to three and three to two, as for instance, 12, 9 and 6 therefore, and in this order, having confirmed both his hand and hearing to the suspended weights, and having established according to them the ratio of the proportions, by an easy artifice he transferred the common suspension of the strings from the diagonal stake to the head of the instrument which he called ... a string-stretcher. Then by the aid of pegs he produced a tension of the strings analogous to that effected by the weights. Employing this method, therefore, as a basis, and as it were an infallible rule, he afterward extended the experiment to other instruments, namely, the striking of pans, to pipes and [...], to monochords, triangles, and the like in all of which he found the same ratio of numbers to obtain. Then he named the sound which participates in the number 6, tonic; that which participates of the number 8, and is four to three, sub-dominant; that which participates of the number 9, and is one tone higher then the sub-dominant, he called, dominant, and 9 to 8; but that which participates of the number 12, octave.

Then he filled up the middle spaces with analogous sounds in diatonic order and formed an octochord from symmetric numbers; from the double, the three to two, the four to three, and from the difference of these, the 8 to 9. Thus he discovered the harmonic progression, which tends by a certain physical necessity from the lowest to the most acute sound, diatonically.

– Iámblichus, *Life of Pythágoras* (translated by K. S. Guthrie)

## Poetry and Philosophy

As I was saying, Eratósthenes contends that the aim of every poet is to entertain, not to instruct. The ancients assert, on the contrary, that poetry is a kind of elementary philosophy, which, taking us in our very boyhood, introduces us to the art of life and instructs us, with pleasure to ourselves, in character, emotions, and actions. And our School goes still further and contends that the wise man alone is a poet. That is the reason why in Greece the various states educate the young, at the very beginning of their education, by means of poetry; not for the mere sake of entertainment, of course, but for the sake of moral discipline. Why, even the musicians, when they give instruction in singing, in lyre-playing, origin flute-playing, lay claim to this virtue, for they maintain that these studies tend to discipline and correct the character. You may hear this contention made not merely by the Pythagoréans, but Aristóxenus also declares the same thing. And Hómer, too, has spoken of the bards as disciplinarians in morality, as when he says of the guard of Clytæmnéstra: "Whom the son of Átreus as he went to Troy strictly charged to keep watch over his wife" …

Rhetoric is, to be sure, wisdom applied to discourse; and Odýsseus displays this gift throughout the entire *Íliad*, in the Trial, in the Prayers, and in the Embassy, where Hómer says: "But when he uttered his great voice from his chest, and words like unto the snowflakes of winter, then could no mortal man contend with Odýsseus." Who, then, can assume that the poet who is capable of introducing other men in the role of orators, or of generals, or in other roles that exhibit the accomplishments of excellence, is himself but one of the buffoons or jugglers, capable only of bewitching and flattering his hearer but not of helping him? Nor can we assume that any excellence of a poet whatever is superior to that which enables him to imitate life through the means of speech. How, then, can a man imitate life if he has no experience of life and is a dolt? Of course we do not speak of the excellence of a poet in the same sense as we speak of that of a carpenter or a blacksmith; for their excellence depends upon no inherent nobility and dignity, whereas the excellence of a poet is inseparably associated with the excellence of the man himself, and it is impossible for one to become a good poet unless he has previously become a good man…

Now inasmuch as Hómer referred his myths to the province of education, he was wont to pay considerable attention to the truth. "And he mingled therein" a false element also, giving his sanction to the truth, but using the false to win the favor of the populace and to out-general the masses. "And as when some skillful man overlays gold upon silver," just so was Hómer wont to add a mythical element to actual occurrences, thus giving flavor and adornment to his style; but he has the same end in view as the historian or the person who narrates facts. So, for instance, he took the Trójan war, an historical fact, and decked it out with his myths; and he did the same in the case of the wanderings of Odýsseus; but to hang an empty story of marvels on something wholly untrue is not Hómer's way of doing things.

– Strábo, *Geography*, I.2.3,5,9 (translated by H. L. Jones)

# CHAPTER XIII.

## THE ENCROACHMENTS OF THE EAST UPON THE WEST

The Lýdian Conquest of Ásia Mínor, I.—The Rise and Conquests of Pérsia, II.
The Pérsian Empire and its Civilization, III.—The Revolt of the Iónian Cities, IV.

## I. THE LÝDIAN CONQUEST OF ÁSIA MÍNOR

### The Kingdom of Crœsus

On the death of Alyáttes, Crœsus, his son, who was thirty-five years old, succeeded to the throne. Of the Greek cities, Éphesus was the first that he attacked. The Ephésians, when he laid siege to the place, made an offering of their city to Diána, by stretching a rope from the town wall to the temple of the goddess, which was distant from the ancient city, then besieged by Crœsus, a space of seven furlongs. They were, as I said, the first Greeks whom he attacked. Afterwards, on some pretext or other, he made war in turn upon every Iónian and Æólian state, bringing forward, where he could, a substantial ground of complaint; where such failed him, advancing some poor excuse.

In this way he made himself master of all the Greek cities in Ásia and forced them to become his tributaries; after which he began to think of building ships, and attacking the islanders. Everything had been got ready for this purpose, when Bías of Priéne (or, as some say, Píttacus the Mytilénean) put a stop to the project. The king had made inquiry of this person, who was lately arrived at Sárdis, if there were any news from Greece; to which he answered, "Yes, sire, the islanders are gathering ten thousand horse, designing an expedition against thee and against thy capital." Crœsus, thinking he spake seriously, broke out, "Ah, might the gods put such a thought into their minds as to attack the sons of the Lýdians with cavalry!" "It seems, oh! king," rejoined the other, "that thou desirest earnestly to catch the islanders on horseback upon the mainland,—thou knowest well what would come of it. But what thinkest thou the islanders desire better, now that they hear thou art about to build ships and sail against them, than to catch the Lýdians at sea, and there revenge on them the wrongs of their brothers upon the mainland, whom thou holdest in slavery?" Crœsus was charmed with the turn of the speech; and thinking there was reason in what was said, gave up his shipbuilding and concluded a league of amity with the Iónians of the isles.

Crœsus afterwards, in the course of many years, brought under his sway almost all the nations to the west of the Hálys.

— Heródotus, *History*, I.26-28 (translated by George Rawlinson)

### Crœsus and Sólon

When all these conquests had been added to the Lýdian empire, and the prosperity of Sárdis was now at its height, there came thither, one after another, all the sages of Greece living at the time, and among them Sólon, the Athénian. He was on his travels, having left Áthens to be absent ten years, under the pretense of wishing to see the world, but really to avoid being forced to repeal any of the laws which, at the request of the Athénians, he had made for them. Without his sanction the Athénians could not repeal them, as they had bound themselves under a heavy curse to be governed for ten years by the laws which should be imposed on them by Sólon.

On this account, as well as to see the world, Sólon set out upon his travels, in the course of which he went to Égypt to the court of Amásis, and also came on a visit to Crœsus at Sárdis.

Crœsus received him as his guest and lodged him in the royal palace. On the third or fourth day after, he bade his servants conduct Sólon over his treasuries, and show him all their greatness and magnificence. When he had seen them all, and, so far as time allowed, inspected them, Crœsus addressed this question to him. "Stranger of Áthens, we have heard much of thy wisdom and of thy travels through many lands, from love of knowledge and a wish to see the world. I am curious therefore to inquire of thee, whom, of all the men that thou hast seen, thou deemest the most happy?" This he asked because he thought himself the happiest of mortals: but Sólon answered him without flattery, according to his true sentiments, "Téllus of Áthens, sire." Full of astonishment at what he heard, Crœsus demanded sharply, "And wherefore dost thou deem Téllus happiest?" To which the other replied, "First, because his country was flourishing in his days, and he himself had sons both beautiful and good, and he lived to see children born to each of them, and these children all grew up; and further because, after a life spent in what our people look upon as comfort, his end was surpassingly glorious. In a battle between the Athénians and their neighbors near Eléusis, he came to the assistance of his countrymen, routed the foe, and died upon the field most gallantly. The Athénians gave him a public funeral on the spot where he fell and paid him the highest honors."

Thus did Sólon admonish Crœsus by the example of Téllus, enumerating the manifold particulars of his happiness. When he had ended, Crœsus inquired a second time, who after Téllus seemed to him the happiest, expecting that at any rate, he would be given the second place. "Cléobis and Bíton," Sólon answered; "they were of Árgive race; their fortune was enough for their wants, and they were besides endowed with so much bodily strength that they had both gained prizes at the Games. Also this tale is told of them: There was a great festival in honor of the goddess Júno at Árgos, to which their mother must needs be taken in a car. Now the oxen did not come home from the field in time: so the youths, fearful of being too late, put the yoke on their own necks, and themselves drew the car in which their mother rode. Five and forty furlongs did they draw her, and stopped before the temple. This deed of theirs was witnessed by the whole assembly of worshippers, and then their life closed in the best possible way. Herein, too, God showed forth most evidently, how much better a thing for man death is than life. For the Árgive men, who stood around the car, extolled the vast strength of the youths; and the Árgive women extolled the mother who was blessed with such a pair of sons; and the mother herself, overjoyed at the deed and at the praises it had won, standing straight before the image, besought the goddess to bestow on Cléobis and Bíton, the sons who had so mightily honored her, the highest blessing to which mortals can attain. Her prayer ended, they offered sacrifice and partook of the holy banquet, after which the two youths fell asleep in the temple. They never woke more, but so passed from the earth. The Árgives, looking on them as among the best of men, caused statues of them to be made, which they gave to the shrine at Délphi."

When Sólon had thus assigned these youths the second place, Crœsus broke in angrily, "What, stranger of Áthens, is my happiness, then, so utterly set at naught by thee, that thou dost not even put me on a level with private men?"

"Oh! Crœsus," replied the other, "thou askedst a question concerning the condition of man, of one who knows that the power above us is full of jealousy, and fond of troubling our lot. A long life gives one to witness much, and experience much oneself, that one would not choose. Seventy years I regard as the limit of the life of man. In these seventy years are contained, without reckoning intercalary months, twenty-five thousand and two hundred days. Add an intercalary month to every other year, that the seasons may come round at the right time, and there will be, besides the seventy years, thirty-five such months, making an addition of one thousand and fifty days. The whole number of the days contained in the seventy years will thus be twenty-six thousand two hundred and fifty, whereof not one but will produce events unlike the rest. Hence man is wholly accident. For thyself, oh! Crœsus, I see that thou art wonderfully rich, and art the lord of many nations; but with respect to that whereon thou questionest me, I have no answer to give, until I hear that thou hast closed thy life happily. For assuredly he who possesses great store of riches is no nearer happiness than he who has what suffices for his daily needs, unless it so hap that luck attend upon him, and so he continue in the enjoyment of all his good things to the end of life. For many of the wealthiest men have been unfavored of fortune, and many whose means were moderate have had excellent luck.

Men of the former class excel those of the latter but in two respects; these last excel the former in many. The wealthy man is better able to content his desires, and to bear up against a sudden buffet of calamity. The other has less ability to withstand these evils (from which, however, his good luck keeps him clear), but he enjoys all these following blessings: he is whole of limb, a stranger to disease, free from misfortune, happy in his children, and comely to look upon. If, in addition to all this, he end his life well, he is of a truth the man of whom thou art in search, the man who may rightly be termed happy. Call him, however, until he die, not happy but fortunate. Scarcely, indeed, can any man unite all these advantages: as there is no country which contains within it all that it needs, but each, while it possesses some things, lacks others, and the best country is that which contains the most; so no single human being is complete in every respect—something is always lacking. He who unites the greatest number of advantages, and retaining them to the day of his death, then dies peaceably, that man alone, sire, is, in my judgment, entitled to bear the name of 'happy.' But in every matter it behooves us to mark well the end: for oftentimes God gives men a gleam of happiness, and then plunges them into ruin."

Such was the speech which Sólon addressed to Crœsus, a speech which brought him neither largesse nor honor. The king saw him depart with much indifference, since he thought that a man must be an arrant fool who made no account of present good, but bade men always wait and mark the end.

— Heródotus, *History*, I.29-33 (translated by George Rawlinson)

## The Death of Átys

After Sólon had gone away a dreadful vengeance, sent of God, came upon Crœsus, to punish him, it is likely, for deeming himself the happiest of men. First he had a dream in the night, which foreshowed him truly the evils that were about to befall him in the person of his son. For Crœsus had two sons, one blasted by a natural defect, being deaf and dumb; the other, distinguished far above all his companions in every pursuit. The name of the last was Átys. It was this son concerning whom he dreamt a dream that he would die by the blow of an iron weapon. When he woke, he considered earnestly with himself, and, greatly alarmed at the dream, instantly made his son take a wife, and whereas in former years the youth had been wont to command the Lýdian forces in the field, he now would not suffer him to accompany them. All the spears and javelins, and weapons used in the wars, he removed out of the male apartments, and laid them in heaps in the chambers of the women, fearing lest perhaps one of the weapons that hung against the wall might fall and strike him.

Now it chanced that while he was making arrangements for the wedding, there came to Sárdis a man under a misfortune, who had upon him the stain of blood. He was by race a Phrýgian, and belonged to the family of the king. Presenting himself at the palace of Crœsus, he prayed to be admitted to purification according to the customs of the country. Now the Lýdian method of purifying is very nearly the same as the Greek. Crœsus granted the request, and went through all the customary rites, after which he asked the suppliant of his birth and country, addressing him as follows: "Who art thou, stranger, and from what part of Phrýgia fleddest thou to take refuge at my hearth? And whom, moreover, what man or what woman, hast thou slain?" "Oh! king," replied the Phrýgian, "I am the son of Górdias, son of Mídas. I am named Adrástus. The man I unintentionally slew was my own brother. For this my father drove me from the land, and I lost all. Then fled I here to thee." "Thou art the offspring," Crœsus rejoined, "of a house friendly to mine, and thou art come to friends. Thou shalt want for nothing so long as thou abidest in my dominions. Bear thy misfortune as easily as thou mayest, so will it go best with thee." Thenceforth Adrástus lived in the palace of the king.

It chanced that at this very same time there was in the Mýsian Olýmpus a huge monster of a boar, which went forth often from this mountain country, and wasted the grain-fields of the Mýsians. Many a time had the Mýsians collected to hunt the beast, but instead of doing him any hurt, they came off always with some loss to themselves. At length they sent ambassadors to Crœsus, who delivered their message to him in these words: "Oh! king, a mighty monster of a boar has appeared in our parts and destroys the labor of our hands. We do our best to take him, but in vain. Now therefore we beseech thee to let thy son accompany us back, with some chosen youths and hounds, that we may rid our country of the animal." Such was the tenor of their prayer.

But Crœsus bethought him of his dream, and answered, "Say no more of my son going with you; that may not be in any wise. He is but just joined in wedlock and is busy enough with that. I will grant you a picked band of Lýdians, and all my huntsmen and hounds; and I will charge those whom I send to use all zeal in aiding you to rid your country of the brute."

With this reply the Mýsians were content; but the king's son, hearing what the prayer of the Mýsians was, came suddenly in, and on the refusal of Crœsus to let him go with them, thus addressed his father: "Formerly, my father, it was deemed the noblest and most suitable thing for me to frequent the wars and hunting-parties, and win myself glory in them; but now thou keepest me away from both, although thou hast never beheld in me either cowardice or lack of spirit. What face meanwhile must I wear as I walk to the forum or return from it? What must the citizens, what must my young bride think of me? What sort of man will she suppose her husband to be? Either, therefore, let me go to the chase of this boar, or give me a reason why it is best for me to do according to thy wishes."

Then Crœsus answered, "My son, it is not because I have seen in thee either cowardice or aught else which has displeased me that I keep thee back; but because a vision which came before me in a dream as I slept, warned me that thou wert doomed to die young, pierced by an iron weapon. It was this which first led me to hasten on thy wedding, and now it hinders me from sending thee upon this enterprise. Fain would I keep watch over thee, if by any means I may cheat fate of thee during my own lifetime. For thou art the one and only son that I possess; the other, whose hearing is destroyed, I regard as if he were not."

"Ah! father," returned the youth, "I blame thee not for keeping watch over me after a dream so terrible; but if thou mistakest, if thou dost not apprehend the dream aright, 'tis no blame for me to show thee wherein thou errest. Now the dream, thou saidst thyself, foretold that I should die stricken by an iron weapon. But what hands has a boar to strike with? What iron weapon does he wield? Yet this is what thou fearest for me. Had the dream said that I should die pierced by a tusk, then thou hadst done well to keep me away; but it said a weapon. Now here we do not combat men, but a wild animal. I pray thee, therefore, let me go with them."

"There thou hast me, my son," said Crœsus, "thy interpretation is better than mine. I yield to it, and change my mind, and consent to let thee go."

Then the king sent for Adrástus, the Phrýgian, and said to him, "Adrástus, when thou wert smitten with the rod of affliction—no reproach, my friend—I purified thee, and have taken thee to live with me in my palace, and have been at every charge. Now, therefore, it behooves thee to requite the good offices which thou hast received at my hands by consenting to go with my son on this hunting party, and to watch over him, if perchance you should be attacked upon the road by some band of daring robbers. Even apart from this, it were right for thee to go where thou mayest make thyself famous by noble deeds. They are the heritage of thy family, and thou too art so stalwart and strong."

Adrástus answered, "Except for thy request, Oh! king, I would rather have kept away from this hunt; for methinks it ill beseems a man under a misfortune such as mine to consort with his happier compeers; and besides, I have no heart to it. On many grounds I had stayed behind; but, as thou urgest it, and I am bound to pleasure thee (for truly it does behoove me to requite thy good offices), I am content to do as thou wishest. For thy son, whom thou givest into my charge, be sure thou shalt receive him back safe and sound, so far as depends upon a guardian's carefulness."

Thus assured, Crœsus let them depart, accompanied by a band of picked youths, and well provided with dogs of chase. When they reached Olýmpus, they scattered in quest of the animal; he was soon found, and the hunters, drawing round him in a circle, hurled their weapons at him. Then the stranger, the man who had been purified of blood, whose name was Adrástus, he also hurled his spear at the boar, but missed his aim, and struck Átys. Thus was the son of Crœsus slain by the point of an iron weapon, and the warning of the vision was fulfilled. Then one ran to Sárdis to bear the tidings to the king, and he came and informed him of the combat and of the fate that had befallen his son.

If it was a heavy blow to the father to learn that his child was dead, it yet more strongly affected him to think that the very man whom he himself once purified had done the deed. In the violence of his grief he called aloud on Júpiter Cathársius to be a witness of what he had suffered at the stranger's hands. Afterwards he invoked the same god as Júpiter Ephístius and Hetǽreus—using the one term because he had unwittingly harbored in his house the man who had now slain his son; and the other, because the stranger, who had been sent as his child's guardian, had turned out his most cruel enemy.

Presently the Lýdians arrived, bearing the body of the youth, and behind them followed the homicide. He took his stand in front of the corpse, and, stretching forth his hands to Crœsus, delivered himself into his power with earnest entreaties that he would sacrifice him upon the body of his son—"his former misfortune was burthen enough; now that he had added to it a second, and had brought ruin on the man who purified him, he could not bear to live." Then Crœsus, when he heard these words, was moved with pity towards Adrástus, notwithstanding the bitterness of his own calamity; and so he answered, "Enough, my friend; I have all the revenge that I require, since thou givest sentence of death against thyself. But in sooth it is not thou who hast injured me, except so far as thou hast unwittingly dealt the blow. Some god is the author of my misfortune, and I was forewarned of it a long time ago." Crœsus after this buried the body of his son, with such honors as befitted the occasion. Adrástus, son of Górdias, son of Mídas, the destroyer of his brother in time past, the destroyer now of his purifier, regarding himself as the most unfortunate wretch whom he had ever known, so soon as all was quiet about the place, slew himself upon the tomb. Crœsus, bereft of his son, gave himself up to mourning for two full years.

— Heródotus, *History*, I.34-45 (translated by George Rawlinson)

## Crœsus Receives a Reply from the Délphic Oracle

The messengers who had the charge of conveying these treasures to the shrines, received instructions to ask the oracles whether Crœsus should go to war with the Pérsians and if so, whether he should strengthen himself by the forces of an ally. Accordingly, when they had reached their destinations and presented the gifts, they proceeded to consult the oracles in the following terms: "Crœsus, of Lýdia and other countries, believing that these are the only real oracles in all the world, has sent you such presents as your discoveries deserved, and now inquires of you whether he shall go to war with the Pérsians, and if so, whether he shall strengthen himself by the forces of a confederate." Both the oracles agreed in the tenor of their reply, which was in each case a prophecy that if Crœsus attacked the Pérsians, he would destroy a mighty empire, and a recommendation to him to look and see who were the most powerful of the Greeks, and to make alliance with them.

At the receipt of these oracular replies Crœsus was overjoyed and, feeling sure now that he would destroy the empire of the Pérsians, he sent once more to Pýtho, and presented to the Déphians, the number of whom he had ascertained, two gold staters apiece. In return for this the Délphians granted to Crœsus and the Lýdians the privilege of precedence in consulting the oracle, exemption from all charges, the most honorable seat at the festivals, and the perpetual right of becoming at pleasure citizens of their town.

— Heródotus, *History*, I.53-56 (translated by George Rawlinson)

## The Pérsians Defeat Crœsus

There were two motives which led Crœsus to attack Cappadócia: firstly, he coveted the land, which he wished to add to his own dominions; but the chief reason was that he wanted to revenge on Cýrus the wrongs of Astýages, and was made confident by the oracle of being able so to do: for Astýages, son of Cyáxares and king of the Medes, who had been dethroned by Cýrus, son of Cambýses, was Crœsus' brother by marriage ... Cýrus had captured this Astýages, who was his mother's father, and kept him prisoner, for a reason which I shall bring forward in another of my history. This capture formed the ground of quarrel between Cýrus and Crœsus, in consequence of which Crœsus sent his servants to ask the oracle if he should attack the Pérsians; and when an evasive answer came, fancying it to be in his favor, carried his arms into the Pérsian territory. When he reached the river Hálys, he transported his army across it, as I maintain, by the bridges which exist there at the present day; but, according to the general belief of the Greeks, by the aid of Tháles the Milésian. The tale is that Crœsus was in doubt how he should get his army across, as the bridges were not made at that time, and that Tháles, who happened to be in the camp, divided the stream and caused it to flow on both sides of the army instead of on the left only. This he effected thus: Beginning some distance above the camp, he dug a deep channel, which he brought round in a semicircle, so that it might pass to rearward of the camp; and that thus the river, diverted from its natural course into the new channel at the point where this left the stream, might flow by the station of the army, and afterwards fall again into the ancient bed. In this way the river was split into two streams, which were both easily fordable...

Having passed the Hálys with the forces under his command, Crœsus entered the district of Cappadócia which is called Ptéria. It lies in the neighborhood of the city of Sinópe upon the Éuxine and is the strongest position in the whole country thereabouts. Here Crœsus pitched his camp and began to ravage the fields of the Sýrians. He besieged and took the chief city of the Ptérians and reduced the inhabitants to slavery: he likewise made himself master of the surrounding villages. Thus he brought ruin on the Sýrians, who were guilty of no offence towards him. Meanwhile, Cýrus had levied an army and marched against Crœsus, increasing his numbers at every step by the forces of the nations that lay in his way. Before beginning his march he had sent heralds to the Iónians, with an invitation to them to revolt from the Lýdian king: they, however, had refused compliance. Cýrus, notwithstanding, marched against the enemy, and encamped opposite them in the district of Ptéria, where the trial of strength took place between the contending powers. The combat was hot and bloody, and upon both sides the number of the slain was great; nor had victory declared in favor of either party, when night came down upon the battlefield. Thus both armies fought valiantly.

Crœsus laid the blame of his ill success on the number of his troops, which fell very short of the enemy; and as on the next day Cýrus did not repeat the attack, he set off on his return to Sárdis, intending to collect his allies and renew the contest in the spring. He meant to call on the Egýptians to send him aid, according to the terms of the alliance which he had concluded with Amásis, previously to his league with the Lacedæmónians. He intended also to summon to his assistance the Babylónians, under their king Labynétus, for they too were bound to him by treaty: and further, he meant to send word to Spárta, and appoint a day for the coming of their succors. Having got together these forces in addition to his own, he would, as soon as the winter was past and springtime come, march once more against the Pérsians. With these intentions Crœsus, immediately on his return, dispatched heralds to his various allies, with a request that they would join him at Sárdis in the course of the fifth month from the time of the departure of his messengers. He then disbanded the army consisting of mercenary troops, which had been engaged with the Pérsians and had since accompanied him to his capital, and let them depart to their homes, never imagining that Cýrus, after a battle in which victory had been so evenly balanced, would venture to march upon Sárdis...

Cýrus, however, when Crœsus broke up so suddenly from his quarters after the battle at Ptéria, conceiving that he had marched away with the intention of disbanding his army, considered a little, and soon saw that it was advisable for him to advance upon Sárdis with all haste, before the Lýdians could get their forces together a second time. Having thus determined, he lost no time in carrying out his plan. He marched forward with such speed that he was himself the first to announce his coming to the Lýdian king. That monarch, placed in the utmost difficulty by the turn of events which had gone so entirely against all his calculations, nevertheless led out the Lýdians to battle. In all Ásia there was not at that time a braver or more warlike people. Their manner of fighting was on horseback; they carried long lances and were clever in the management of their steeds.

The two armies met in the plain before Sárdis. It is a vast flat, bare of trees, watered by the Hýllus and a number of other streams, which all flow into one larger than the rest, called the Hérmus. This river rises in the sacred mountain of the Dindyménian Mother and falls into the sea near the town of Phocǽa.

When Cýrus beheld the Lýdians arranging themselves in order of battle on this plain, fearful of the strength of their cavalry, he adopted a device which Hárpagus, one of the Medes, suggested to him. He collected together all the camels that had come in the train of his army to carry the provisions and the baggage, and taking off their loads, he mounted riders upon them accoutered as horsemen. These he commanded to advance in front of his other troops against the Lýdian horse; behind them were to follow the foot soldiers, and last of all the cavalry. When his arrangements were complete, he gave his troops orders to slay all the other Lýdians who came in their way without mercy, but to spare Crœsus and not kill him, even if he should be seized and offer resistance. The reason why Cýrus opposed his camels to the enemy's horse was because the horse has a natural dread of the camel and cannot abide either the sight or the smell of that animal. By this stratagem he hoped to make Crœsus's horse useless to him, the horse being what he chiefly depended on for victory. The two armies then joined battle, and immediately the Lýdian war-horses, seeing and smelling the camels, turned round and galloped off; and so it came to pass that all Crœsus's hopes withered away. The Lýdians, however, behaved manfully. As soon as they understood what was happening, they leaped off their horses, and engaged with the Pérsians on foot. The combat was long; but at last, after a great slaughter on both sides, the Lýdians turned and fled. They were driven within their walls and the Pérsians laid siege to Sárdis.

— Heródotus, *History*, I.73-80 (translated by George Rawlinson)


## The Fall of Sárdis and Capture of Crœsus

With respect to Crœsus himself, this is what befell him at the taking of the town. He had a son, of whom I made mention above, a worthy youth, whose only defect was that he was deaf and dumb. In the days of his prosperity Crœsus had done the utmost that be could for him, and among other plans which he had devised, had sent to Délphi to consult the oracle on his behalf. The answer which he had received from the Pýthoness ran thus:

Lýdian, wide-ruling monarch, thou wondrous simple Crœsus,
Wish not ever to hear in thy palace the voice thou hast prayed for
Uttering intelligent sounds. Far better thy son should be silent!
Ah! woe worth the day when thine ear shall first list to his accents.

When the town was taken, one of the Pérsians was just going to kill Crœsus, not knowing who he was. Crœsus saw the man coming, but under the pressure of his affliction, did not care to avoid the blow, not minding whether or no he died beneath the stroke. Then this son of his, who was voiceless, beholding the Pérsian as he rushed towards Crœsus, in the agony of his fear and grief burst into speech, and said, "Man, do not kill Crœsus." This was the first time that he had ever spoken a word, but afterwards he retained the power of speech for the remainder of his life.

— Heródotus, *History*, I.84-85 (translated by George Rawlinson)

## Crœsus Before King Cýrus

Thus was Sárdis taken by the Pérsians, and Crœsus himself fell into their hands, after having reigned fourteen years, and been besieged in his capital fourteen days; thus too did Crœsus fulfill the oracle, which said that he should destroy a mighty empire by destroying his own. Then the Pérsians who had made Crœsus prisoner brought him before Cýrus. Now a vast pile had been raised by his orders, and Crœsus, laden with fetters, was placed upon it, and with him twice seven of the sons of the Lýdians. I know not whether Cýrus was minded to make an offering of the first-fruits to some god or other, or whether he had vowed a vow and was performing it, or whether, as may well be, he had heard that Crœsus was a holy man, and so wished to see if any of the heavenly powers would appear to save him from being burnt alive. However it might be, Cýrus was thus engaged, and Crœsus was already on the pile, when it entered his mind in the depth of his woe that there was a divine warning in the words which had come to him from the lips of Sólon, "No one while he lives is happy."

When this thought smote him he fetched a long breath, and breaking his deep silence, groaned out aloud, thrice uttering the name of Sólon. Cýrus caught the sounds, and bade the interpreters inquire of Crœsus who it was he called on. They drew near and asked him, but he held his peace, and for a long time made no answer to their questionings, until at length, forced to say something, he exclaimed, "One I would give much to see converse with every monarch." Not knowing what he meant by this reply, the interpreters begged him to explain himself; and as they pressed for an answer, and grew to be troublesome, he told them how, a long time before, Sólon, an Athénian, had come and seen all his splendor, and made light of it; and how whatever he had said to him had fallen out exactly as he foreshowed, although it was nothing that especially concerned him, but applied to all mankind alike, and most to those who seemed to themselves happy. Meanwhile, as he thus spoke, the pile was lighted, and the outer portion began to blaze. Then Cýrus, hearing from the interpreters what Crœsus had said, relented, bethinking himself that he too was a man, and that it was a fellow-man, and one who had once been as blessed by fortune as himself, that he was burning alive; afraid, moreover, of retribution, and full of the thought that whatever is human is insecure. So he bade them quench the blazing fire as quickly as they could, and take down Crœsus and the other Lýdians, which they tried to do, but the flames were not to be mastered.

Then, the Lýdians say that Crœsus, perceiving by the efforts made to quench the fire that Cýrus had relented, and seeing also that all was in vain, and that the men could not get the fire under, called with a loud voice upon the god Apóllo, and prayed him, if he ever received at his hands any acceptable gift, to come to his aid, and deliver him from his present danger. As thus with tears he besought the god, suddenly, though up to that time the sky had been clear and the day without a breath of wind, dark clouds gathered, and the storm burst over their heads with rain of such violence, that the flames were speedily extinguished. Cýrus, convinced by this that Crœsus was a good man and a favorite of heaven, asked him after he was taken off the pile, "Who it was that had persuaded him to lead an army into his country, and so become his foe rather than continue his friend?" to which Crœsus made answer as follows: "What I did, oh! king, was to thy advantage and to my own loss. If there be blame, it rests with the god of the Greeks, who encouraged me to begin the war. No one is so foolish as to prefer war to peace, in which, instead of sons burying their fathers, fathers bury their sons. But the gods willed it so."

Thus did Crœsus speak. Cýrus then ordered his fetters to be taken off, and made him sit down near himself, and paid him much respect, looking upon him, as did also the courtiers, with a sort of wonder. Crœsus, wrapped in thought, uttered no word. After a while, happening to turn and perceive the Pérsian soldiers engaged in plundering the town, he said to Cýrus, "May I now tell thee, oh! king, what I have in my mind, or is silence best?" Cýrus bade him speak his mind boldly. Then he put this question: "What is it, oh! Cýrus, which those men yonder are doing so busily?" "Plundering thy city," Cýrus answered, "and carrying off thy riches." "Not my city," rejoined the other, "nor my riches. They are not mine anymore. It is thy wealth which they are pillaging."

Cýrus, struck by what Crœsus had said, bade all the court to withdraw, and then asked Crœsus what he thought it best for him to do as regarded the plundering. Crœsus answered, "Now that the gods have made me thy slave, oh! Cýrus, it seems to me that it is my part, if I see anything to thy advantage, to show it to thee. Thy subjects, the Pérsians, are a poor people with a proud spirit. If then thou lettest them pillage and possess themselves of great wealth, I will tell thee what thou hast to expect at their hands. The man who gets the most, look to having him rebel against thee. Now then, if my words please thee, do thus, oh! king: Let some of thy bodyguards be placed as sentinels at each of the city gates, and let them take their booty from the soldiers as they leave the town, and tell them that they do so because the tenths are due to Júpiter. So wilt thou escape the hatred they would feel if the plunder were taken away from them by force; and they, seeing that what is proposed is just, will do it willingly."

Cýrus was beyond measure pleased with this advice, so excellent did it seem to him. He praised Crœsus highly and gave orders to his bodyguard to do as he had suggested. Then, turning to Crœsus, he said, "Oh! Crœsus, I see that thou are resolved both in speech and act to show thyself a virtuous prince: ask me, therefore, whatever thou wilt as a gift at this moment." Crœsus replied, "Oh! my lord, if thou wilt suffer me to send these fetters to the god of the Greeks, whom I once honored above all other gods, and ask him if it is his wont to deceive his benefactors—that will be the highest favor thou canst confer on me." Cýrus upon this inquired what charge he had to make against the god. Then Crœsus gave him a full account of all his projects, and of the answers of the oracle, and of the offerings which he had sent, on which he dwelt especially, and told him how it was the encouragement given him by the oracle which had led him to make war upon Pérsia. All this he related, and at the end again besought permission to reproach the god with his behavior.

— Heródotus, *History*, I.86-90 (translated by George Rawlinson)


## II. THE RISE AND CONQUESTS OF PÉRSIA

## The Iónian Greeks Beg Their Former Liberties

Immediately after the conquest of Lýdia by the Pérsians, the Iónian and Æólian Greeks sent ambassadors to Cýrus at Sárdis and prayed to become his lieges on the footing which they had occupied under Crœsus. Cýrus listened attentively to their proposals and answered them by a fable.

"There was a certain piper," he said, "who was walking one day by the seaside, when he espied some fish; so he began to pipe to them, imagining they would come out to him upon the land. But as he found at last that his hope was vain, he took a net, and enclosing a great draught of fishes, drew them ashore. The fish then began to leap and dance; but the piper said, 'Cease your dancing now, as you did not choose to come and dance when I piped to you.'" Cýrus gave this answer to the Iónians and Æólians, because, when he urged them by his messengers to revolt from Crœsus, they refused; but now, when his work was done, they came to offer their allegiance. It was in anger, therefore, that he made them this reply. The Iónians, on hearing it, set to work to fortify their towns, and held meetings at the Paniónium, which were attended by all excepting the Milésians, with whom Cýrus had concluded a separate treaty, by which he allowed them the terms they had formerly obtained from Crœsus. The other Iónians resolved, with one accord, to send ambassadors to Spárta to implore assistance.

— Heródotus, *History*, I.141 (translated by George Rawlinson)

## Cýrus Conquers Bábylon

... Cýrus, with the first approach of the ensuing spring, marched forward against Bábylon. The Babylónians, encamped without their walls, awaited his coming. A battle was fought at a short distance from the city, in which the Babylónians were defeated by the Pérsian king, whereupon they withdrew within their defenses. Here they shut themselves up, and made light of his siege, having laid in a store of provisions for many years in preparation against this attack; for when they saw Cýrus conquering nation after nation, they were convinced that he would never stop, and that their turn would come at last.

Cýrus was now reduced to great perplexity, as time went on and he made no progress against the place. In this distress either some one made the suggestion to him, or he bethought himself of a plan, which he proceeded to put in execution. He placed a portion of his army at the point where the river enters the city, and another body at the back of the place where it issues forth, with orders to march into the town by the bed of the stream, as soon as the water became shallow enough. He then himself drew off with the unwarlike portion of his host, and made for the place where Nitocris dug the basin for the river, where he did exactly what she had done formerly: he turned the Euphrátes by a canal into the basin, which was then a marsh, on which the river sank to such an extent that the natural bed of the stream became fordable. Hereupon the Pérsians who had been left for the purpose at Bábylon by the, riverside, entered the stream, which had now sunk so as to reach about midway up a man's thigh, and thus got into the town.

Had the Babylónians been apprised of what Cýrus was about, or had they noticed their danger, they would never have allowed the Pérsians to enter the city, but would have destroyed them utterly; for they would have made fast all the street-gates which gave upon the river, and mounting upon the walls along both sides of the stream, would so have caught the enemy, as it were, in a trap. But, as it was, the Pérsians came upon them by surprise and so took the city. Owing to the vast size of the place, the inhabitants of the central parts (as the residents at Bábylon declare) long after the outer portions of the town were taken, knew nothing of what had chanced, but as they were engaged in a festival, continued dancing and reveling until they learnt the capture but too certainly. Such, then, were the circumstances of the first taking of Bábylon.

— Heródotus, *History*, I.189-191 (translated by George Rawlinson)

## Cambýses Conquers Égypt

Psammenítus, son of Amásis, lay encamped at the mouth of the Nile, called the Pelúsiac, awaiting Cambýses. For Cambýses, when he went up against Égypt, found Amásis no longer in life: he had died after ruling Égypt forty and four years, during all which time no great misfortune had befallen him. When he died, his body was embalmed, and buried in the tomb which he had himself caused to be made in the temple. After his son Psammenítus had mounted the throne, a strange prodigy occurred in Égypt—rain fell at Egýptian Thebes, a thing which never happened before, and which, to the present time, has never happened again, as the Thébans themselves testify. In Upper Égypt it does not usually rain at all; but on this occasion, rain fell at Thebes in small drops.

The Pérsians crossed the desert, and, pitching their camp close to the Egýptians, made ready for battle. Hereupon the mercenaries in the pay of Psammenítus, who were Greeks and Cárians, full of anger against Phánes for having brought a foreign army upon Égypt, bethought themselves of a mode whereby they might be revenged on him. Phánes had left sons in Égypt. The mercenaries took these, and leading them to the camp, displayed them before the eyes of their father; after which they brought out a bowl, and, placing it in the space between the two hosts, they led the sons of Phánes, one by one, to the vessel, and slew them over it. When the last was dead, water and wine were poured into the bowl, and all the soldiers tasted of the blood, and so they went to the battle. Stubborn was the fight which followed, and it was not till vast numbers had been slain upon both sides, that the Egýptians turned and fled.

— Heródotus, *History*, II.10-11 (translated by George Rawlinson)

## III. THE PÉRSIAN EMPIRE AND ITS CIVILIZATION

# A Description of Bábylon

Assýria possesses a vast number of great cities, whereof the most renowned and strongest at this time was Bábylon, whither, after the fall of Níneveh, the seat of government had been removed. The following is a description of the place: The city stands on a broad plain, and is an exact square, a hundred and twenty furlongs in length each way, so that the entire circuit is four hundred and eighty furlongs. While such is its size, in magnificence there is no other city that approaches to it. It is surrounded, in the first place, by a broad and deep moat, full of water, behind which rises a wall fifty royal cúbits in width, and two hundred in height. (The royal cúbit is longer by three fingers' breadth than the common cúbit.)

And here I may not omit to tell the use to which the mold dug out of the great moat was turned, nor the manner wherein the wall was wrought. As fast as they dug the moat the soil which they got from the cutting was made into bricks, and when a sufficient number were completed they baked the bricks in kilns. Then they set to building, and began with bricking the borders of the moat, after which they proceeded to construct the wall itself, using throughout for their cement hot bitumen, and interposing a layer of wattled reeds at every thirtieth course of the bricks. On the top, along the edges of the wall, they constructed buildings of a single chamber facing one another, leaving between them room for a four-horse chariot to turn. In the circuit of the wall are a hundred gates, all of brass, with brazen lintels and side-posts. The bitumen used in the work was brought to Bábylon from the Is, a small stream which flows into the Euphrátes at the point where the city of the same name stands, eight days' journey from Bábylon. Lumps of bitumen are found in great abundance in this river.

The city is divided into two portions by the river which runs through the midst of it. This river is the Euphrátes, a broad, deep, swift stream, which rises in Arménia, and empties itself into the Erythræan sea. The city wall is brought down on both sides to the edge of the stream: thence, from the corners of the wall, there is carried along each bank of the river a fence of burnt bricks. The houses are mostly three and four stories high; the streets all run in straight lines, not only those parallel to the river, but also the cross streets which lead down to the waterside. At the river end of these cross streets are low gates in the fence that skirts the stream, which are, like the great gates in the outer wall, of brass, and open on the water.

The outer wall is the main defense of the city. There is, however, a second inner wall, of less thickness than the first, but very little inferior to it in strength. The center of each division of the town was occupied by a fortress. In the one stood the palace of the kings, surrounded by a wall of great strength and size: in the other was the sacred precinct of Júpiter Bélus, a square enclosure two furlongs each way, with gates of solid brass; which was also remaining in my time. In the middle of the precinct there was a tower of solid masonry, a furlong in length and breadth, upon which was raised a second tower, and on that a third, and so on up to eight. The ascent to the top is on the outside, by a path which winds round all the towers. When one is about half-way up, one finds a resting-place and seats, where persons are wont to sit some time on their way to the summit. On the topmost tower there is a spacious temple, and inside the temple stands a couch of unusual size, richly adorned, with a golden table by its side. There is no statue of any kind set up in the place...

Below, in the same precinct, there is a second temple, in which is a sitting figure of Júpiter, all of gold. Before the figure stands a large golden table, and the throne whereon it sits, and the base on which the throne is placed, are likewise of gold. The Chaldéans told me that all the gold together was eight hundred talents' weight. Outside the temple are two altars, one of solid gold, on which it is only lawful to offer sucklings; the other a common altar, but of great size, on which the full-grown animals are sacrificed. It is also on the great altar that the Chaldéans burn the frankincense, which is offered to the amount of a thousand talents' weight, every year, at the festival of the God. In the time of Cýrus there was likewise in this temple a figure of a man, twelve cúbits high, entirely of solid gold. I myself did not see this figure, but I relate what the Chaldéans report concerning it. Daríus, the son of Hystáspes, plotted to carry the statue off, but had not the hardihood to lay his hands upon it. Xérxes, however, the son of Daríus, killed the priest who forbade him to move the statue, and took it away. Besides the ornaments which I have mentioned, there are a large number of private offerings in this holy precinct.

— Heródotus, *History*, I.178-183 (translated by George Rawlinson)

## Religious Rites of the Pérsians

The customs which I know the Pérsians to observe are the following: they have no images of the gods, no temples nor altars, and consider the use of them a sign of folly. This comes, I think, from their not believing the gods to have the same nature with men, as the Greeks imagine. Their wont, however, is to ascend the summits of the loftiest mountains, and there to offer sacrifice to Júpiter, which is the name they give to the whole circuit of the firmament. They likewise offer to the sun and moon, to the earth, to fire, to water, and to the winds. These are the only gods whose worship has come down to them from ancient times. At a later period they began the worship of Uránia, which they borrowed from the Arábians and Assýrians...

To these gods the Pérsians offer sacrifice in the following manner: they raise no altar, light no fire, pour no libations; there is no sound of the flute, no putting on of chaplets, no consecrated barley-cake; but the man who wishes to sacrifice brings his victim to a spot of ground which is pure from pollution, and there calls upon the name of the god to whom he intends to offer. It is usual to have the turban encircled with a wreath, most commonly of myrtle. The sacrificer is not allowed to pray for blessings on himself alone, but he prays for the welfare of the king, and of the whole Pérsian people, among whom he is of necessity included. He cuts the victim in pieces, and having boiled the flesh, he lays it out upon the tenderest herbage that he can find, trefoil especially. When all is ready, one of the Mági comes forward and chants a hymn, which they say recounts the origin of the gods. It is not lawful to offer sacrifice unless there is a Mágus present. After waiting a short time the sacrificer carries the flesh of the victim away with him, and makes whatever use of it he may please.

— Heródotus, *History*, I.131-132 (translated by George Rawlinson)

## The Scýthians and Ámazons

It is reported of the Saurómatæ, that when the Greeks fought with the Ámazons ... that the Greeks after gaining the battle of the Thermódon, put to sea, taking with them on board three of their vessels all the Ámazons whom they had made prisoners; and that these women upon the voyage rose up against the crews, and massacred them to a man. As however they were quite strange to ships, and did not know how to use either rudder, sails, or oars, they were carried, after the death of the men, where the winds and the waves listed. At last they reached the shores of the Pálus Mæótis [marshes of the Sea of Azov] and came to a place called Crémni or "the Cliffs," which is in the country of the free Scýthians. Here they went ashore, and proceeded by land towards the inhabited regions; the first herd of horses which they fell in with they seized, and mounting upon their backs, fell to plundering the Scýthian territory.

The Scyths could not tell what to make of the attack upon them. The dress, the language, the nation itself, were alike unknown whence the enemy had come even, was a marvel. Imagining, however, that they were all men of about the same age, they went out against them, and fought a battle. Some of the bodies of the slain fell into their hands, whereby they discovered the truth. Hereupon they deliberated, and made a resolve to kill no more of them, but to send against them a detachment of their youngest men, as near as they could guess equal to the women in number, with orders to encamp in their neighborhood, and do as they saw them do—when the Ámazons advanced against them, they were to retire, and avoid a fight—when they halted, the young men were to approach and pitch their camp near the camp of the enemy. All this they did on account of their strong desire to obtain children from so notable a race.

So the youths departed, and obeyed the orders which had been given them. The Ámazons soon found out that they had not come to do them any harm; and so they on their part ceased to offer the Scýthians any molestation. And now day after day the camps approached nearer to one another; both parties led the same life, neither having anything but their arms and horses, so that they were forced to support themselves by hunting and pillage. At last an incident brought two of them together. The man easily gained the good graces of the woman, who bade him by signs (for they did not understand each other's language) to bring a friend the next day to the spot where they had met, promising on her part to bring with her another woman. He did so, and the woman kept her word. When the rest of the youths heard what had taken place, they also sought and gained the favor of the other Ámazons.

The two camps were then joined in one, the Scýthians living with the Ámazons as their wives; and the men were unable to learn the tongue of the women, but the women soon caught up the tongue of the men. When they could thus understand one another, the Scyths addressed the Ámazons in these words: "We have parents, and properties, let us therefore give up this mode of life, and return to our nation, and live with them. You shall be our wives there no less than here, and we promise you to have no others." But the Ámazons said, "We could not live with your women; our customs are quite different from theirs. To draw the bow, to hurl the javelin, to bestride the horse, these are our arts. Of womanly employments we know nothing. Your women, on the contrary, do none of these things; but stay at home in their wagons, engaged in womanish tasks, and never go out to hunt, or to do anything. We should never agree together. But if you truly wish to keep us as your wives, and would conduct yourselves with strict justice towards us, go you home to your parents, bid them give you your inheritance, and then come back to us, and let us and you live together by ourselves."

The youths approved of the advice and followed it. They went and got the portion of goods which fell to them, returned with it, and rejoined their wives, who then addressed them in these words following: "We are ashamed, and afraid to live in the country where we now are. Not only have we stolen you from your fathers, but we have done great damage to Scýthia by our ravages. As you like us for wives, grant the request we make of you. Let us leave this country together and go and dwell beyond the Tánaïs [the Don River]." Again the youths complied. Crossing the Tánaïs they journeyed eastward a distance of three days' march from that stream, and again northward a distance of three days' march from the Pálus Mæótis. Here they came to the country where they now live and took up their abode in it. The women of the Saurómatæ have continued from that day to the present to observe their ancient customs, frequently hunting on horseback with their husbands, sometimes even unaccompanied; in war taking the field; and wearing the very same dress as the men.

The Saurómatæ speak the language of Scýthia, but have never spoken it correctly, because the Ámazons learnt it imperfectly at the first. Their marriage-law lays it down that no girl shall wed till she has killed a man in battle. Sometimes it happens that a woman dies unmarried at an advanced age, having never been able in her whole lifetime to fulfil the condition.

— Heródotus, *History*, IV.109-117 (translated by George Rawlinson)


## IV. THE REVOLT OF THE IÓNIAN CITIES

## The Athénians and Iónians Burn Sárdis

The Iónians sailed with this fleet to Éphesus, and, leaving their ships at Coréssus in the Ephésian territory, took guides from the city, and went up the country with a great host. They marched along the course of the river Caýster, and, crossing over the ridge of Tmólus, came down upon Sárdis and took it, no man opposing them; the whole city fell into their hands, except only the citadel, which Artaphérnes defended in person, having with him no contemptible force.

Though, however, they took the city, they did not succeed in plundering it; for, as the houses in Sárdis were most of them built of reeds, and even the few which were of brick had a reed thatching for their roof, one of them was no sooner fired by a soldier than the flames ran speedily from house to house, and spread over the whole place. As the fire raged, the Lýdians and such Pérsians as were in the city, enclosed on every side by the flames, which had seized all the skirts of the town, and finding themselves unable to get out, came in crowds into the market-place, and gathered themselves upon the banks of the Pactólus. This stream, which comes down from Mount Tmólus, and brings the Sárdians a quantity of gold-dust, runs directly through the marketplace of Sárdis, and joins the Hérmus, before that river reaches the sea. So the Lýdians and Pérsians, brought together in this way in the market-place and about the Pactólus, were forced to stand on their defense; and the Iónians, when they saw the enemy in part resisting, in part pouring towards them in dense crowds, took fright, and drawing off to the ridge which is called Tmólus when night came, went back to their ships.

Sárdis however was burnt, and, among other buildings, a temple of the native goddess Cýbele was destroyed; which was the reason afterwards alleged by the Pérsians for setting on fire the temples of the Greeks. As soon as what had happened was known, all the Pérsians who were stationed on this side the Hálys drew together and brought help to the Lýdians. Finding however, when they arrived, that the Iónians had already withdrawn from Sárdis, they set off, and, following close upon their track, came up with them at Éphesus. The Iónians drew out against them in battle array; and a fight ensued, wherein the Greeks had very greatly the worse. Vast numbers were slain by the Pérsians...

So ended this encounter. Afterwards the Athénians quite forsook the Iónians, and, though Aristágoras besought them much by his ambassadors, refused to give him any further help. Still the Iónians, notwithstanding this desertion, continued unceasingly their preparations to carry on the war against the Pérsian king, which their late conduct towards him had rendered unavoidable. Sailing into the Héllespont, they brought Byzántium, and all the other cities in that quarter, under their sway. Again, quitting the Héllespont, they went to Cária, and won the greater part of the Cárians to their side; while Cáunus, which had formerly refused to join with them, after the burning of Sárdis, came over likewise.

All the Cýprians too, excepting those of Ámathus, of their own proper motion espoused the Iónian cause... King Daríus received tidings of the taking and burning of Sárdis by the Athénians and Iónians; and at the same time he learnt that the author of the league, the man by whom the whole matter had been planned and contrived, was Aristágoras the Milésian. It is said that he no sooner understood what had happened, than, laying aside all thought concerning the Iónians, who would, he was sure, pay dear for their rebellion, he asked, "Who the Athénians were?" and, being informed, called for his bow, and placing an arrow on the string, shot upward into the sky, saying, as he let fly the shaft: "Grant me, Júpiter, to revenge myself on the Athénians!" After this speech, he bade one of his servants every day, when his dinner was spread, three times repeat these words to him: "Master, remember the Athénians."

— Heródotus, *History*, V.100-105 (translated by George Rawlinson)

## The Defeat of the Iónian Fleet and the Sack of Milétus

The Phœnícians soon afterwards sailed to the attack; and the Iónians likewise put themselves in line and went out to meet them. When they had now neared one another, and joined battle, which of the Iónians fought like brave men and which like cowards, I cannot declare with any certainty, for charges are brought on all sides; but the tale goes that the Sámians, according to the agreement which they had made with Æáces, hoisted sail, and quitting their post bore away for Sámos, except eleven ships, whose captains gave no heed to the orders of the commanders, but remained and took part in the battle. The state of Sámos, in consideration of this action, granted to these men, as an acknowledgment of their bravery, the honor of having their names, and the names of their fathers, inscribed upon a pillar, which still stands in the marketplace. The Lésbians also, when they saw the Sámians, who were drawn up next them, begin to flee, themselves did the like; and the example, once set, was followed by the greater number of the Iónians.

Of those who remained and fought, none were so rudely handled as the Chíans, who displayed prodigies of valor, and disdained to play the part of cowards. They furnished to the common fleet, as I mentioned above, one hundred ships, having each of them forty armed citizens, and those picked men, on board; and when they saw the greater portion of the allies betraying the common cause, they for their part, scorning to imitate the base conduct of these traitors, although they were left almost alone and unsupported, a very few friends continuing to stand by them, notwithstanding went on with the fight, and ofttimes cut the line of the enemy, until at last, after they had taken very many of their adversaries' ships, they ended by losing more than half of their own. Hereupon, with the remainder of their vessels, the Chíans fled away to their own country...

Dionýsius, the Phocǽan, when he perceived that all was lost, having first captured three ships from the enemy, himself took to flight. He would not, however, return to Phocǽa, which he well knew must fall again, like the rest of Iónia, under the Pérsian yoke; but straightway, as he was, he set sail for Phœnícia, and there sunk a number of merchantmen, and gained a great booty; after which he directed his course to Sícily, where he established himself as a corsair, and plundered the Carthagínians and Tyrrhénians, but did no harm to the Greeks.

The Pérsians, when they had vanquished the Iónians in the sea-fight, besieged Milétus both by land and sea, driving mines under the walls, and making use of every known device, until at length they took both the citadel and the town, six years from the time when the revolt first broke out under Aristágoras. All the inhabitants of the city they reduced to slavery... Those of the Milésians whose lives were spared, being carried prisoners to Súsa, received no ill treatment at the hands of King Daríus, but were established by him in Ámpe, a city on the shores of the Erythræan sea, near the spot where the Tígris flows into it. Milétus itself, and the plain about the city, were kept by the Pérsians for themselves, while the hill-country was assigned to the Cárians of Pédasus

— Heródotus, *History*, VI.14-20 (translated by George Rawlinson)

## The Subjugation of the Iónians

The naval armament of the Pérsians wintered at Milétus, and in the following year proceeded to attack the islands off the coast, Chíos, Lésbos, and Ténedos, which were reduced without difficulty. Whenever they became masters of an island, the barbarians, in every single instance, netted the inhabitants. Now the mode in which they practice this netting is the following. Men join hands, so as to form a line across from the north coast to the south, and then march through the island from end to end and hunt out the inhabitants. In like manner the Pérsians took also the Iónian towns upon the mainland, not however netting the inhabitants, as it was not possible.

And now their generals made good all the threats wherewith they had menaced the Iónians before the battle. For no sooner did they get possession of the towns than they choose out all the best favored boys and made them eunuchs, while the most beautiful of the girls they tore from their homes and sent as presents to the king, at the same time burning the cities themselves, with their temples. Thus were the Iónians for the third time reduced to slavery; once by the Lýdians, and a second, and now a third time, by the Pérsians.

— Heródotus, *History*, VI.81-82 (translated by George Rawlinson)

## Miltíades Escapes to Áthens

He now no sooner heard that the Phœnícians were attacking Ténedos than he loaded five tríremes with his goods and chattels and set sail for Áthens. Cárdia was the point from which he took his departure; and as he sailed down the gulf of Mélas, along the shore of the Chersonésus, he came suddenly upon the whole Phœnícian fleet. However, he himself escaped, with four of his vessels, and got into Ímbrus, one tríreme only falling into the hands of his pursuers. This vessel was under the command of his eldest son Metíochus, whose mother was not the daughter of the Thrácian king Olórus, but a different woman. Metíochus and his ship were taken; and when the Phœnícians found out that he was a son of Miltíades they resolved to convey him to the king, expecting thereby to rise high in the royal favor. For they remembered that it was Miltíades who counselled the Iónians to hearken when the Scyths prayed them to break up the bridge and return home. Daríus, however, when the Phœnícians brought Metíochus into his presence, was so far from doing him any hurt, that he loaded him with benefits. He gave him a house and estate, and also a Pérsian wife, by whom there were children born to him who were accounted Pérsians. As for Miltíades himself, from Ímbrus he made his way in safety to Áthens.

— Heródotus, *History*, VI.41 (translated by George Rawlinson)

# CHAPTER XIV.

## THE INVASIONS OF GREECE BY DARÍUS AND XÉRXES

The First Invasion Under Daríus, I.—Interval Between the First and Second Invasions, II.
The Second Pérsian Invasion Under Xérxes. III.


## I. THE FIRST INVASION UNDER DARÍUS

### The Failed Naval Expedition of the Pérsians

At this time the Pérsians did no more hurt to the Iónians; but on the contrary, before the year was out, they carried into effect the following measures, which were greatly to their advantage. Artaphérnes, sátrap of Sárdis, summoned deputies from all the Iónian cities, and forced them to enter into agreements with one another, not to harass each other by force of arms, but to settle their disputes by reference. He likewise took the measurement of their whole country in parasangs—such is the name which the Pérsians give to a distance of thirty furlongs—and settled the tributes which the several cities were to pay, at a rate that has continued unaltered from the time when Artaphérnes fixed it down to the present day. The rate was very nearly the same as that which had been paid before the revolt. Such were the peaceful dealings of the Pérsians with the Iónians.

The next spring Daríus superseded all the other generals, and sent down Mardónius ... to the coast, and with him a vast body of men, some fit for sea, others for land service. Mardónius was a youth at this time and had only lately married ... the king's daughter. When Mardónius, accompanied by this numerous host, reached Cilícia, he took ship and proceeded along shore with his fleet, while the land army marched under other leaders towards the Héllespont. In the course of his voyage along the coast of Ásia he came to Iónia; and here I have a marvel to relate which will greatly surprise those Greeks who cannot believe that Ótanes advised the seven conspirators to make Pérsia a commonwealth. Mardónius put down all the despots throughout Iónia, and in lieu of them established democracies. Having so done, he hastened to the Héllespont, and when a vast multitude of ships had been brought together, and likewise a powerful land force, he conveyed his troops across the strait by means of his vessels and proceeded through Éurope against Erétria and Áthens.

At least these towns served as a pretext for the expedition, the real purpose of which was to subjugate as great a number as possible of the Grécian cities; and this became plain when the Thásians, who did not even lift a hand in their defense, were reduced by the sea force, while the land army added the Macedónians to the former slaves of the king. All the tribes on the hither side of Macedónia had been reduced previously. From Thásos the fleet stood across to the mainland, and sailed along shore to Acánthus, whence an attempt was made to double Mount Áthos. But here a violent north wind sprang up, against which nothing could contend, and handled a large number of the ships with much rudeness, shattering them and driving them aground upon Áthos. It is said the number of the ships destroyed was little short of three hundred; and the men who perished were more than twenty thousand. For the sea about Áthos abounds in monsters beyond all others; and so a portion were seized and devoured by these animals, while others were dashed violently against the rocks; some, who did not know how to swim, were engulfed; and some died of the cold.

— Heródotus, *History*, VI.42-44 (translated by George Rawlinson)

## The Pérsians Advance Toward Erétria and Áthens

Meantime the Pérsian pursued his own design, from day to day exhorted by his servant to "remember the Athénians," and likewise urged continually by the Pisistrátidæ, who were ever accusing their countrymen. Moreover, it pleased him well to have a pretext for carrying war into Greece, that so he might reduce all those who had refused to give him earth and water. As for Mardónius, since his expedition had succeeded so ill, Daríus took the command of the troops from him, and appointed other generals in his stead, who were to lead the host against Erétria and Áthens; to wit, Dátis, who was by descent a Mede, and Artaphérnes, the son of Artaphérnes, his own nephew. These men received orders to carry Áthens and Erétria away captive, and to bring the prisoners into his presence.

So the new commanders took their departure from the court and went down to Cilícia, to the Aléian plain, having with them a numerous and well appointed land army. Encamping here, they were joined by the sea force which had been required of the several states, and at the same time by the horse transports which Daríus had, the year before, commanded his tributaries to make ready. Aboard these the horses were embarked; and the troops were received by the ships of war; after which the whole fleet, amounting in all to six hundred tríremes, made sail for Iónia. Thence, instead of proceeding with a straight course along the shore to the Héllespont and to Thrace, they loosed from Sámos and voyaged across the Icárian sea through the midst of the islands; mainly, as I believe, because they feared the danger of doubling Mount Áthos, where the year before they had suffered so grievously on their passage; but a constraining cause also was their former failure to take Náxos.

When the Pérsians, therefore, approaching from the Icárian Sea, cast anchor at Náxos, which, recollecting what there befell them formerly, they had determined to attack before any other state, the Náxians, instead of encountering them, took to flight, and hurried off to the hills. The Pérsians however succeeded in laying hands on some, and them they carried away captive, while at the same time they burnt all the temples together with the town. This done, they left Náxos, and sailed away to the other islands.

While the Pérsians were thus employed, the Délians likewise quitted Délos, and took refuge in Ténos. And now the expedition drew near, when Dátis sailed forward in advance of the other ships; commanding them, instead of anchoring at Délos, to rendezvous at Rhénea, over against Délos, while he himself proceeded to discover whither the Délians had fled; after which he sent a herald to them with this message:

"Why are ye fled, O holy men? Why have ye judged me so harshly and so wrongfully? I have surely sense enough, even had not the king so ordered, to spare the country which gave birth to the two gods—to spare, I say, both the country and its inhabitants. Come back therefore to your dwellings; and once more inhabit your island."

Such was the message which Dátis sent by his herald to the Délians. He likewise placed upon the altar three hundred talents' weight of frankincense and offered it.

— Heródotus, *History*, VI.94-97 (translated by George Rawlinson)

## Daríus Sacks Erétria

After this he sailed with his whole host against Erétria, taking with him both Iónians and Æólians. When he was departed, Délos (as the Délians told me) was shaken by an earthquake, the first and last shock that has been felt to this day. And truly this was a prodigy whereby the god warned men of the evils that were coming upon them. For in the three following generations of Daríus the son of Hystáspes, Xérxes the son of Daríus, and Artaxérxes the son of Xérxes, more woes befell Greece than in the twenty generations preceding Daríus—woes caused in part by the Pérsians, but in part arising from the contentions among their own chief men respecting the supreme power...

The barbarians, after loosing from Délos, proceeded to touch at the other islands, and took troops from each, and likewise carried off a number of the children as hostages. Going thus from one to another, they came at last to Carýstus; but here the hostages were refused by the Carýstians, who said they would neither give any, nor consent to bear arms against the cities of their neighbors, meaning Áthens and Erétria. Hereupon the Pérsians laid siege to Carýstus, and wasted the country round, until at length the inhabitants were brought over and agreed to do what was required of them.

Meanwhile the Erétrians, understanding that the Pérsian armament was coming against them, besought the Athénians for assistance. Nor did the Athénians refuse their aid, but assigned to them as auxiliaries the four thousand landholders to whom they had allotted the estates of the Chalcídian Hippóbatæ. At Erétria, however, things were in no healthy state; for though they had called in the aid of the Athénians, yet they were not agreed among themselves how they should act; some of them were minded to leave the city and to take refuge in the heights of Eubœa, while others, who looked to receiving a reward from the Pérsians, were making ready to betray their country. So when these things came to the ears of Æschines ... one of the first men in Erétria, he made known the whole state of affairs to the Athénians who were already arrived, and besought them to return home to their own land, and not perish with his countrymen. And the Athénians hearkened to his counsel, and ... in this way escaped the danger.

The Pérsian fleet now drew near and anchored at three places in the territory of Erétria. Once masters of these posts, they proceeded forthwith to disembark their horses, and made ready to attack the enemy. But the Erétrians were not minded to sally forth and offer battle; their only care, after it had been resolved not to quit the city, was, if possible, to defend their walls. And now the fortress was assaulted in good earnest, and for six days there fell on both sides vast numbers, but on the seventh day Euphórbus ... betrayed the place to the Pérsians. These were no sooner entered within the walls than they plundered and burnt all the temples that there were in the town, in revenge for the burning of their own temples at Sárdis; moreover, they did according to the orders of Daríus, and carried away captive all the inhabitants

— Heródotus, *History*, VI.98-101 (translated by George Rawlinson)


## Phidíppides Carries a Message to the Spártans

It was this Miltíades who now commanded the Athénians, after escaping from the Chersonésus, and twice nearly losing his life. First he was chased as far as Ímbrus by the Phœnícians, who had a great desire to take him and carry him up to the king; and when he had avoided this danger, and, having reached his own country, thought himself to be altogether in safety, he found his enemies waiting for him, and was cited by them before a court and impeached for his tyranny in the Chersonésus. But he came off victorious here likewise and was thereupon made general of the Athénians by the free choice of the people.

And first, before they left the city, the generals sent off to Spárta [150 miles] a herald, one Phidíppides, who was by birth an Athénian, and by profession and practice a trained runner. This man, according to the account which he gave to the Athénians on his return, when he was near Mount Parthénium, above Tégea, fell in with the god Pan, who called him by his name, and bade him ask the Athénians "wherefore they neglected him so entirely, when he was kindly disposed towards them, and had often helped them in times past, and would do so again in time to come?" The Athénians, entirely believing in the truth of this report, as soon as their affairs were once more in good order, set up a temple to Pan under the Acrópolis, and, in return for the message which I have recorded, established in his honor yearly sacrifices and a torch-race.

On the occasion of which we speak when Phidíppides was sent by the Athénian generals, and, according to his own account, saw Pan on his journey, he reached Spárta on the very next day after quitting the city of Áthens. Upon his arrival he went before the rulers, and said to them:

"Men of Lacedǽmon, the Athénians beseech you to hasten to their aid, and not allow that state, which is the most ancient in all Greece, to be enslaved by the barbarians. Erétria, look you, is already carried away captive; and Greece weakened by the loss of no mean city."

Thus did Phidíppides deliver the message committed to him. And the Spártans wished to help the Athénians, but were unable to give them any present succor, as they did not like to break their established law. It was then the ninth day of the first decade; and they could not march out of Spárta on the ninth, when the moon had not reached the full. So they waited for the full of the moon.

— Heródotus, *History*, VI.104-106 (translated by George Rawlinson)

## Miltíades Urges a Stand at Márathon

The Athénian generals were divided in their opinions; and some advised not to risk a battle, because they were too few to engage such a host as that of the Medes, while others were for fighting at once; and among these last was Miltíades. He therefore, seeing that opinions were thus divided, and that the less worthy counsel appeared likely to prevail, resolved to go to the Pólemarch, and have a conference with him. For the man on whom the lot fell to be Pólemarch at Áthens was entitled to give his vote with the ten generals, since anciently the Athénians allowed him an equal right of voting with them. The Pólemarch at this juncture was Callímachus... To him therefore Miltíades went, and said:

"With thee it rests, Callímachus, either to bring Áthens to slavery, or, by securing her freedom, to leave behind thee to all future generations a memory beyond even Harmódius and Aristogíton. For never since the time that the Athénians became a people were they in so great a danger as now. If they bow their necks beneath the yoke of the Medes, the woes which they will have to suffer when given into the power of Híppias are already determined on; if, on the other hand, they fight and overcome, Áthens may rise to be the very first city in Greece. How it comes to pass that these things are likely to happen, and how the determining of them in some sort rests with thee, I will now proceed to make clear.

"We generals are ten in number, and our votes are divided; half of us wish to engage, half to avoid a combat. Now, if we do not fight, I look to see a great disturbance at Áthens which will shake men's resolutions, and then I fear they will submit themselves; but if we fight the battle before any unsoundness show itself among our citizens, let the gods but give us fair play, and we are well able to overcome the enemy. On thee therefore we depend in this matter, which lies wholly in thine own power. Thou hast only to add thy vote to my side and thy country will be free, and not free only, but the first state in Greece. Or, if thou preferrest to give thy vote to them who would decline the combat, then the reverse will follow."

Miltíades by these words gained Callímachus; and the addition of the Pólemarch's vote caused the decision to be in favor of fighting. Hereupon all those generals who had been desirous of hazarding a battle, when their turn came to command the army, gave up their right to Miltíades. He however, though he accepted their offers, nevertheless waited, and would not fight until his own day of command arrived in due course.

— Heródotus, *History*, VI.109-110 (translated by George Rawlinson)

# The Battle of Márathon

Then at length, when his own turn was come, the Athénian battle was set in array, and this was the order of it. Callímachus the Pólemarch led the right wing; for it was at that time a rule with the Athénians to give the right wing to the Pólemarch. After this followed the tribes, according as they were numbered, in an unbroken line; while last of all came the Platǽans, forming the left wing. And ever since that day it has been a custom with the Athénians, in the sacrifices and assemblies held each fifth year at Áthens, for the Athénian herald to implore the blessing of the gods on the Platǽans conjointly with the Athénians. Now, as they marshalled the host upon the field of Márathon, in order that the Athénian front might be of equal length with the Médian, the ranks of the center were diminished, and it became the weakest part of the line, while the wings were both made strong with a depth of many ranks.

So when the battle was set in array, and the victims showed themselves favorable, instantly the Athénians, so soon as they were let go, charged the barbarians at a run. Now the distance between the two armies was little short of eight furlongs. The Pérsians, therefore, when they saw the Greeks coming on at speed, made ready to receive them, although it seemed to them that the Athénians were bereft of their senses, and bent upon their own destruction; for they saw a mere handful of men coming on at a run without either horsemen or archers. Such was the opinion of the barbarians; but the Athénians in close array fell upon them and fought in a manner worthy of being recorded. They were the first of the Greeks, so far as I know, who introduced the custom of charging the enemy at a run, and they were likewise the first who dared to look upon the Médian garb, and to face men clad in that fashion. Until this time the very name of the Medes had been a terror to the Greeks to hear.

The two armies fought together on the plain of Márathon for a length of time; and in the mid battle, where the Pérsians themselves and the Sácæ had their place, the barbarians were victorious, and broke and pursued the Greeks into the inner country; but on the two wings the Athénians and the Platǽans defeated the enemy. Having so done, they suffered the routed barbarians to fly at their ease, and joining the two wings in one, fell upon those who had broken their own center, and fought and conquered them. These likewise fled, and now the Athénians hung upon the runaways and cut them down, chasing them all the way to the shore, on reaching which they laid hold of the ships and called aloud for fire.

It was in the struggle here that Callímachus the Pólemarch, after greatly distinguishing himself, lost his life; Stesiláüs too, the son of Thrasiláüs, one of the generals, was slain; and Cynǽgirus, the son of Euphórion, having seized on a vessel of the enemy's by the ornament at the stern, had his hand cut off by the blow of an axe, and so perished; as likewise did many other Athénians of note and name.

Nevertheless, the Athénians secured in this way seven of the vessels; while with the remainder the barbarians pushed off and, taking aboard their Erétrian prisoners from the island where they had left them, doubled Cape Súnium, hoping to reach Áthens before the return of the Athénians. The Alcmæónidæ were accused by their countrymen of suggesting this course to them; they had, it was said, an understanding with the Pérsians, and made a signal to them, by raising a shield, after they were embarked in their ships.

The Pérsians accordingly sailed round Súnium. But the Athénians with all possible speed marched away to the defense of their city, and succeeded in reaching Áthens before the appearance of the barbarians: and as their camp at Márathon had been pitched in a precinct of Hércules, so now they encamped in another precinct of the same god at Cynosárges. The barbarian fleet arrived, and lay to off Phálerum, which was at that time the haven of Áthens; but after resting awhile upon their oars, they departed and sailed away to Ásia.

There fell in this battle of Márathon, on the side of the barbarians, about six thousand and four hundred men; on that of the Athénians, one hundred and ninety-two. Such was the number of the slain on the one side and the other.

— Heródotus, *History*, VI.111-117 (translated by George Rawlinson)

## The Trial and Death of Miltíades

After the blow struck at Márathon, Miltíades, who was previously held in high esteem by his countrymen, increased yet more in influence. Hence, when he told them that he wanted a fleet of seventy ships, with an armed force, and money, without informing them what country he was going to attack, but only promising to enrich them if they would accompany him, seeing that it was a right wealthy land, where they might easily get as much gold as they cared to have—when he told them this, they were quite carried away, and gave him the whole armament which he required.

So Miltíades, having got the armament, sailed against Páros, with the object, as he alleged, of punishing the Párians for having gone to war with Áthens, inasmuch as a tríreme of theirs had come with the Pérsian fleet to Márathon. This, however, was a mere pretense; the truth was, that Miltíades owed the Párians a grudge, because Lyságoras, the son of Tísias, who was a Párian by birth, had told tales against him to Hydárnes the Pérsian. Arrived before the place against which his expedition was designed, he drove the Párians within their walls, and forthwith laid siege to the city. At the same time, he sent a herald to the inhabitants, and required of them a hundred talents, threatening that, if they refused, he would press the siege, and never give it over till the town was taken. But the Párians, without giving his demand a thought, proceeded to use every means that they could devise for the defense of their city, and even invented new plans for the purpose, one of which was, by working at night, to raise such parts of the wall as were likely to be carried by assault to double their former height.

Thus far all the Greeks agree in their accounts of this business; what follows is related upon the testimony of the Párians only. Miltíades had come to his wit's end, when one of the prisoners, a woman named Tímo, who was by birth a Párian, and had held the office of under-priestess in the temple of the infernal goddesses, came and conferred with him. This woman, they say, being introduced into the presence of Miltíades, advised him, if he set great store by the capture of the place, to do something which she could suggest to him. When therefore she had told him what it was she meant, he betook himself to the hill which lies in front of the city, and there leapt the fence enclosing the precinct of Céres Thesmophória, since he was not able to open the door. After leaping into the place he went straight to the sanctuary, intending to do something within it—either to remove some of the holy things which it was not lawful to stir, or to perform some act or other, I cannot say what—and had just reached the door, when suddenly a feeling of horror came upon him, and he returned back the way he had come; but in jumping down from the outer wall, he strained his thigh, or, as some say, struck the ground with his knee.

So Miltíades returned home sick, without bringing the Athénians any money, and without conquering Páros, having done no more than to besiege the town for six-and-twenty days, and ravage the remainder of the island. The Párians, however, when it came to their knowledge that Timo, the under-priestess of the goddesses, had advised Miltíades what he should do, were minded to punish her for her crime; they therefore sent messengers to Délphi, as soon as the siege was at an end, and asked the god if they should put the under-priestess to death. "She had discovered," they said, "to the enemies of her country how they might bring it into subjection and had exhibited to Miltíades mysteries which it was not lawful for a man to know." But the Pýthoness forbade them, and said, "Tímo was not in fault; it was decreed that Miltíades should come to an unhappy end; and she was sent to lure him to his destruction." Such was the answer given to the Párians by the Pýthoness.

The Athénians, upon the return of Miltíades from Páros, had much debate concerning him; and Xanthíppus, the son of Áriphron, who spoke more freely against him than all the rest, impleaded him before the people, and brought him to trial for his life, on the charge of having dealt deceitfully with the Athénians. Miltíades, though he was present in court, did not speak in his own defense; for his thigh had begun to mortify, and disabled him from pleading his cause. He was forced to lie on a couch while his defense was made by his friends, who dwelt at most length on the fight at Márathon, while they made mention also of the capture of Lémnos, telling how Miltíades took the island, and, after executing vengeance on the Pelásgians, gave up his conquest to Áthens. The judgment of the people was in his favor so far as to spare his life; but for the wrong he had done them they fined him fifty talents. Soon afterwards his thigh completely gangrened and mortified: and so Miltíades died; and the fifty talents were paid by his son Címon.

— Heródotus, *History*, VI.132-136 (translated by George Rawlinson)


## II. INTERVAL BETWEEN THE FIRST AND SECOND INVASIONS (490-480 B.C.)

### Demarátus Stripped of His Kingship

At last, as there came to be much strife concerning this matter, the Spártans made a decree that the Délphic oracle should be asked to say whether Demarátus were Aríston's son or no. Cleómenes set them upon this plan; and no sooner was the decree passed than he made a friend of Cóbon, the son of Aristophántus, a man of the greatest weight among the Délphians; and this Cóbon prevailed upon Periálla, the prophetess, to give the answer which Cleómenes wished. Accordingly, when the sacred messengers came and put their question, the Pýthoness returned for answer "that Demarátus was not Aríston's son." Some time afterwards all this became known; and Cóbon was forced to fly from Délphi; while Periálla the prophetess was deprived of her office.

— Heródotus, *History*, VI.66 (translated by George Rawlinson)

### Demarátus Turns to Pérsia

Demarátus, having learnt all that he wished to know, took with him provision for the journey, and went into Élis, pretending that he purposed to proceed to Délphi, and there consult the oracle. The Lacedæmónians, however, suspecting that he meant to fly his country, sent men in pursuit of him; but Demarátus hastened, and leaving Élis before they arrived, sailed across to Zacýnthus. The Lacedæmónians followed, and sought to lay hands upon him, and to separate him from his retinue; but the Zacýnthians would not give him up to them: so he escaping, made his way afterwards by sea to Ásia, and presented himself before King Daríus, who received him generously, and gave him both lands and cities. Such was the chance which drove Demarátus to Ásia, a man distinguished among the Lacedæmónians for many noble deeds and wise counsels, and who alone of all the Spártan kings brought honor to his country by winning at Olýmpia the prize in the four-horse chariot-race.

After Demarátus was deposed, Leotýchides, the son of Ménares, received the kingdom. He had a son, Zeuxídamus, called Cyníscus by many of the Spártans. This Zeuxídamus did not reign at Spárta, but died before his father, leaving a son, Archidámus. Leotýchides, when Zeuxídamus was taken from him, married a second wife, named Eurýdame, the sister of Mínius and daughter of Diactórides. By her he had no male offspring, but only a daughter called Lámpito, whom he gave in marriage to Archidámus, Zeuxídamus' son.

Even Leotýchides, however, did not spend his old age in Spárta, but suffered a punishment whereby Demarátus was fully avenged. He commanded the Lacedæmónians when they made war against Théssaly, and might have conquered the whole of it, but was bribed by a large sum of money. It chanced that he was caught in the fact, being found sitting in his tent on a gauntlet, quite full of silver. Upon this he was brought to trial and banished from Spárta; his house was razed to the ground; and he himself fled to Tégea, where he ended his days. But these events took place long afterwards.

— Heródotus, *History*, VI.70-72 (translated by George Rawlinson)

## Xérxes Assumes the Throne

Now when tidings of the battle that had been fought at Márathon reached the ears of King Daríus, the son of Hystáspes, his anger against the Athénians, which had been already roused by their attack upon Sárdis, waxed still fiercer, and he became more than ever eager to lead an army against Greece. Instantly he sent off messengers to make proclamation through the several states that fresh levies were to be raised, and these at an increased rate; while ships, horses, provisions, and transports were likewise to be furnished. So the men published his commands; and now all Ásia was in commotion by the space of three years, while everywhere, as Greece was to be attacked, the best and bravest were enrolled for the service, and had to make their preparations accordingly.

After this, in the fourth year, the Egýptians whom Cambýses had enslaved revolted from the Pérsians; whereupon Daríus was more hot for war than ever, and earnestly desired to march an army against both adversaries.

Now, as he was about to lead forth his levies against Égypt and Áthens, a fierce contention for the sovereign power arose among his sons; since the law of the Pérsians was that a king must not go out with his army, until he has appointed one to succeed him upon the throne. Daríus, before he obtained the kingdom, had had three sons born to him from his former wife, who was a daughter of Góbryas; while, since he began to reign, Atóssa, the daughter of Cýrus, had borne him four. Artabazánes was the eldest of the first family, and Xérxes of the second. These two, therefore, being the sons of different mothers, were now at variance. Artabazánes claimed the crown as the eldest of all the children, because it was an established custom all over the world for the eldest to have the pre-eminence; while Xérxes, on the other hand, urged that he was sprung from Atóssa, the daughter of Cýrus, and that it was Cýrus who had won the Pérsians their freedom.

Before Daríus had pronounced on the matter, it happened that Demarátus, the son of Aríston, who had been deprived of his crown at Spárta, and had afterwards, of his own accord, gone into banishment, came up to Súsa, and there heard of the quarrel of the princes. Hereupon, as report says, he went to Xérxes, and advised him, in addition to all that he had urged before, to plead that at the time when he was born Daríus was already king, and bore rule over the Pérsians; but when Artabazánes came into the world, he was a mere private person. It would therefore be neither right nor seemly that the crown should go to another in preference to himself. "For at Spárta," said Demarátus, by way of suggestion, "the law is that if a king has sons before he comes to the throne, and another son is born to him afterwards, the child so born is heir to his father's kingdom." Xérxes followed this counsel, and Daríus, persuaded that he had justice on his side, appointed him his successor...

Daríus, when he had thus appointed Xérxes his heir, was minded to lead forth his armies; but he was prevented by death while his preparations were still proceeding. He died in the year following the revolt of Égypt and the matters here related, after having reigned in all six-and-thirty years, leaving the revolted Egýptians and the Athénians alike unpunished. At his death the kingdom passed to his son Xérxes.

— Heródotus, *History*, VII.1-4 (translated by George Rawlinson)

# The Character of Themístocles

It is confessed by all that from his youth [Themístocles] was of a vehement and impetuous nature, of a quick apprehension and a strong and aspiring bent for action and great affairs. The holidays and intervals in his studies he did not spend in play or idleness, as other children, but would be always inventing or arranging some oration or declamation to himself, the subject of which was generally the excusing or accusing his companions, so that his master would often say to him, "You, my boy, will be nothing small, but great one way or other, for good or else for bad." He received reluctantly and carelessly instructions given him to improve his manners and behavior, or to teach him any pleasing or graceful accomplishment, but whatever was said to improve him in sagacity, or in management of affairs, he would give attention to, beyond one of his years, from confidence in his natural capacities for such things. And thus afterwards, when in company where people engaged themselves in what are commonly thought the liberal and elegant amusements, he was obliged to defend himself against the observations of those who considered themselves highly accomplished, by the somewhat arrogant retort, that he certainly could not make use of any stringed instrument, could only, were a small and obscure city put into his hands, make it great and glorious...

In the first essays of his youth he was not regular nor happily balanced; he allowed himself to follow mere natural character, which, without the control of reason and instruction, is apt to hurry, upon either side, into sudden and violent courses, and very often to break away and determine upon the worst; as he afterwards owned himself, saying, that the wildest colts make the best horses, if they only get properly trained and broken in. But those who upon this fasten stories of their own invention, as of his being disowned by his father, and that his mother died for grief of her son's ill fame, certainly calumniate him; and there are others who relate, on the contrary, how that to deter him from public business, and to let him see how the vulgar behave themselves towards their leaders when they have at last no farther use of them, his father showed him the old galleys as they lay forsaken and cast about upon the sea-shore.

Yet it is evident that his mind was early imbued with the keenest interest in public affairs, and the most passionate ambition for distinction. Eager from the first to obtain the highest place, he unhesitatingly accepted the hatred of the most powerful and influential leaders in the city, but more especially of Aristídes, the son of Lysímachus, who always opposed him... Not but that the incompatibility of their lives and manners may seem to have increased the difference, for Aristídes was of a mild nature, and of a nobler sort of character, and, in public matters, acting always with a view, not to glory or popularity, but to the best interests of the state consistently with safety and honesty, he was often forced to oppose Themístocles, and interfere against the increase of his influence, seeing him stirring up the people to all kinds of enterprises, and introducing various innovations.

For it is said that Themístocles was so transported with the thoughts of glory, and so inflamed with the passion for great actions, that, though he was still young when the battle of Márathon was fought against the Pérsians, upon the skillful conduct of the general, Miltíades, being everywhere talked about, he was observed to be thoughtful, and reserved, alone by himself; he passed the nights without sleep, and avoided all his usual places of recreation, and to those who wondered at the change, and inquired the reason of it, he gave the answer, that "the trophy of Miltíades would not let him sleep." And when others were of opinion that the battle of Márathon would be an end to the war, Themístocles thought that it was but the beginning of far greater conflicts, and for these, to the benefit of all Greece, he kept himself in continual readiness, and his city also in proper training, foreseeing from far before what would happen.

– Plútarch, *Life of Themístocles* (translated by John Dryden)

## Themístocles and His Love of Honor

He was, indeed, by nature, a great lover of honor, as is evident from the anecdotes recorded of him. When chosen admiral by the Athénians, he would not quite conclude any single matter of business, either public or private, but deferred all till the day they were to set sail, that, by dispatching a great quantity of business all at once, and having to meet a great variety of people, he might make an appearance of greatness and power. Viewing the dead bodies cast up by the sea, he perceived bracelets and necklaces of gold about them, yet passed on, only showing them to a friend that followed him, saying, "Take you these things, for you are not Themístocles." ... He said that the Athénians did not honor him or admire him, but made, as it were, a sort of plane-tree of him; sheltered themselves under him in bad weather, and, as soon as it was fine, plucked his leaves and cut his branches.

When the Seríphian told him that he had not obtained this honor by himself, but by the greatness of his city, he replied, "You speak truth; I should never have been famous if I had been of Seríphus; nor you, had you been of Áthens." When another of the generals, who thought he had performed considerable service for the Athénians, boastingly compared his actions with those of Themístocles, he told him that once upon a time the Day after the Festival found fault with the Festival: "On you there is nothing but hurry and trouble and preparation, but, when I come, everybody sits down quietly and enjoys himself;" which the Festival admitted was true, but "if I had not come first, you would not have come at all." "Even so," he said, "if Themístocles had not come before, where had you been now?" Laughing at his own son, who got his mother, and, by his mother's means, his father also, to indulge him, he told him that he had the most power of any one in Greece: "For the Athénians command the rest of Greece, I command the Athénians, your mother commands me, and you command your mother." Loving to be singular in all things, when he had land to sell, he ordered the crier to give notice that there were good neighbors near it. Of two who courted his daughter, he preferred the man of worth to the one who was rich, saying he desired a man without riches, rather than riches without a man. Such was the character of his sayings.

– Plútarch, *Life of Themístocles* (translated by John Dryden)

## Themístocles Prepares the Athénians

And, first of all, the Athénians being accustomed to divide amongst themselves the revenue proceeding from the silver mines at Láurium, he was the only man that dared propose to the people that this distribution should cease, and that with the money ships should be built to make war against the Ægínetans, who were the most flourishing people in all Greece, and by the number of their ships held the sovereignty of the sea; and Themístocles thus was more easily able to persuade them, avoiding all mention of danger from Daríus or the Pérsians, who were at a great distance, and their coming very uncertain, and at that time not much to be feared; but, by a seasonable employment of the emulation and anger felt by the Athénians against the Ægínetans, he induced them to preparation. So that with this money a hundred ships were built, with which they afterwards fought against Xérxes. And, henceforward, little by little, turning and drawing the city down towards the sea, in the belief, that, whereas by land they were not a fit match for their next neighbors, with their ships they might be able to repel the Pérsians and command Greece, thus, as Pláto says, from steady soldiers he turned them into mariners and seamen tossed about the sea, and gave occasion for the reproach against him, that he took away from the Athénians the spear and the shield, and bound them to the bench and the oar...

Themístocles is said to have been eager in the acquisition of riches, according to some, that he might be the more liberal; for loving to sacrifice often, and to be splendid in his entertainment of strangers, he required a plentiful revenue; yet he is accused by others of having been parsimonious and sordid to that degree that he would sell provisions which were sent to him as a present...

He went beyond all men in the passion for distinction. When he was still young and unknown in the world, he entreated Épicles of Hermióniæ, who had a good hand at the lute and was much sought after by the Athénians, to come and practice at home with him, being ambitious of having people inquire after his house and frequent his company. When he came to the Olýmpic games, and was so splendid in his equipage and entertainments, in his rich tents and furniture, that he strove to outdo Címon, he displeased the Greeks, who thought that such magnificence might be allowed in one who was a young man and of a great family but was a great piece of insolence in one as yet undistinguished, and without title or means for making any such display. In a dramatic contest, the play he paid for won the prize, which was then a matter that excited much emulation; he put up a tablet in record of it, with an inscription...

He was well liked by the common people, would salute every particular citizen by his own name, and always show himself a just judge in questions of business between private men; he said to Simónides, the poet of Céos, who desired something of him, when he was commander of the army, that was not reasonable, "Simónides, you would be no good poet if you wrote false measure, nor should I be a good magistrate if for favor I made false law." And at another time, laughing at Simónides, he said, that he was a man of little judgment to speak against the Corínthians, who were inhabitants of a great city, and to have his own picture drawn so often, having so ill-looking a face.

Gradually growing to be great, and winning the favor of the people, he at last gained the day with his faction over that of Aristídes and procured his banishment by ostracism. When the king of Pérsia was now advancing against Greece, and the Athénians were in consultation who should be general, and many withdrew themselves of their own accord, being terrified with the greatness of the danger, there was one Epícydes, a popular speaker, ... a man of an eloquent tongue, but of a faint heart, and a slave to riches, who was desirous of the command, and was looked upon to be in a fair way to carry it by the number of votes; but Themístocles, fearing that, if the command should fall into such hands, all would be lost, bought off Epicýdes and his pretensions, it is said, for a sum of money.

– Plútarch, *Life of Themístocles* (translated by John Dryden)


III. THE SECOND PÉRSIAN INVASION UNDER XÉRXES


# The Canal Through the Isthmus at Áthos

Reckoning from the recovery of Égypt, Xérxes spent four full years in collecting his host and making ready all things that were needful for his soldiers. It was not till the close of the fifth year that he set forth on his march, accompanied by a mighty multitude. For of all the armaments whereof any mention has reached us, this was by far the greatest...

All these expeditions, and others, if such there were, are as nothing compared with this. For was there a nation in all Ásia which Xérxes did not bring with him against Greece? Or was there a river, except those of unusual size, which sufficed for his troops to drink? One nation furnished ships; another was arrayed among the foot-soldiers; a third had to supply horses; a fourth, transports for the horse and men likewise for the transport service; a fifth, ships of war towards the bridges; a sixth, ships and provisions.

And in the first place, because the former fleet had met with so great a disaster about Áthos, preparations were made, by the space of about three years, in that quarter. A fleet of tríremes lay

... in the Chersonésus; and from this station detachments were sent by the various nations whereof the army was composed, which relieved one another at intervals, and worked at a trench beneath the lash of taskmasters; while the people dwelling about Áthos bore likewise a part in the labor. Two Pérsians ... superintended the undertaking.

Áthos is a great and famous mountain, inhabited by men, and stretching far out into the sea. Where the mountain ends towards the mainland it forms a peninsula; and in this place there is a neck of land about twelve furlongs across, the whole extent whereof, from the sea of the Acánthians to that over against Toróne, is a level plain, broken only by a few low hills. Here, upon this isthmus where Áthos ends, is Sand, a Greek city. Inside of Sand, and upon Áthos itself, are a number of towns, which Xérxes was now employed in disjoining from the continent...

Now the manner in which they dug was the following: a line was drawn across by the city of Sand; and along this the various nations parceled out among themselves the work to be done. When the trench grew deep, the workmen at the bottom continued to dig, while others handed the earth, as it was dug out, to laborers placed higher up upon ladders, and these taking it, passed it on farther, till it came at last to those at the top, who carried it off and emptied it away. All the other nations, therefore, except the Phœnícians, had double labor; for the sides of the trench fell in continually, as could not but happen, since they made the width no greater at the top than it was required to be at the bottom. But the Phœnícians showed in this the skill which they are wont to exhibit in all their undertakings. For in the portion of the work which was allotted to them they began by making the trench at the top twice as wide as the prescribed measure, and then as they dug downwards approached the sides nearer and nearer together, so that when they reached the bottom their part of the work was of the same width as the rest.

— Heródotus, *History*, VII.20-24 (translated by George Rawlinson)

## The Bridge Across the Héllespont

Towards this tongue of land then, the men to whom the business was assigned carried out a double bridge from Abýdos; and while the Phœnícians constructed one line with cables of white flax, the Egýptians in the other used ropes made of papýrus. Now it is seven furlongs across from Abýdos to the opposite coast. When, therefore, the channel had been bridged successfully, it happened that a great storm arising broke the whole work to pieces and destroyed all that had been done.

So when Xérxes heard of it he was full of wrath, and straightway gave orders that the Héllespont should receive three hundred lashes, and that a pair of fetters should be cast into it. Nay, I have even heard it said that he bade the branders take their irons and therewith brand the Héllespont. It is certain that he commanded those who scourged the waters to utter, as they lashed them, these barbarian and wicked words: "Thou bitter water, thy lord lays on thee this punishment because thou hast wronged him without a cause, having suffered no evil at his hands. Verily King Xérxes will cross thee, whether thou wilt or no. Well dost thou deserve that no man should honor thee with sacrifice; for thou art of a truth a treacherous and unsavory river." While the sea was thus punished by his orders, he likewise commanded that the overseers of the work should lose their heads.

Then they, whose business it was, executed the unpleasing task laid upon them; and other master-builders were set over the work, who accomplished it in the way which I will now describe.

They joined together tríremes and fifty-oared ships, 360 to support the bridge on the side of the Éuxine Sea, and 314 to sustain the other; and these they placed at right angles to the sea, and in the direction of the current of the Héllespont, relieving by these means the tension of the shore cables. Having joined the vessels, they moored them with anchors of unusual size, that the vessels of the bridge towards the Éuxine might resist the winds which blow from within the straits, and that those of the more western bridge facing the Ægéan might withstand the winds which set in from the south and from the south-east. A gap was left in the pentecónters in no fewer than three places, to afford a passage for such light craft as chose to enter or leave the Éuxine. When all this was done, they made the cables taut from the shore by the help of wooden capstans. This time, moreover, instead of using the two materials separately, they assigned to each bridge six cables, two of which were of white flax, while four were of papýrus. Both cables were of the same size and quality; but the flaxen were the heavier, weighing not less than a talent the cúbit. When the bridge across the channel was thus complete, trunks of trees were sawn into planks, which were cut to the width of the bridge, and these were laid side by side upon the tightened cables, and then fastened on the top. This done, brushwood was brought, and arranged upon the planks, after which earth was heaped upon the brushwood, and the whole trodden down into a solid mass. Lastly a bulwark was set up on either side of this causeway, of such a height as to prevent the sumpter-beasts and the horses from seeing over it and taking fright at the water.

— Heródotus, *History*, VII.34-36 (translated by George Rawlinson)

## Xérxes Reviews His Army and Fleet

On reaching the Scamánder, which was the first stream, of all that they had crossed since they left Sárdis, whose water failed them and did not suffice to satisfy the thirst of men and cattle, Xérxes ascended into the Pérgamus of Príam, since he had a longing to behold the place. When he had seen everything, and inquired into all particulars, he made an offering of a thousand oxen to the Trójan Minérva, while the Mágians poured libations to the heroes who were slain at Troy. The night after, a panic fell upon the camp: but in the morning they set off with daylight, and ... so reached Abýdos.

Arrived here, Xérxes wished to look upon all his host; so as there was a throne of white marble upon a hill near the city, which they of Abýdos had prepared beforehand, by the king's bidding, for his especial use, Xérxes took his seat on it, and, gazing thence upon the shore below, beheld at one view all his land forces and all his ships. While thus employed, he felt a desire to behold a sailing-match among his ships, which accordingly took place, and was won by the Phœnícians of Sídon, much to the joy of Xérxes, who was delighted alike with the race and with his army.

And now, as he looked and saw the whole Héllespont covered with the vessels of his fleet, and all the shore and every plain about Abýdos as full as possible of men, Xérxes congratulated himself on his good fortune; but after a little while he wept.

Then Artabánus, the king's uncle (the same who at the first so freely spake his mind to the king, and advised him not to lead his army against Greece), when he heard that Xérxes was in tears, went to him, and said:

"How different, sire, is what thou art now doing, from what thou didst a little while ago! Then thou didst congratulate thyself; and now, behold! thou weepest."

"There came upon me," replied he, "a sudden pity, when I thought of the shortness of man's life, and considered that of all this host, so numerous as it is, not one will be alive when a hundred years are gone by."

— Heródotus, *History*, VII.40-46 (translated by George Rawlinson)

## Xérxes Questions Demarátus

Now after Xérxes had sailed down the whole line and was gone ashore, he sent for Demarátus the son of Aríston, who had accompanied him in his march upon Greece, and bespake him thus:

"Demarátus, it is my pleasure at this time to ask thee certain things which I wish to know. Thou art a Greek, and, as I hear from the other Greeks with whom I converse, no less than from thine own lips, thou art a native of a city which is not the meanest or the weakest in their land. Tell me, therefore, what thinkest thou? Will the Greeks lift a hand against us? Mine own judgment is, that even if all the Greeks and all the barbarians of the West were gathered together in one place, they would not be able to abide my onset, not being really of one mind. But I would fain know what thou thinkest hereon."

Thus Xérxes questioned; and the other replied in his turn: "O king! is it thy will that I give thee a true answer, or dost thou wish for a pleasant one?"

Then the king bade him speak the plain truth and promised that he would not on that account hold him in less favor than heretofore.

So Demarátus, when he heard the promise, spake as follows:

"O king! since thou biddest me at all risks speak the truth, and not say what will one day prove me to have lied to thee, thus I answer. Want has at all times been a fellow-dweller with us in our land, while valor is an ally whom we have gained by dint of wisdom and strict laws. Her aid enables us to drive out want and escape thraldom. Brave are all the Greeks who dwell in any Dórian land; but what I am about to say does not concern all, but only the Lacedæmónians. First then, come what may, they will never accept thy terms, which would reduce Greece to slavery; and further, they are sure to join battle with thee, though all the rest of the Greeks should submit to thy will. As for their numbers, do not ask how many they are, that their resistance should be a possible thing; for if a thousand of them should take the field, they will meet thee in battle, and so will any number, be it less than this, or be it more."

— Heródotus, *History*, VII.102 (translated by George Rawlinson)

## Áthens Receives an Oracle from Délphi

To return, however, to my main subject, the expedition of the Pérsian king, though it was in name directed against Áthens, threatened really the whole of Greece. And of this the Greeks were aware some time before; but they did not all view the matter in the same light. Some of them had given the Pérsian earth and water, and were bold on this account, deeming themselves thereby secured against suffering hurt from the barbarian army; while others, who had refused compliance, were thrown into extreme alarm. For whereas they considered all the ships in Greece too few to engage the enemy, it was plain that the greater number of states would take no part in the war, but warmly favored the Medes.

And here I feel constrained to deliver an opinion, which most men, I know, will dislike, but which, as it seems to me to be true, I am determined not to withhold. Had the Athénians, from fear of the approaching danger, quitted their country, or had they without quitting it submitted to the power of Xérxes, there would certainly have been no attempt to resist the Pérsians by sea; in which case the course of events by land would have been the following. Though the Peloponnésians might have carried ever so many breastworks across the Ísthmus, yet their allies would have fallen off from the Lacedæmónians, not by voluntary desertion, but because town after town must have been taken by the fleet of the barbarians; and so the Lacedæmónians would at last have stood alone, and, standing alone, would have displayed prodigies of valor and died nobly. Either they would have done thus, or else, before it came to that extremity, seeing one Greek state after another embrace the cause of the Medes, they would have come to terms with King Xérxes—and thus, either way Greece would have been brought under Pérsia. For I cannot understand of what possible use the walls across the Ísthmus could have been, if the king had had the mastery of the sea. If then a man should now say that the Athénians were the saviors of Greece, he would not exceed the truth. For they truly held the scales; and whichever side they espoused must have carried the day.

They too it was who, when they had determined to maintain the freedom of Greece, roused up that portion of the Greek nation which had not gone over to the Medes; and so, next to the gods, they repulsed the invader. Even the terrible oracles which reached them from Délphi, and struck fear into their hearts, failed to persuade them to fly from Greece. They had the courage to remain faithful to their land and await the coming of the foe.

When the Athénians, anxious to consult the oracle, sent their messengers to Délphi, hardly had the envoys completed the customary rites about the sacred precinct, and taken their seats inside the sanctuary of the god, when the Pýthoness, Aristoníce by name, thus prophesied:

Wretches, why sit ye here? Fly, fly to the ends of creation, quitting your homes, and the crags which your city crowns with her circlet. Neither the head, nor the body is firm in its place, nor at bottom firm the feet, nor the hands; nor resteth the middle uninjured. All—all ruined and lost. Since fire, and impetuous Áres, speeding along in a Sýrian chariot, hastes to destroy her. Not alone shalt thou suffer; full many the towers he will level, Many the shrines of the gods he will give to a fiery destruction. Even now they stand with dark sweat horribly dripping, trembling and quaking for fear; and lo! from the high roofs trickleth black blood, sign prophetic of hard distresses impending. Get ye away from the temple; and brood on the ills that await ye!

When the Athénian messengers heard this reply, they were filled with the deepest affliction: whereupon Tímon, the son of Andróbulus, one of the men of most mark among the Délphians, seeing how utterly cast down they were at the gloomy prophecy, advised them to take an olive-branch, and entering the sanctuary again, consult the oracle as suppliants. The Athénians followed this advice, and going in once more, said: "O king! we pray thee reverence these boughs of supplication which we bear in our hands, and deliver to us something more comforting concerning our country. Else we will not leave thy sanctuary, but will stay here till we die." Upon this the priestess gave them a second answer, which was the following:

Pállas has not been able to soften the lord of Olýmpus, though she has often prayed him, and urged him with excellent counsel. Yet once more I address thee in words firmer than adamant. When the foe shall have taken whatever the limit of Cécrops holds within it, and all which divine Cithǽron, shelters, then far-seeing Jove grants this to the prayers of Athéna: Safe shall the wooden wall continue for thee and thy children. Wait not the tramp of the horse, nor the footmen mightily moving over the land, but turn your back to the foe, and retire ye. Yet shall a day arrive when ye shall meet him in battle. Holy Sálamis, thou shalt destroy the offspring of women, when men scatter the seed, or when they gather the harvest.

This answer seemed, as indeed it was, gentler than the former one; so the envoys wrote it down, and went back with it to Áthens. When, however, upon their arrival, they produced it before the people, and inquiry began to be made into its true meaning, many and various were the interpretations which men put on it; two, more especially, seemed to be directly opposed to one another. Certain of the old men were of opinion that the god meant to tell them the citadel would escape; for this was anciently defended by a palisade; and they supposed that barrier to be the "wooden wall" of the oracle. Others maintained that the fleet was what the god pointed at; and their advice was that nothing should be thought of except the ships, which had best be at once got ready. Still such as said the "wooden wall" meant the fleet, were perplexed by the last two lines of the oracle:

Holy Sálamis, thou shall destroy the offspring of women, when men scatter the seed, or when they gather the harvest.

These words caused great disturbance among those who took the wooden wall to be the ships; since the interpreters understood them to mean that, if they made preparations for a sea-fight, they would suffer a defeat off Sálamis.

Now there was at Áthens a man who had lately made his way into the first rank of citizens: his true name was Themístocles; but he was known more generally as the son of Néocles. This man came forward and said that the interpreters had not explained the oracle altogether aright, "For if," he argued, "the clause in question had really respected the Athénians, it would not have been expressed so mildly; the phrase used would have been 'Luckless Sálamis,' rather than 'Holy Sálamis,' had those to whom the island belonged been about to perish in its neighborhood. Rightly taken, the response of the god threatened the enemy, much more than the Athénians." He therefore counselled his countrymen to make ready to fight on board their ships, since they were the wooden wall in which the god told them to trust. When Themístocles had thus cleared the matter, the Athénians embraced his view, preferring it to that of the interpreters. The advice of these last had been against engaging in a sea-fight. "All the Athénians could do," they said, "was, without lifting a hand in their defense, to quit Áttica, and make a settlement in some other country."

— Heródotus, *History*, VII.138-144 (translated by George Rawlinson)

## Xérxes Returns the Greek Spies

So when these resolutions had been agreed upon, and the quarrels between the states made up, first of all they sent into Ásia three men as spies. These men reached Sárdis, and took note of the king's forces, but, being discovered, were examined by order of the generals who commanded the land army, and, having been condemned to suffer death, were led out to execution. Xérxes, however, when the news reached him, disapproving the sentence of the generals, sent some of his bodyguard with instructions, if they found the spies still alive, to bring them into his presence. The messengers found the spies alive, and brought them before the king, who, when he heard the purpose for which they had come, gave orders to his guards to take them round the camp, and show them all the footmen and all the horse, letting them gaze at everything to their hearts' content; then, when they were satisfied, to send them away unharmed to whatever country they desired.

For these orders Xérxes gave afterwards the following reasons. "Had the spies been put to death," he said, "the Greeks would have continued ignorant of the vastness of his army, which surpassed the common report of it; while he would have done them a very small injury by killing three of their men. On the other hand, by the return of the spies to Greece, his power would become known; and the Greeks," he expected, "would make surrender of their freedom before he began his march, by which means his troops would be saved all the trouble of an expedition." This reasoning was like to that which he used upon another occasion. While he was staying at Abýdos, he saw some grain-ships, which were passing through the Héllespont from the Éuxine, on their way to Ægína and the Peloponnésus. His attendants, hearing that they were the enemy's, were ready to capture them, and looked to see when Xérxes would give the signal. He, however, merely asked "whither the ships were bound?" and when they answered, "For thy foes, master, with grain on board," "We too are bound thither," he rejoined, "laden, among other things, with grain. What harm is it, if they carry our provisions for us?" So the spies, when they had seen everything, were dismissed, and came back to Éurope.

— Heródotus, *History*, VII.146-147 (translated by George Rawlinson)

## Gélo's Condition for Aid

Thus spake the envoys; and Gélo replied with vehemence: "Greeks, ye have had the face to come here with selfish words, and exhort me to join in league with you against the barbarian. Yet when I erewhile asked you to join with me in fighting barbarians, what time the quarrel broke out between me and Cárthage; and when I earnestly besought you to revenge on the men of Egésta their murder of Doriéus, the son of Anaxándridas, promising to assist you in setting free the trading places from which you receive great profits and advantages, you neither came hither to give me succor, nor yet to revenge Doriéus; but, for any efforts on your part to hinder it, these countries might at this time have been entirely under the barbarians. Now, however, that matters have

112

prospered and gone well with me, while the danger has shifted its ground and at present threatens yourselves, lo! you call Gélo to mind. But though ye slighted me then, I will not imitate you now: I am ready to give you aid, and to furnish as my contribution two hundred tríremes, twenty thousand men-at-arms, two thousand cavalry, and an equal number of archers, slingers, and light horsemen, together with grain for the whole Grécian army so long as the war shall last. These services, however, I promise on one condition: that ye appoint me chief captain and commander of the Grécian forces during the war with the barbarian. Unless ye agree to this, I will neither send succors, nor come myself."

Syágrus, when he heard these words, was unable to contain himself, and exclaimed: "Surely a groan would burst from Pélops' son, Agamémnon, did he hear that her leadership was snatched from Spárta by Gélo and the men of Sýracuse. Speak then no more of any such condition, as that we should yield thee the chief command; but if thou art minded to come to the aid of Greece, prepare to serve under Lacedæmónian generals. Wilt thou not serve under a leader? Then, prithee, withhold thy succors."

Hereupon Gélo, seeing the indignation which showed itself in the words of Syágrus, delivered to the envoys his final offer: "Spártan stranger," he said, "reproaches cast forth against a man are wont to provoke him to anger; but the insults which thou hast uttered in thy speech shall not persuade me to outstep good breeding in my answer. Surely if you maintain so stoutly your right to the command, it is reasonable that I should be still more stiff in maintaining mine, forasmuch as I am at the head of a far larger fleet and army. Since, however, the claim which I have put forward is so displeasing to you, I will yield, and be content with less. Take, if it please you, the command of the land force, and I will be admiral of the fleet; or assume, if you prefer it, the command by sea, and I will be leader upon the land. Unless you are satisfied with these terms, you must return home by yourselves, and lose this great alliance." Such was the offer which Gélo made.

Hereat broke in the Athénian envoy, before the Spártan could answer, and thus addressed Gélo: "King of the Syracúsans! Greece sent us here to thee to ask for an army, and not to ask for a general. Thou, however, dost not promise to send us any army at all, if thou art not made leader of the Greeks; and this command is what alone thou sticklest for. Now when thy request was to have the whole command, we were content to keep silence; for well we knew that we might trust the Spártan envoy to make answer for us both. But since, after failing in thy claim to lead the whole armament, thou hast now put forward a request to have the command of the fleet, know that, even should the Spártan envoy consent to this, we will not consent. The command by sea, if the Lacedæmónians do not wish for it, belongs to us. While they like to keep this command, we shall raise no dispute; but we will not yield our right to it in favor of anyone else. Where would be the advantage of our having raised up a naval force greater than that of any other Greek people, if nevertheless we should suffer Syracúsans to take the command away from us? from us, I say, who are Athénians, the most ancient nation in Greece, the only Greeks who have never changed their abode, the people who are said by the poet Hómer to have sent to Troy the man best able of all the Greeks to array and marshal an army, so that we may be allowed to boast somewhat."

Gélo replied, "Athénian stranger, ye have, it seems, no lack of commanders; but ye are likely to lack men to receive their orders. As ye are resolved to yield nothing and claim everything, ye had best make haste back to Greece, and say that the spring of her year is lost to her." The meaning of this expression was the following: as the spring is manifestly the finest season of the year, so (he meant to say) were his troops the finest of the Greek army. Greece, therefore, deprived of his alliance, would be like a year with the spring taken from it.

— Heródotus, *History*, VII.158-162 (translated by George Rawlinson)

## Thermópylæ and Artemísium

The opinion which prevailed was that they should guard the pass of Thermópylæ; since it was narrower than the Thessálian defile, and at the same time nearer to them. Of the pathway, by which the Greeks who fell at Thermópylæ were intercepted, they had no knowledge, until, on their arrival at Thermópylæ, it was discovered to them by the Trachínians. This pass then it was determined that they should guard, in order to prevent the barbarians from penetrating into Greece through it; and at the same time it was resolved that the fleet should proceed to Artemísium, in the region of Histiǽotis, for, as those places are near to one another, it would be easy for the fleet and army to hold communication. The two places may be thus described.

Artemísium is where the sea of Thrace contracts into a narrow channel, running between the isle of Scíathus and the mainland of Magnésia. When this narrow strait is passed you come to the line of coast called Artemísium; which is a portion of Eubœa and contains a temple of Ártemis. As for the entrance into Greece by Tráchis, it is, at its narrowest point, about fifty feet wide. This however is not the place where the passage is most contracted; for it is still narrower a little above and a little below Thermópylæ. At Alpéni, which is lower down than that place, it is only wide enough for a single carriage; and up above, at the river Phœnix, near the town called Ánthela, it is the same. West of Thermópylæ rises a lofty and precipitous hill, impossible to climb, which runs up into the chain of Œta; while to the east the road is shut in by the sea and by marshes. In this place are the warm springs, which the natives call "The Cauldrons"; and above them stands an altar sacred to Hércules. A wall had once been carried across the opening; and in this there had of old times been a gateway. These works were made by the Phócians, through fear of the Thessálians, at the time when the latter came from Thesprótia to establish themselves in the land of Æólis, which they still occupy. As the Thessálians strove to reduce Phócis, the Phócians raised the wall to protect themselves, and likewise turned the hot springs upon the pass, that so the ground might be broken up by watercourses, using thus all possible means to hinder the Thessálians from invading their country. The old wall had been built in very remote times; and the greater part of it had gone to decay through age. Now however the Greeks resolved to repair its breaches, and here make their stand against the barbarian. At this point there is a village very nigh the road, Alpéni by name, from which the Greeks reckoned on getting grain for their troops

— Heródotus, *History*, VII.175-176 (translated by George Rawlinson)

## Leónidas Guards the Pass to Thermópylæ

The Greeks who at this spot awaited the coming of Xérxes were the following: From Spárta, three hundred men-at-arms; from Arcádia, a thousand Tégeans and Mantinéans, five hundred of each people; a hundred and twenty Orchoménians, from the Arcádian Orchómenus; and a thousand from other cities: from Córinth, four hundred men; from Phlíus, two hundred; and from Mycénæ eighty. Such was the number from the Peloponnésus. There were also present, from Bœótia, seven hundred Théspians and four hundred Thébans.

Besides these troops, the Lócrians of Ópus and the Phócians had obeyed the call of their countrymen, and sent, the former all the force they had, the latter a thousand men. For envoys had gone from the Greeks at Thermópylæ among the Lócrians and Phócians, to call on them for assistance, and to say: "They were themselves but the vanguard of the host, sent to precede the main body, which might every day be expected to follow them. The sea was in good keeping, watched by the Athénians, the Ægínetans, and the rest of the fleet. There was no cause why they should fear; for after all the invader was not a god but a man; and there never had been, and never would be, a man who was not liable to misfortunes from the very day of his birth, and those misfortunes greater in proportion to his own greatness. The assailant, therefore, being only a mortal, must needs fall from his glory." Thus urged, the Lócrians and the Phócians had come with their troops to Tráchis.

The various nations had each captains of their own under whom they served; but the one to whom all especially looked up, and who had the command of the entire force, was the Lacedæmónian, Leónidas ... Leónidas had come to be king of Spárta quite unexpectedly.

Having two elder brothers, Cleómenes and Doriéus, he had no thought of ever mounting the throne. However, when Cleómenes died without male offspring, as Doriéus was likewise deceased, having perished in Sícily, the crown fell to Leónidas, who was older than Cleómbrotus, the youngest of the sons of Anaxándridas, and, moreover, was married to the daughter of Cleómenes. He had now come to Thermópylæ, accompanied by the three hundred men which the law assigned him, whom he had himself chosen from among the citizens, and who were all of them fathers with sons living. On his way he had taken the troops from Thebes, whose number I have already mentioned, and who were under the command of Leontíades the son of Eurýmachus. The reason why he made a point of taking troops from Thebes, and Thebes only, was that the Thébans were strongly suspected of being well inclined to the Medes. Leónidas therefore called on them to come with him to the war, wishing to see whether they would comply with his demand, or openly refuse, and disclaim the Greek alliance. They, however, though their wishes leant the other way, nevertheless sent the men.

The force with Leónidas was sent forward by the Spártans in advance of their main body, that the sight of them might encourage the allies to fight, and hinder them from going over to the Medes, as it was likely they might have done had they seen that Spárta was backward. They intended presently, when they had celebrated the Carnéan festival, which was what now kept them at home, to leave a garrison in Spárta, and hasten in full force to join the army. The rest of the allies also intended to act similarly; for it happened that the Olýmpic festival fell exactly at this same period. None of them looked to see the contest at Thermópylæ decided so speedily; wherefore they were content to send forward a mere advanced guard. Such accordingly were the intentions of the allies.

The Greek forces at Thermópylæ, when the Pérsian army drew near to the entrance of the pass, were seized with fear; and a council was held to consider about a retreat. It was the wish of the Peloponnésians generally that the army should fall back upon the Peloponnésus, and there guard the Ísthmus. But Leónidas, who saw with what indignation the Phócians and Lócrians heard of this plan, gave his voice for remaining where they were, while they sent envoys to the several cities to ask for help, since they were too few to make a stand against an army like that of the Medes.

— Heródotus, *History*, VII.202-207 (translated by George Rawlinson)

## Xérxes Observes the Spártan Detachment

While this debate was going on, Xérxes sent a mounted spy to observe the Greeks, and note how many they were, and see what they were doing. He had heard, before he came out of Théssaly, that a few men were assembled at this place, and that at their head were certain Lacedæmónians, under Leónidas, a descendant of Hércules. The horseman rode up to the camp, and looked about him, but did not see the whole army; for such as were on the further side of the wall (which had been rebuilt and was now carefully guarded) it was not possible for him to behold; but he observed those on the outside, who were encamped in front of the rampart. It chanced that at this time the Lacedæmónians held the outer guard, and were seen by the spy, some of them engaged in gymnastic exercises, others combing their long hair. At this the spy greatly marveled, but he counted their number, and when he had taken accurate note of everything, he rode back quietly; for no one pursued after him, nor paid any heed to his visit. So he returned, and told Xérxes all that he had seen.

Upon this, Xérxes, who had no means of surmising the truth—namely, that the Spártans were preparing to do or die manfully—but thought it laughable that they should be engaged in such employments, sent and called to his presence Demarátus the son of Aríston, who still remained with the army. When he appeared, Xérxes told him all that he had heard, and questioned him concerning the news, since he was anxious to understand the meaning of such behavior on the part of the Spártans. Then Demarátus said:

"I spake to thee, O king! concerning these men long since, when we had but just begun our march upon Greece; thou, however, didst only laugh at my words, when I told thee of all this, which I saw would come to pass. Earnestly do I struggle at all times to speak truth to thee, sire; and now listen to it once more. These men have come to dispute the pass with us; and it is for this that they are now making ready. It is their custom, when they are about to hazard their lives, to adorn their heads with care. Be assured, however, that if thou canst subdue the men who are here and the Lacedæmónians who remain in Spárta, there is no other nation in all the world which will venture to lift a hand in their defense. Thou hast now to deal with the first kingdom and town in Greece, and with the bravest men."

Then Xérxes, to whom what Demarátus said seemed altogether to surpass belief, asked further, "How it was possible for so small an army to contend with his?" "O king!" Demarátus answered, "let me be treated as a liar, if matters fall not out as I say."

— Heródotus, *History*, VII.208-209 (translated by George Rawlinson)

## The Spártans Withstand the Pérsians at Thermópylæ

But Xérxes was not persuaded any the more. Four whole days he suffered to go by, expecting that the Greeks would run away. When, however, he found on the fifth that they were not gone, thinking that their firm stand was mere impudence and recklessness, he grew wroth, and sent against them the Medes and Císsians, with orders to take them alive and bring them into his presence. Then the Medes rushed forward and charged the Greeks, but fell in vast numbers: others however took the places of the slain, and would not be beaten off, though they suffered terrible losses. In this way it became clear to all, and especially to the king, that though he had plenty of combatants, he had but very few warriors. The struggle, however, continued during the whole day.

Then the Medes, having met so rough a reception, withdrew from the fight; and their place was taken by the band of Pérsians under Hydárnes, whom the king called his "Immortals." They, it was thought, would soon finish the business. But when they joined battle with the Greeks, it was with no better success than the Médian detachment—things went much as before—the two armies fighting in a narrow space, and the barbarians using shorter spears than the Greeks, and having no advantage from their numbers. The Lacedæmónians fought in a way worthy of note, and showed themselves far more skillful in fight than their adversaries, often turning their backs, and making as though they were all flying away, on which the barbarians would rush after them with much noise and shouting, when the Spártans at their approach would wheel round and face their pursuers, in this way destroying vast numbers of the enemy. Some Spártans likewise fell in these encounters, but only a very few. At last the Pérsians, finding that all their efforts to gain the pass availed nothing, and that, whether they attacked by divisions or in any other way, it was to no purpose, withdrew to their own quarters. During these assaults, it is said that Xérxes, who was watching the battle, thrice leaped from the throne on which he sat, in terror for his army.

The next day the combat was renewed, but with no better success on the part of the barbarians. The Greeks were so few that the barbarians hoped to find them disabled, by reason of their wounds, from offering any further resistance; and so they once more attacked them. But the Greeks were drawn up in detachments according to their cities and bore the brunt of the battle in turns—all except the Phócians, who had been stationed on the mountain to guard the pathway. So, when the

Pérsians found no difference between that day and the preceding, they again retired to their quarters.

— Heródotus, History, VII.210-212 (translated by George Rawlinson)

## Ephiáltes Betrays the Pass

Now, as the king was in great strait, and knew not how he should deal with the emergency, Ephiáltes, the son of Eurydémus, a man of Mális, came to him and was admitted to a conference. Stirred by the hope of receiving a rich reward at the king's hands, he had come to tell him of the pathway which led across the mountain to Thermópylæ; by which disclosure he brought destruction on the band of Greeks who had there withstood the barbarians...

Great was the joy of Xérxes on this occasion; and as he approved highly of the enterprise which Ephiáltes undertook to accomplish, he forthwith sent upon the errand Hydárnes, and the Pérsians under him. The troops left the camp about the time of the lighting of the lamps. The pathway along which they went was first discovered by the Málians of these parts, who soon afterwards led the Thessálians by it to attack the Phócians, at the time when the Phócians fortified the pass with a wall, and so put themselves under covert from danger. And ever since, the path has always been put to an ill use by the Málians...

The Pérsians took this path, and, crossing the Asópus, continued their march through the whole of the night, having the mountains of Œta on their right hand, and on their left those of Tráchis. At dawn of day they found themselves close to the summit. Now the hill was guarded, as I have already said, by a thousand Phócian men-at-arms, who were placed there to defend the pathway, and at the same time to secure their own country. They had been given the guard of the mountain path, while the other Greeks defended the pass below, because they had volunteered for the service, and had pledged themselves to Leónidas to maintain the post.

The ascent of the Pérsians became known to the Phócians in the following manner: During all the time that they were making their way up, the Greeks remained unconscious of it, inasmuch as the whole mountain was covered with groves of oak; but it happened that the air was very still, and the leaves which the Pérsians stirred with their feet made, as it was likely they would, a loud rustling, whereupon the Phócians jumped up and flew to seize their arms. In a moment the barbarians came in sight, and, perceiving men arming themselves, were greatly amazed; for they had fallen in with an enemy when they expected no opposition. Hydárnes, alarmed at the sight, and fearing lest the Phócians might be Lacedæmónians, inquired of Ephiáltes to what nation these troops belonged. Ephiáltes told him the exact truth, whereupon he arrayed his Pérsians for battle. The Phócians, galled by the showers of arrows to which they were exposed, and imagining themselves the special object of the Pérsian attack, fled hastily to the crest of the mountain, and there made ready to meet death; but while their mistake continued, the Pérsians, with Ephiáltes and Hydárnes, not thinking it worth their while to delay on account of Phócians, passed on and descended the mountain with all possible speed.

— Heródotus, History, VII.213,215-218 (translated by George Rawlinson)

## Leónidas Resolves to Make a Stand

The Greeks at Thermópylæ received the first warning of the destruction which the dawn would bring on them from the seer Megístias, who read their fate in the victims as he was sacrificing. After this, deserters came in, and brought the news that the Pérsians were marching round by the hills; it was still night when these men arrived. Last of all, the scouts came running down from the heights, and brought in the same accounts, when the day was just beginning to break. Then the Greeks held a council to consider what they should do, and here opinions were divided. Some were strong against quitting their post, while others contended to the contrary. So when the council had broken up, part of the troops departed and went their ways homeward to their several states; part however resolved to remain, and to stand by Leónidas to the last.

It is said that Leónidas himself sent away the troops who departed, because he tendered their safety, but thought it unseemly that either he or his Spártans should quit the post which they had been especially sent to guard. For my own part, I incline to think that Leónidas gave the order, because he perceived the allies to be out of heart and unwilling to encounter the danger to which his own mind was made up. He therefore commanded them to retreat, but said that he himself could not draw back with honor, knowing that, if he stayed, glory awaited him, and that Spárta in that case would not lose her prosperity. For when the Spártans, at the very beginning of the war, sent to consult the oracle concerning it, the answer which they received from the Pýthoness was "that either Spárta must be overthrown by the barbarians, or one of her kings must perish." The prophecy was delivered in hexámeter verse, and ran thus:

O ye men who dwell in the streets of broad Lacedǽmon! Either your glorious town shall be sacked by the children of Pérseus, or, in exchange, must all through the whole Lacónian country mourn for the loss of a king, descendant of great Héracles. He cannot be withstood by the courage of bulls nor of lions. Strive as they may, he is mighty as Jove. There is nought that shall stay him, till he have got for his prey your king, or your glorious city.

The remembrance of this answer, I think, and the wish to secure the whole glory for the Spártans, caused Leónidas to send the allies away. This is more likely than that they quarreled with him and took their departure in such unruly fashion. To me it seems no small argument in favor of this view, that the seer also who accompanied the army, Megístias, the Acarnánian—said to have been of the blood of Melámpus, and the same who was led by the appearance of the victims to warn the Greeks of the danger which threatened them—received orders to retire (as it is certain he did) from Leónidas, that he might escape the coming destruction. Megístias, however, though bidden to depart, refused, and stayed with the army; but he had an only son present with the expedition, whom he now sent away.

So the allies, when Leónidas ordered them to retire, obeyed him and forthwith departed. Only the Théspians and the Thébans remained with the Spártans; and of these the Thébans were kept back by Leónidas as hostages, very much against their will. The Théspians, on the contrary, stayed entirely of their own accord, refusing to retreat, and declaring that they would not forsake Leónidas and his followers. So they abode with the Spártans, and died with them. Their leader was Demóphilus, the son of Diádromes.

— Heródotus, *History*, VII.219-222 (translated by George Rawlinson)

## The Spártans and Théspians Destroyed

At sunrise Xérxes made libations, after which he waited until the time when the forum is wont to fill, and then began his advance. Ephiáltes had instructed him thus, as the descent of the mountain is much quicker, and the distance much shorter, than the way round the hills, and the ascent. So the barbarians under Xérxes began to draw nigh; and the Greeks under Leónidas, as they now went forth determined to die, advanced much further than on previous days, until they reached the more open portion of the pass. Hitherto they had held their station within the wall, and from this had gone forth to fight at the point where the pass was the narrowest. Now they joined battle beyond the defile, and carried slaughter among the barbarians, who fell in heaps. Behind them the captains of the squadrons, armed with whips, urged their men forward with continual blows. Many were thrust into the sea, and there perished; a still greater number were trampled to death by their own soldiers; no one heeded the dying. For the Greeks, reckless of their own safety and desperate, since they knew that, as the mountain had been crossed, their destruction was nigh at hand, exerted themselves with the most furious valor against the barbarians.

By this time the spears of the greater number were all shivered, and with their swords they hewed down the ranks of the Pérsians; and here, as they strove, Leónidas fell fighting bravely, together with many other famous Spártans... And now there arose a fierce struggle between the Pérsians and the Lacedæmónians over the body of Leónidas, in which the Greeks four times drove back the enemy, and at last by their great bravery succeeded in bearing off the body. This combat was scarcely ended when the Pérsians with Ephiáltes approached; and the Greeks, informed that they drew nigh, made a change in the manner of their fighting. Drawing back into the narrowest part of the pass, and retreating even behind the cross wall, they posted themselves upon a hillock, where they stood all drawn up together in one close body, except only the Thébans. The hillock whereof I speak is at the entrance of the straits, where the stone lion stands which was set up in honor of Leónidas. Here they defended themselves to the last, such as still had swords using them, and the others resisting with their hands and teeth; till the barbarians, who in part had pulled down the wall and attacked them in front, in part had gone round and now encircled them upon every side, overwhelmed and buried the remnant which was left beneath showers of missile weapons.

Thus nobly did the whole body of Lacedæmónians and Théspians behave; but nevertheless one man is said to have distinguished himself above all the rest, to wit, Dienéces the Spártan. A speech which he made before the Greeks engaged the Medes, remains on record. One of the Trachínians told him, "Such was the number of the barbarians, that when they shot forth their arrows the sun would be darkened by their multitude." Dienéces, not at all frightened at these words, but making light of the Médian numbers, answered "Our Trachínian friend brings us excellent tidings. If the Medes darken the sun, we shall have our fight in the shade." Other sayings too of a like nature are reported to have been left on record by this same person...

The slain were buried where they fell; and in their honor, nor less in honor of those who died before Leónidas sent the allies away, an inscription was set up, which said:

Here did four thousand men from Pélops' land
Against three hundred myriads bravely stand.

This was in honor of all. Another was for the Spártans alone:

Go, stranger, and to Lacedæmon tell
That here, obeying her behests, we fell.

This was for the Lacedæmónians. The seer had the following:

The great Megístias' tomb you here may view,
Whom slew the Medes, fresh from Sperchíus' fords.
Well the wise seer the coming death foreknew,
Yet scorned he to forsake his Spártan lords.

These inscriptions, and the pillars likewise, were all set up by the Amphíctyons, except that in honor of Megístias, which was inscribed to him (on account of their sworn friendship) by Simónides.

— Heródotus, *History*, VII.223-226,228 (translated by George Rawlinson)

## The Message of Demarátus to the Spártans

I return now to a point in my History, which at the time I left incomplete. The Lacedæmónians were the first of the Greeks to hear of the king's design against their country; and it was at this time that they sent to consult the Délphic oracle and received the answer of which I spoke a while ago. The discovery was made to them in a very strange way. Demarátus, the son of Arístón, after he took refuge with the Medes, was not, in my judgment, which is supported by probability, a well-wisher to the Lacedæmónians. It may be questioned, therefore, whether he did what I am about to mention from good-will or from insolent triumph. It happened that he was at Súsa at the time when Xérxes determined to lead his army into Greece; and in this way becoming acquainted with his design, he resolved to send tidings of it to Spárta. So as there was no other way of effecting his purpose, since the danger of being discovered was great, Demarátus framed the following contrivance. He took a pair of tablets, and, clearing the wax away from them, wrote what the king was purposing to do upon the wood whereof the tablets were made; having done this, he spread the wax once more over the writing, and so sent it. By these means, the guards placed to watch the roads, observing nothing but a blank tablet, were sure to give no trouble to the bearer. When the tablet reached Lacedæmon, there was no one, I understand, who could find out the secret, till Górgo, the daughter of Cleómenes and wife of Leónidas, discovered it, and told the others. "If they would scrape the wax off the tablet," she said, "they would be sure to find the writing upon the wood." The Lacedæmónians took her advice, found the writing, and read it; after which they sent it round to the other Greeks. Such then is the account which is given of this matter.

— Heródotus, *History*, VII.239 (translated by George Rawlinson)

## Themístocles Bribes the Greek Commanders

At the present time the Greeks, on their arrival at Artemísium, when they saw the number of the ships which lay at anchor near Áphetæ, and the abundance of troops everywhere, feeling disappointed that matters had gone with the barbarians so far otherwise than they had expected, and full of alarm at what they saw, began to speak of drawing back from Artemísium towards the inner parts of their country. So when the Eubœans heard what was in debate, they went to Eurybíades, and besought him to wait a few days, while they removed their children and their slaves to a place of safety. But, as they found that they prevailed nothing, they left him and went to Themístocles, the Athénian commander, to whom they gave a bribe of thirty talents, on his promise that the fleet should remain and risk a battle in defense of Eubœa.

And Themístocles succeeded in detaining the fleet in the way which I will now relate. He made over to Eurybíades five talents out of the thirty paid him, which he gave as if they came from himself; and having in this way gained over the admiral, he addressed himself to Adeimántus, the Corínthian leader, who was the only remonstrant now, and who still threatened to sail away from Artemísium and not wait for the other captains. Addressing himself to this man, Themístocles said with an oath: "Thou forsake us? By no means! I will pay thee better for remaining than the Mede would for leaving thy friends." And straightway he sent on board the ship of Adeimántus a present of three talents of silver. So these two captains were won by gifts, and came over to the views of Themístocles, who was thereby enabled to gratify the wishes of the Eubœans. He likewise made his own gain on the occasion; for he kept the rest of the money, and no one knew of it. The commanders who took the gifts thought that the sums were furnished by Áthens and had been sent to be used in this way.

— Heródotus, *History*, VIII.4-5 (translated by George Rawlinson)

## Artemísium and the Storm off Eubœa

When the Pérsian commanders and crews saw the Greeks thus boldly sailing towards them with their few ships, they thought them possessed with madness, and went out to meet them, expecting (as indeed seemed likely enough) that they would take all their vessels with the greatest ease. The Greek ships were so few, and their own so far outnumbered them, and sailed so much better, that they resolved, seeing their advantage, to encompass their foe on every side. And now such of the Iónians as wished well to the Grécian cause and served in the Pérsian fleet unwillingly, seeing their countrymen surrounded, were sorely distressed; for they felt sure that not one of them would ever make his escape, so poor an opinion had they of the strength of the Greeks. On the other hand, such as saw with pleasure the attack on Greece, now vied eagerly with each other which should be the first to make prize of an Athénian ship, and thereby to secure himself a rich reward from the king. For through both the hosts none were so much accounted of as the Athénians.

The Greeks, at a signal, brought the sterns of their ships together into a small compass, and turned their prows on every side towards the barbarians; after which, at a second signal, although enclosed within a narrow space, and closely pressed upon by the foe, yet they fell bravely to work, and captured thirty ships of the barbarians, at the same time taking prisoner Phílaon, the son of Chérsis, and brother of Górgus king of Sálamis, a man of much repute in the fleet. The first who made prize of a ship of the enemy was Lycomédes, an Athénian, who was afterwards adjudged the meed of valor. Victory however was still doubtful when night came on and put a stop to the combat. The Greeks sailed back to Artemísium; and the barbarians returned to Áphetæ, much surprised at the result, which was far other than they had looked for. In this battle only one of the Greeks who fought on the side of the king deserted and joined his countrymen. This was Antidórus of Lémnos, whom the Athénians rewarded for his desertion by the present of a piece of land in Sálamis.

Evening had barely closed in when a heavy rain—it was about midsummer—began to fall, which continued the whole night, with terrible thunderings and lightnings from Mount Pélion: the bodies of the slain and the broken pieces of the damaged ships were drifted in the direction of Áphetæ, and floated about the prows of the vessels there, disturbing the action of the oars. The barbarians, hearing the storm, were greatly dismayed, expecting certainly to perish, as they had fallen into such a multitude of misfortunes. For before they were well recovered from the tempest and the wreck of their vessels off Mount Pélion, they had been surprised by a sea-fight which had taxed all their strength, and now the sea-fight was scarcely over when they were exposed to floods of rain, and the rush of swollen streams into the sea, and violent thunderings.

If, however, they who lay at Áphetæ passed a comfortless night, far worse were the sufferings of those who had been sent to make the circuit of Eubœa; inasmuch as the storm fell on them out at sea, whereby the issue was indeed calamitous. They were sailing along near the Hollows of Eubœa, when the wind began to rise and the rain to pour: overpowered by the force of the gale, and driven they knew not whither, at the last they fell upon rocks, Heaven so contriving, in order that the Pérsian fleet might not greatly exceed the Greek, but be brought nearly to its level. This squadron, therefore, was entirely lost about the Hollows of Eubœa.

The barbarians at Áphetæ were glad when day dawned, and remained in quiet at their station, content if they might enjoy a little peace after so many sufferings. Meanwhile there came to the aid of the Greeks a reinforcement of fifty-three ships from Áttica. Their arrival, and the news (which reached Artemísium about the same time) of the complete destruction by the storm of the ships sent to sail round Eubœa, greatly cheered the spirits of the Greek sailors. So they waited again till the same hour as the day before, and, once more putting out to sea, attacked the enemy. This time they fell in with some Cilícian vessels, which they sank; when night came on, they withdrew to Artemísium.

121

The third day was now come, and the captains of the barbarians, ashamed that so small a number of ships should harass their fleet, and afraid of the anger of Xérxes, instead of waiting for the others to begin the battle, weighed anchor themselves, and advanced against the Greeks about the hour of noon, with shouts encouraging one another. Now it happened that these sea-fights took place on the very same days with the combats at Thermópylæ; and as the aim of the struggle was in the one case to maintain the pass, so in the other it was to defend the Eurípus. While the Greeks, therefore, exhorted one another not to let the barbarians burst in upon Greece, these latter shouted to their fellows to destroy the Grécian fleet, and get possession of the channel.

And now the fleet of Xérxes advanced in good order to the attack, while the Greeks on their side remained quite motionless at Artemísium. The Pérsians therefore spread themselves, and came forward in a half-moon, seeking to encircle the Greeks on all sides, and thereby prevent them from escaping. The Greeks, when they saw this, sailed out to meet their assailants; and the battle forthwith began. In this engagement the two fleets contended with no clear advantage to either, for the armament of Xérxes injured itself by its own greatness, the vessels falling into disorder, and oft-times running foul of one another; yet still they did not give way, but made a stout fight, since the crews felt it would indeed be a disgrace to turn and fly from a fleet so inferior in number. The Greeks therefore suffered much, both in ships and men; but the barbarians experienced a far larger loss of each. So the fleets separated after such a combat as I have described.

— Heródotus, *History*, VIII.10-16 (translated by George Rawlinson)

## Áthens is Sacked

When the captains from these various nations were come together at Sálamis, a council of war was summoned; and Eurybíades proposed that any one who liked to advise, should say which place seemed to him the fittest, among those still in the possession of the Greeks, to be the scene of a naval combat. Áttica, he said, was not to be thought of now; but he desired their counsel as to the remainder. The speakers mostly advised that the fleet should sail away to the Ísthmus, and there give battle in defense of the Peloponnésus; and they urged as a reason for this, that if they were worsted in a sea-fight at Sálamis, they would be shut up in an island where they could get no help; but if they were beaten near the Ísthmus, they could escape to their homes.

As the captains from the Peloponnésus were thus advising, there came an Athénian to the camp, who brought word that the barbarians had entered Áttica, and were ravaging and burning everything. For the division of the army under Xérxes was just arrived at Áthens from its march through Bœótia, where it had burnt Théspiæ and Platǽa—both which cities were forsaken by their inhabitants, who had fled to the Peloponnésus—and now it was laying waste all the possessions of the Athénians. Théspiæ and Platǽa had been burnt by the Pérsians, because they knew from the Thébans that neither of those cities had espoused their side.

Since the passage of the Héllespont and the commencement of the march upon Greece, a space of four months had gone by; one, while the army made the crossing, and delayed about the region of the Héllespont; and three while they proceeded thence to Áttica, which they entered in the Árchonship of Callíades. They found the city forsaken; a few people only remained in the temple, either keepers of the treasures, or men of the poorer sort. These persons having fortified the citadel with planks and boards, held out against the enemy. It was in some measure their poverty which had prevented them from seeking shelter in Sálamis; but there was likewise another reason which in part induced them to remain. They imagined themselves to have discovered the true meaning of the oracle uttered by the Pýthoness, which promised that "the wooden wall" should never be taken—the wooden wall, they thought, did not mean the ships, but the place where they had taken refuge.

The Pérsians encamped upon the hill over against the citadel, which is called Mars' hill by the Athénians, and began the siege of the place, attacking the Greeks with arrows whereto pieces of lighted tow were attached, which they shot at the barricade. And now those who were within the citadel found themselves in a most woeful case; for their wooden rampart betrayed them; still, however, they continued to resist. It was in vain that the Pisistrátidæ came to them and offered terms of surrender—they stoutly refused all parley, and among their other modes of defense, rolled down huge masses of stone upon the barbarians as they were mounting up to the gates: so that Xérxes was for a long time very greatly perplexed, and could not contrive any way to take them.

At last, however, in the midst of these many difficulties, the barbarians made discovery of an access. For verily the oracle had spoken truth; and it was fated that the whole mainland of Áttica should fall beneath the sway of the Pérsians. Right in front of the citadel, but behind the gates and the common ascent—where no watch was kept, and no one would have thought it possible that any foot of man could climb—a few soldiers mounted from the sanctuary of Agláurus, Cécrops' daughter, notwithstanding the steepness of the precipice. As soon as the Athénians saw them upon the summit, some threw themselves headlong from the wall, and so perished; while others fled for refuge to the inner part of the temple. The Pérsians rushed to the gates and opened them, after which they massacred the suppliants, When all were slain, they plundered the temple, and fired every part of the citadel.

Xérxes, thus completely master of Áthens, dispatched a horseman to Súsa, with a message to Artabánus, informing him of his success hitherto. The day after, he collected together all the Athénian exiles who had come into Greece in his train, and bade them go up into the citadel, and there offer sacrifice after their own fashion. I know not whether he had had a dream which made him give this order, or whether he felt some remorse on account of having set the temple on fire. However this may have been, the exiles were not slow to obey the command given them.

— Heródotus, *History*, VIII.49-54 (translated by George Rawlinson)

## Themístocles Urges a Sea Battle at Sálamis

Meanwhile, at Sálamis, the Greeks no sooner heard what had befallen the Athénian citadel, than they fell into such alarm that some of the captains did not even wait for the council to come to a vote, but embarked hastily on board their vessels, and hoisted sail as though they would take to flight immediately. The rest, who stayed at the council board, came to a vote that the fleet should give battle at the Ísthmus. Night now drew on; and the captains, dispersing from the meeting, proceeded on board their respective ships.

Themístocles, as he entered his own vessel, was met by Mnesíphilus, an Athénian, who asked him what the council had resolved to do. On learning that the resolve was to stand away for the Ísthmus, and there give battle on behalf of the Peloponnésus, Mnesíphilus exclaimed:

"If these men sail away from Sálamis, thou wilt have no fight at all for the one fatherland; for they will all scatter themselves to their own homes; and neither Eurybíades nor any one else will be able to hinder them, nor to stop the breaking up of the armament. Thus will Greece be brought to ruin through evil counsels. But haste thee now; and, if there be any possible way, seek to unsettle these resolves—mayhap thou mightest persuade Eurybíades to change his mind, and continue here."

The suggestion greatly pleased Themístocles; and without answering a word, he went straight to the vessel of Eurybíades. Arrived there, he let him know that he wanted to speak with him on a matter touching the public service. So Eurybíades bade him come on board and say whatever he wished. Then Themístocles, seating himself at his side, went over all the arguments which he had heard from Mnesíphilus, pretending as if they were his own, and added to them many new ones besides; until at last he persuaded Eurybíades, by his importunity, to quit his ship and again collect the captains to council.

As soon as they were come, and before Eurybíades had opened to them his purpose in assembling them together, Themístocles, as men are wont to do when they are very anxious, spoke much to divers of them; whereupon the Corínthian captain, Adeimántus, the son of Ocýtus, observed: "Themístocles, at the Games they who start too soon are scourged." "True," rejoined the other in his excuse, "but they who wait too late are not crowned."

Thus he gave the Corínthian at this time a mild answer; and towards Eurybíades himself he did not now use any of those arguments which he had urged before, or say aught of the allies betaking themselves to flight if once they broke up from Sálamis; it would have been ungraceful for him, when the confederates were present, to make accusation against any: but he had recourse to quite a new sort of reasoning, and addressed him as follows:

"With thee it rests, O Eurybíades! to save Greece, if thou wilt only hearken unto me, and give the enemy battle here, rather than yield to the advice of those among us, who would have the fleet withdrawn to the Ísthmus. Hear now, I beseech thee, and judge between the two courses. At the Ísthmus thou wilt fight in an open sea, which is greatly to our disadvantage, since our ships are heavier and fewer in number than the enemy's; and further, thou wilt in any case lose Sálamis, Mégara, and Ægína, even if all the rest goes well with us. The land and sea force of the Pérsians will advance together; and thy retreat will but draw them towards the Peloponnésus, and so bring all Greece into peril. If, on the other hand, thou doest as I advise, these are the advantages which thou wilt so secure: in the first place, as we shall fight in a narrow sea with few ships against many, if the war follows the common course, we shall gain a great victory; for to fight in a narrow space is favorable to us—in an open sea, to them. Again, Sálamis will in this case be preserved, where we have placed our wives and children.

"Nay, that very point by which ye set most store, is secured as much by this course as by the other; for whether we fight here or at the Ísthmus, we shall equally give battle in defense of the Peloponnésus. Assuredly ye will not do wisely to draw the Pérsians upon that region. For if things turn out as I anticipate, and we beat them by sea, then we shall have kept your Ísthmus free from the barbarians, and they will have advanced no further than Áttica, but from thence have fled back in disorder; and we shall, moreover, have saved Mégara, Ægína, and Sálamis itself, where an oracle has said that we are to overcome our enemies. When men counsel reasonably, reasonable success ensues; but when in their counsels they reject reason, the god does not choose to follow the wanderings of human fancies."

When Themístocles had thus spoken, Adeimántus the Corínthian again attacked him, and bade him be silent, since he was a man without a city; at the same time he called on Eurybíades not to put the question at the instance of one who had no country, and urged that Themístocles should show of what state he was envoy, before he gave his voice with the rest. This reproach he made, because the city of Áthens had been taken, and was in the hands of the barbarians. Hereupon Themístocles spake many bitter things against Adeimántus and the Corínthians generally; and for proof that he had a country, reminded the captains, that with two hundred ships at his command, all fully manned for battle, he had both city and territory as good as theirs; since there was no Grécian state which could resist his men if they were to make a descent.

After this declaration, he turned to Eurybíades, and addressing him with still greater warmth and earnestness: "If thou wilt stay here," he said, "and behave like a brave man, all will be well; if not, thou wilt bring Greece to ruin. For the whole fortune of the war depends on our ships. Be thou persuaded by my words. If not, we will take our families on board, and go, just as we are, to Síris, in Ítaly, which is ours from of old, and which the prophecies declare we are to colonize some day or other. You, when you have lost allies like us, will hereafter call to mind what I have now said."

At these words of Themístocles, Eurybíades changed his determination; principally, as I believe, because he feared that if he withdrew the fleet to the Ísthmus, the Athénians would sail away, and knew that without the Athénians, the rest of their ships could be no match for the fleet of the enemy. He therefore decided to remain and give battle at Sálamis.

— Heródotus, *History*, VIII.56-64 (translated by George Rawlinson)

## Themístocles Forces the Fight at Sálamis

The same night the land army of the barbarians began its march towards the Peloponnésus, where, however, all that was possible had been done to prevent the enemy from forcing an entrance by land. As soon as ever news reached the Peloponnésus of the death of Leónidas and his companions at Thermópylæ, the inhabitants flocked together from the various cities, and encamped at the Ísthmus, under the command of Cleómbrotus, son of Anaxándridas, and brother of Leónidas. Here their first care was to block up the Scirónian Way; after which it was determined in council to build a wall across the Ísthmus. As the number assembled amounted to many tens of thousands, and there was not one who did not give himself to the work, it was soon finished. Stones, bricks, timber, baskets filled full of sand, were used in the building; and not a moment was lost by those who gave their aid; for they labored without ceasing either by night or day.

Now the nations who gave their aid, and who had flocked in full force to the Ísthmus, were the following: the Lacedæmónians, all the tribes of the Arcádians, the Éleans, the Corínthians, the Sicyónians, the Epidáurians, the Phliásians, the Trœzénians, and the Hermiónians. These all gave their aid, being greatly alarmed at the danger which threatened Greece. But the other inhabitants of the Peloponnésus took no part in the matter; though the Olýmpic and Carnéan festivals were now over...

So the Greeks at the Ísthmus toiled unceasingly, as though in the greatest peril; since they never imagined that any great success would be gained by the fleet. The Greeks at Sálamis, on the other hand, when they heard what the rest were about, felt greatly alarmed; but their fear was not so much for themselves as for the Peloponnésus. At first they conversed together in low tones, each man with his fellow, secretly, and marveled at the folly shown by Eurybíades; but presently the smothered feeling broke out, and another assembly was held; whereat the old subjects provoked much talk from the speakers, one side maintaining that it was best to sail to the Peloponnésus and risk battle for that, instead of abiding at Sálamis and fighting for a land already taken by the enemy; while the other, which consisted of the Athénians, Ægínetans, and Megárians, was urgent to remain and have the battle fought where they were.

Then Themístocles, when he saw that the Peloponnésians would carry the vote against him, went out secretly from the council, and, instructing a certain man what he should say, sent him on board a merchant ship to the fleet of the Medes. The man's name was Sicínnus; he was one of Themístocles' household slaves and acted as tutor to his sons; in after times, when the Théspians were admitting persons to citizenship, Themístocles made him a Théspian, and a rich man to boot. The ship brought Sicínnus to the Pérsian fleet, and there he delivered his message to the leaders in these words:

"The Athénian commander has sent me to you privily, without the knowledge of the other Greeks. He is a well-wisher to the king's cause and would rather success should attend on you than on his countrymen; wherefore he bids me tell you that fear has seized the Greeks and they are meditating a hasty flight. Now then it is open to you to achieve the best work that ever ye wrought, if only ye will hinder their escaping. They no longer agree among themselves, so that they will not now make any resistance. Nay, it is likely ye may see a fight already begun between such as favor and such as oppose your cause." The messenger, when he had thus expressed himself, departed and was seen no more.

Then the captains, believing all that the messenger had said, proceeded to land a large body of Pérsian troops on the islet of Psyttaléa, which lies between Sálamis and the mainland; after which, about the hour of midnight, they advanced their western wing towards Sálamis, so as to enclose the Greeks. At the same time the force stationed about Céos and Cynosúra moved forward and filled the whole strait as far as Munýchia with their ships. This advance was made to prevent the Greeks from escaping by flight, and to block them up in Sálamis, where it was thought that vengeance might be taken upon them for the battles fought near Artemísium. The Pérsian troops were landed on the islet of Psyttaléa, because, as soon as the battle began, the men and wrecks were likely to be drifted thither, as the isle lay in the very path of the coming fight - and they would thus be able to save their own men and destroy those of the enemy. All these movements were made in silence, that the Greeks might have no knowledge of them; and they occupied the whole night, so that the men had no time to get their sleep.

— Heródotus, *History*, VIII.71-76 (translated by George Rawlinson)

## Aristídes Joins with Themístocles

Meanwhile, among the captains at Sálamis, the strife of words grew fierce. As yet they did not know that they were encompassed, but imagined that the barbarians remained in the same places where they had seen them the day before.

In the midst of their contention, Aristídes, the son of Lysímachus, who had crossed from Ægína, arrived in Sálamis. He was an Athénian, and had been ostracized by the commonalty; yet I believe, from what I have heard concerning his character, that there was not in all Áthens a man so worthy or so just as he. He now came to the council, and, standing outside, called for Themístocles. Now Themístocles was not his friend, but his most determined enemy. However, under the pressure of the great dangers impending, Aristídes forgot their feud, and called Themístocles out of the council, since he wished to confer with him. He had heard before his arrival of the impatience of the Peloponnésians to withdraw the fleet to the Ísthmus. As soon therefore as Themístocles came forth, Aristídes addressed him in these words:

"Our rivalry at all times, and especially at the present season, ought to be a struggle, which of us shall most advantage our country. Let me then say to thee, that so far as regards the departure of the Peloponnésians from this place, much talk and little will be found precisely alike. I have seen with my own eyes that which I now report: that, however much the Corínthians or Eurybíades himself may wish it, they cannot now retreat; for we are enclosed on every side by the enemy. Go in to them, and make this known."

"Thy advice is excellent," answered the other; "and thy tidings are also good. That which I earnestly desired to happen, thine eyes have beheld accomplished. Know that what the Medes have now done was at my instance; for it was necessary, as our men would not fight here of their own free will, to make them fight whether they would or no. But come now, as thou hast brought the good news, go in and tell it. For if I speak to them, they will think it a feigned tale, and will not believe that the barbarians have enclosed us around. Therefore do thou go to them, and inform them how matters stand. If they believe thee, it will be for the best; but if otherwise, it will not harm. For it is impossible that they should now flee away, if we are indeed shut in on all sides, as thou sayest."

Then Aristídes entered the assembly, and spoke to the captains: he had come, he told them, from Ægína, and had but barely escaped the blockading vessels—the Greek fleet was entirely enclosed by the ships of Xérxes—and he advised them to get themselves in readiness to resist the foe. Having said so much, he withdrew. And now another contest arose; for the greater part of the captains would not believe the tidings.

But while they still doubted, a Ténian tríreme, commanded by Panǽtius the son of Sosímenes, deserted from the Pérsians and joined the Greeks, bringing full intelligence. For this reason the Ténians were inscribed upon the tripod at Délphi among those who overthrew the barbarians. With this ship, which deserted to their side at Sálamis, and the Lémnian vessel which came over before at Artemísium, the Greek fleet was brought to the full number of 380 ships; otherwise it fell short by two of that amount.

— Heródotus, *History*, VIII.78-82 (translated by George Rawlinson)

## The Greek Victory at Sálamis

The fleet had scarce left the land when they were attacked by the barbarians. At once most of the Greeks began to back water, and were about touching the shore, when Aménias of Pallíne, one of the Athénian captains, darted forth in front of the line, and charged a ship of the enemy. The two vessels became entangled, and could not separate, whereupon the rest of the fleet came up to help Aménias and engaged with the Pérsians. Such is the account which the Athénians give of the way in which the battle began; but the Æginetans maintain that the vessel which had been to Ægína for the Æácidæ was the one that brought on the fight. It is also reported, that a phantom in the form of a woman appeared to the Greeks, and, in a voice that was heard from end to end of the fleet, cheered them on to the fight; first, however, rebuking them, and saying, "Strange men, how long are ye going to back water?"

Against the Athénians, who held the western extremity of the line towards Eléusis, were placed the Phœnícians; against the Lacedæmónians, whose station was eastward towards the Pirǽus, the Iónians. Of these last a few only followed the advice of Themístocles, to fight backwardly; the greater number did far otherwise...

Far the greater number of the Pérsian ships engaged in this battle were disabled, either by the Athénians or by the Æginetans. For as the Greeks fought in order and kept their line, while the barbarians were in confusion and had no plan in anything that they did, the issue of the battle could scarce be other than it was. Yet the Pérsians fought far more bravely here than at Eubœa, and indeed surpassed themselves; each did his utmost through fear of Xérxes, for each thought that the king's eye was upon himself.

What part the several nations, whether Greek or barbarian, took in the combat, I am not able to say for certain; Artemísia, however, I know, distinguished herself in such a way as raised her even higher than she stood before in the esteem of the king. For after confusion had spread throughout the whole of the king's fleet, and her ship was closely pursued by an Athénian tríreme, she, having no way to fly, since in front of her were a number of friendly vessels, and she was nearest of all the Pérsians to the enemy, resolved on a measure which in fact proved her safety. Pressed by the Athénian pursuer, she bore straight against one of the ships of her own party, a Calýndian, which had Damasíthymus, the Calýndian king, himself on board. I cannot say whether she had had any quarrel with the man while the fleet was at the Héllespont, or no—neither can I decide whether she of set purpose attacked his vessel, or whether it merely chanced that the Calýndian ship came in her way—but certain it is that she bore down upon his vessel and sank it, and that thereby she had the good fortune to procure herself a double advantage. For the commander of the Athénian tríreme, when he saw her bear down on one of the enemy's fleet, thought immediately that her vessel was a Greek, or else had deserted from the Pérsians, and was now fighting on the Greek side; he therefore gave up the chase, and turned away to attack others.

Thus in the first place she saved her life by the action, and was enabled to get clear off from the battle; while further, it fell out that in the very act of doing the king an injury she raised herself to a greater height than ever in his esteem. For as Xérxes beheld the fight, he remarked (it is said) the destruction of the vessel, whereupon the bystanders observed to him: "Seest thou, master, how well Artemísia fights, and how she has just sunk a ship of the enemy?" Then Xérxes asked if it were really Artemísia's doing; and they answered, "Certainly; for they knew her ensign": while all made sure that the sunken vessel belonged to the opposite side. Everything, it is said, conspired to prosper the queen - it was especially fortunate for her that not one of those on board the Calýndian ship survived to become her accuser. Xérxes, they say, in reply to the remarks made to him, observed, "My men have behaved like women, my women like men!"

There fell in this combat Ariabígnes, one of the chief commanders of the fleet, who was son of Daríus and brother of Xérxes; and with him perished a vast number of men of high repute, Pérsians, Medes, and allies. Of the Greeks there died only a few; for, as they were able to swim, all those that were not slain outright by the enemy escaped from the sinking vessels and swam across to Sálamis. But on the side of the barbarians more perished by drowning than in any other way, since they did not know how to swim. The great destruction took place when the ships which had been first engaged began to fly; for they who were stationed in the rear, anxious to display their valor before the eyes of the king, made every effort to force their way to the front, and thus became entangled with such of their own vessels as were retreating...

When the rout of the barbarians began, and they sought to make their escape to Phálerum, the Ægínetans, awaiting them in the channel, performed exploits worthy to be recorded. Through the whole of the confused struggle the Athénians employed themselves in destroying such ships as either made resistance or fled to shore, while the Ægínetans dealt with those which endeavored to escape down the strait; so that the Pérsian vessels were no sooner clear of the Athénians than forthwith they fell into the hands of the Ægínetan squadron.

— Heródotus, *History*, VIII.84-91 (translated by George Rawlinson)

## Xérxes Plans to Depart

Xérxes, when he saw the extent of his loss, began to be afraid lest the Greeks might be counselled by the Iónians, or without their advice might determine to sail straight to the Héllespont and break down the bridges there; in which case he would be blocked up in Éurope, and run great risk of perishing. He therefore made up his mind to fly; but, as he wished to hide his purpose alike from the Greeks and from his own people, he set to work to carry a mound across the channel to Sálamis, and at the same time began fastening a number of Phœnícian merchant ships together, to serve at once for a bridge and a wall. He likewise made many warlike preparations, as if he were about to engage the Greeks once more at sea. Now, when these things were seen, all grew fully persuaded that the king was bent on remaining and intended to push the war in good earnest. Mardónius, however, was in no respect deceived; for long acquaintance enabled him to read all the king's thoughts. Meanwhile, Xérxes, though engaged in this way, sent off a messenger to carry intelligence of his misfortune to Pérsia.

Nothing mortal travels so fast as these Pérsian messengers. The entire plan is a Pérsian invention; and this is the method of it. Along the whole line of road there are men (they say) stationed with horses, in number equal to the number of days which the journey takes, allowing a man and horse to each day; and these men will not be hindered from accomplishing at their best speed the distance which they have to go, either by snow, or rain, or heat, or by the darkness of night. The first rider delivers his dispatch to the second and the second passes it to the third; and so it is borne from hand to hand along the whole line, like the light in the torch-race, which the Greeks celebrate to Vúlcan. The Pérsians give the riding post in this manner, the name of "Angárum."

At Súsa, on the arrival of the first message, which said that Xérxes was master of Áthens, such was the delight of the Pérsians who had remained behind, that they forthwith strewed all the streets with myrtle boughs, and burnt incense, and fell to feasting and merriment. In like manner, when the second message reached them, so sore was their dismay, that they all with one accord rent their garments, and cried aloud, and wept and wailed without stint. They laid the blame of the disaster on Mardónius; and their grief on the occasion was less on account of the damage done to their ships, than owing to the alarm which they felt about the safety of the king. Hence their trouble did not cease till Xérxes himself, by his arrival, put an end to their fears.

— Heródotus, *History*, VIII.97 (translated by George Rawlinson)

## Xérxes Leaves Mardónius and an Army of 300,000

King Xérxes and his army waited but a few days after the sea-fight, and then withdrew into Bœótia by the road which they had followed on their advance. It was the wish of Mardónius to escort the king a part of the way; and as the time of year was no longer suitable for carrying on war, he thought it best to winter in Théssaly, and wait for the spring before he attempted the Peloponnésus. After the army was come into Théssaly, Mardónius made choice of the troops that were to stay with him; and, first of all, he took the whole body called the "Immortals," except only their leader, Hydárnes, who refused to quit the person of the king. Next, he chose the Pérsians who wore breastplates, and the thousand picked horse; likewise the Medes, the Sácans, the Báctrians, and the Índians, foot and horse equally. These nations he took entire: from the rest of the allies he culled a few men, taking either such as were remarkable for their appearance, or else such as had performed, to his knowledge, some valiant deed. The Pérsians furnished him with the greatest number of troops, men who were adorned with chains and armlets. Next to them were the Medes, who in number equaled the Pérsians, but in valor fell short of them. The whole army, reckoning the horsemen with the rest, amounted to 300,000 men.

At the time when Mardónius was making choice of his troops, and Xérxes still continued in Théssaly, the Lacedæmónians received a message from the Délphic oracle, bidding them seek satisfaction at the hands of Xérxes for the death of Leónidas, and take whatever he chose to give them. So the Spártans sent a herald with all speed into Théssaly, who arrived while the entire Pérsian army was still there. This man, being brought before the king, spake as follows:

"King of the Medes, the Lacedæmónians and the Herácleids of Spárta require of thee the satisfaction due for bloodshed, because thou slewest their king, who fell fighting for Greece."

Xérxes laughed, and for a long time spake not a word. At last, however, he pointed to Mardónius, who was standing by him, and said: "Mardónius here shall give them the satisfaction they deserve to get." And the herald accepted the answer, and forthwith went his way.

— Heródotus, *History*, VIII.97-103,113-114 (translated by George Rawlinson)

## Áthens Rejects the Alliance of Mardónius

"We know, as well as thou dost, that the power of the Mede is many times greater than our own: we did not need to have that cast in our teeth. Nevertheless, we cling so to freedom that we shall offer what resistance we may. Seek not to persuade us into making terms with the barbarian; say what thou wilt, thou wilt never gain our assent. Return rather at once and tell Mardónius that our answer to him is this: 'So long as the sun keeps his present course, we will never join alliance with Xérxes. Nay, we shall oppose him unceasingly, trusting in the aid of those gods and heroes whom he has lightly esteemed, whose houses and whose images he has burnt with fire.' Come not thou again to us with words like these; nor, thinking to do us a service, persuade us to unholy actions. Thou art the guest and friend of our nation; we would not that thou shouldst receive hurt at our hands."

— Heródotus, *History*, VIII.140-143 (translated by George Rawlinson)

# CHAPTER XV.

## EFFECTS OF THE PÉRSIAN WARS UPON GREEK CULTURE

The New Spirit in Literature, I.—Improvements in Art; Sculpture, II.—State of Philosophy and Science, III.

### I. THE NEW SPIRIT IN LITERATURE

## The Reversal of Greece's Fortune

A man may justly feel perplexed when he stops to consider the inconsistency that is to be found in the life of mankind; for no thing which we consider to be good is ever found to have been given to human beings unadulterated, nor is there any evil in an absolute form without some admixture of advantage. Proofs of this will be obtained if we give thought to the events of the past, especially to those of outstanding importance. For instance, the campaign of Xérxes, the king of the Pérsians, against Greece aroused the greatest fear among the Greeks by reason of the immensity of his armaments, since the war they were entering might well decide their slavery, and since the Greek cities of Ásia had already been enslaved, all men assumed that those of Greece would also suffer a similar fate.

But the war, contrary to expectation, came to an amazing end, and not only were the peoples of Greece freed of the dangers threatening them, but they also won for themselves great glory, and every city of Héllas enjoyed such an abundant prosperity that all men were filled with wonder at the complete reversal of their fortune. For from this time over the next fifty years Greece made great advance in prosperity. In these years, for example, plenty brought increase to the arts, and the greatest artists of whom we have record, including the sculptor Phídias, flourished at that time; and there was likewise great advance in education, and philosophy and oratory had a high place of honor among all Greeks, and especially the Athénians. For the philosophers were Sócrates and Pláto and Áristotle, and the orators were Péricles and Isócrates and his pupils; and there were likewise men who have become renowned for generalship: Miltíades, Themístocles, Aristídes, Címon, Myrónides, and others more than these, regarding whom it would be a long task to write.

First place belonged to the Athénians, who had advanced so far in both fame and prowess that their name was known throughout practically the entire inhabited world; for they increased their leadership to such a degree that, by their own resources and without the aid of Lacedæmónians or Peloponnésians, they overcame great Pérsian armaments both on land and on sea, and humbled the famed leadership of the Pérsians to such an extent that they forced them by the terms of a treaty to liberate all the cities of Ásia.

— Diodórus Sículus, *Library of History*, XII.1-2 (translated by C. H. Oldfather)

## Those Who Died at Thermópylæ

Of those who at Thermópylæ were slain,
    Glorious the doom, and beautiful the lot;
Their tomb an altar: men from tears refrain
    To honor them, and praise, but mourn them not.

Such sepulcher, nor drear decay
Nor all-destroying time shall waste; this right have they.

Within their grave the home-bred glory
      Of Greece was laid: this witness gives
Leónidas the Spártan, in whose story
      A wreath of famous virtue ever lives.

— Simónides, *Of Those Who Died at Thermópylæ* (translated by John Sterling)

## The Origin of Rhodes

Ancient sayings of men relate,
That when Zeus and the Immortals divided earth,
Rhodes was not yet apparent in the deep sea;
But in salt depths the island was hid.
And, Hélios being absent, no one claimed for him his lot;
So they left him without any region for his share,
The pure god. And Zeus was about to make a second drawing of lots
For him warned. But he did not permit him;
For he said that within the white sea he had seen a certain land
springing up from the bottom,
Capable of feeding many men, and suitable for flocks.
And straightway he commanded golden-filleted Lachésis
To stretch forth her hands, and not contradict
The great oath of the gods, but with the son of Crónos
Assent that, to the bright air being sent by his nod,
It should hereafter be his prize. And his words were fully performed,
Meeting with truth. The island sprang from the watery
Sea; and the genial Father of penetrating beams,
Ruler of fire-breathing horses, has it.

— Píndar, *Olýmpian Odes*, VII.100-129 (translated by Henry David Thoreau)

## Æsculápius

As many, therefore, as came suffering
From spontaneous ulcers, or wounded
In their limbs with glittering steel,
Or with the far-cast stone,
Or by the summer's heat o'ercome in body,
Or by winter, relieving he saved from
Various ills; some cherishing
With soothing strains,
Others having drunk refreshing draughts, or applying
Remedies to the limbs, others by cutting off he made erect.
But even wisdom is bound by gain,
And gold appearing in the hand persuaded even him, with its bright reward,
To bring a man from death
Already overtaken. But the Crónian, smiting
With both hands, quickly took away
The breath from his breasts;
And the rushing thunderbolt hurled him to death.
It is necessary for mortal minds
To seek what is reasonable from the divinities,

Knowing what is before the feet, of what destiny we are.
Do not, my soul, aspire to the life
Of the Immortals, but exhaust the practicable means.

> — Píndar, *Pýthian Odes*, III.83-110 (translated by Henry David Thoreau)

## The Height of Glory

Fortunate and celebrated
By the wise is that man
Who, conquering by his hands or virtue
Of his feet, takes the highest prizes
Through daring and strength,
And living still sees his youthful son
Deservedly obtaining Pýthian crowns.
The brazen heaven is not yet accessible to him.
But whatever glory we
Of mortal race may reach,
He goes beyond, even to the boundaries
Of navigation. But neither in ships, nor going on foot,
Couldst thou find the wonderful way to the contests of the Hyperbóreans.

> — Píndar, *Pýthian Odes*, X.33-48 (translated by Henry David Thoreau)

## The Youth of Achílles

One with native virtues
Greatly prevails; but he who
Possesses acquired talents, an obscure man,
Aspiring to various things, never with fearless
Foot advances, but tries
A myriad virtues with inefficient mind.
Yellow-haired Achílles, meanwhile, remaining in the house of Phílyra,
Being a boy played
Great deeds; often brandishing
Iron-pointed javelins in his hands,
Swift as the winds, in fight he wrought death to savage lions;
And he slew boars, and brought their bodies
Palpitating to Crónian Centáurus,
As soon as six years old. And all the while
Ártemis and bold Athéna admired him,
Slaying stags without dogs or treacherous nets;
For he conquered them on foot.

> — Píndar, *Némean Odes*, III.69-90 (translated by Henry David Thoreau)

## The Origins of Tragedy and Comedy

Poetry in general seems to have sprung from two causes, each of them lying deep in our nature. First, the instinct of imitation is implanted in man from childhood, one difference between him and other animals being that he is the most imitative of living creatures, and through imitation learns his earliest lessons; and no less universal is the pleasure felt in things imitated. We have evidence of this in the facts of experience. Objects which in themselves we view with pain, we delight to contemplate when reproduced with minute fidelity: such as the forms of the most ignoble animals and of dead bodies. The cause of this again is, that to learn gives the liveliest pleasure, not only to philosophers but to men in general, whose capacity, however, of learning is more limited. Thus the reason why men enjoy seeing a likeness is, that in contemplating it they find themselves learning or inferring, and perhaps saying, 'Ah, that is he.' For if you happen not to have seen the original, the pleasure will be due not to the imitation as such, but to the execution, the coloring, or some such other cause.

Imitation, then, is one instinct of our nature. Next, there is the instinct for 'harmony' and rhythm, meters being manifestly sections of rhythm. Persons, therefore, starting with this natural gift developed by degrees their special aptitudes, till their rude improvisations gave birth to Poetry.

Poetry now diverged in two directions, according to the individual character of the writers. The graver spirits imitated noble actions, and the actions of good men. The more trivial sort imitated the actions of meaner persons, at first composing satires, as the former did hymns to the gods and the praises of famous men. A poem of the satirical kind cannot indeed be put down to any author earlier than Hómer; though many such writers probably there were. But from Hómer onward, instances can be cited—his own *Margítes*, for example, and other similar compositions. The appropriate meter was also here introduced; hence the measure is still called the iámbic or lampooning measure, being that in which people lampooned one another. Thus the older poets were distinguished as writers of heroic or of lampooning verse...

... Whether Tragedy has as yet perfected its proper types or not; and whether it is to be judged in itself, or in relation also to the audience—this raises another question. Be that as it may, Tragedy—as also Comedy—was at first mere improvisation. The one originated with the authors of the Díthyramb, the other with those of the phallic songs, which are still in use in many of our cities. Tragedy advanced by slow degrees; each new element that showed itself was in turn developed. Having passed through many changes, it found its natural form, and there it stopped.

Æschylus first introduced a second actor; he diminished the importance of the Chorus and assigned the leading part to the dialogue. Sóphocles raised the number of actors to three and added scene-painting. Moreover, it was not till late that the short plot was discarded for one of greater compass, and the grotesque diction of the earlier satyric form for the stately manner of Tragedy. The iámbic measure then replaced the trochaic tetrameter, which was originally employed when the poetry was of the satyric order and had greater with dancing. Once dialogue had come in, Nature herself discovered the appropriate measure. For the iámbic is, of all measures, the most colloquial. We see it in the fact that conversational speech runs into iámbic lines more frequently than into any other kind of verse; rarely into hexámeters, and only when we drop the colloquial intonation. The additions to the number of 'episodes' or acts, and the other accessories of which tradition tells, must be taken as already described; for to discuss them in detail would, doubtless, be a large undertaking.

Comedy is, as we have said, an imitation of characters of a lower type—not, however, in the full sense of the word bad, the ludicrous being merely a subdivision of the ugly. It consists in some defect or ugliness which is not painful or destructive. To take an obvious example, the comic mask is ugly and distorted, but does not imply pain.

The successive changes through which Tragedy passed, and the authors of these changes, are well known, whereas Comedy has had no history, because it was not at first treated seriously. It was late before the Árchon granted a comic chorus to a poet; the performers were till then voluntary. Comedy had already taken definite shape when comic poets, distinctively so called, are heard of. Who furnished it with masks, or prologues, or increased the number of actors—these and other similar details remain unknown. As for the plot, it came originally from Sícily; but of Athénian writers Crátes was the first who abandoning the 'iámbic' or lampooning form, generalized his themes and plots.

Epic poetry agrees with Tragedy in so far as it is an imitation in verse of characters of a higher type. They differ in that Epic poetry admits but one kind of meter and is narrative in form. They differ, again, in their length: for Tragedy endeavors, as far as possible, to confine itself to a single revolution of the sun, or but slightly to exceed this limit, whereas the Epic action has no limits of time. This, then, is a second point of difference; though at first the same freedom was admitted in Tragedy as in Epic poetry.

Of their constituent parts some are common to both, some peculiar to Tragedy: whoever, therefore knows what is good or bad Tragedy, knows also about Epic poetry. All the elements of an Epic poem are found in Tragedy, but the elements of a Tragedy are not all found in the Epic poem.

– Áristotle, *Poetics*, IV-V (translated by S. H. Butcher)

## II. IMPROVEMENTS IN ART; SCULPTURE

# The Tomb of Mausólus

Scópas had for rivals and contemporaries, Bryáxis, Timótheus, and Leóchares, artists whom we are bound to mention together, from the fact that they worked together at the Mausoleum; such being the name of the tomb that was erected by his wife Artemísia in honor of Mausólus, a petty king of Cária, who died in the second year of the hundred and seventh Olýmpiad. It was through the exertions of these artists more particularly, that this work came to be reckoned one of the Seven Wonders of the World. The circumference of this building is, in all, four hundred and forty feet, and the breadth from north to south sixty-three, the two fronts being not so wide in extent. It is twenty-five cúbits in height and is surrounded with six-and-thirty columns, the outer circumference being known as the "Ptéron." The east side was sculptured by Scópas, the north by Bryáxis, the south by Timótheus, and the west by Leóchares; but, before their task was completed, Queen Artemísia died. They did not leave their work, however, until it was finished, considering that it was at once a memorial of their own fame and of the sculptor's art: and, to this day even, it is undecided which of them has excelled. A fifth artist also took part in the work; for above the Ptéron there is a pýramid erected, equal in height to the building below, and formed of four and twenty steps, which gradually taper upwards towards the summit; a platform, crowned with a representation of a four-horse chariot by Pýthis. This addition makes the total height of the work one hundred and forty feet.

– Plíny the Elder, *The Natural History*, 36.4 (translated by John Bostock and H. T. Riley)

## III. STATE OF PHILOSOPHY AND SCIENCE

# The Philosophy of Heraclítus

Here is a general summary of his doctrines. All things are composed of fire, and into fire they are again resolved; further, all things come about by destiny, and existent things are brought into harmony by the clash of opposing currents; again, all things are filled with souls and divinities. He has also given an account of all the orderly happenings in the universe and declares the sun to be no larger than it appears. Another of his sayings is: "Of soul thou shalt never find boundaries, not if thou trackest it on every path; so deep is its cause." Self-conceit he used to call a falling sickness (epilepsy) and eyesight a lying sense. Sometimes, however, his utterances are clear and distinct, so that even the dullest can easily understand and derive therefrom elevation of soul. For brevity and weightiness his exposition is incomparable.

Coming now to his particular tenets, we may state them as follows: Fire is the element; all things are exchanged for fire and come into being by rarefaction and condensation; but of this he gives no clear explanation. All things come into being by conflict of opposites, and the sum of things flows like a stream. Further, all that exists is limited and forms one world. And it is alternately born from fire and again resolved into fire in fixed cycles to all eternity, and this is determined by destiny. Of the opposites that which tends to birth or creation is called war and strife, and that which tends to destruction by fire is called concord and peace. Change he called a pathway up and down, and this determines the birth of the world.

For fire by contracting turns into moisture, and this condensing turns into water; water again when congealed turns into earth. This process he calls the downward path. Then again earth is liquified, and thus gives rise to water, and from water the rest of the series is derived. He reduces nearly everything to exhalation from the sea. This process is the upward path. Exhalations arise from earth as well as from sea; those from sea are bright and pure, those from earth dark. Fire is fed by the bright exhalations, the moist element by the others. He does not make clear the nature of the surrounding element. He says, however, that there are in it bowls with their concavities turned towards us, in which the bright exhalations collect and produce flames. These are the stars. The flame of the sun is the brightest and the hottest; the other stars are further from the earth and for that reason give it less light and heat. The moon, which is nearer to the earth, traverses a region which is not pure. The sun, however, moves in a clear and untroubled region, and keeps a proportionate distance from us. That is why it gives us more heat and light. Eclipses of the sun and moon occur when the bowls are turned upwards; the monthly phases of the moon are due to the bowl turning round in its place little by little. Day and night, months, seasons and years, rains and winds and other similar phenomena are accounted for by the various exhalations. Thus the bright exhalation, set aflame in the hollow orb of the sun, produces day, the opposite exhalation when it has got the mastery causes night; the increase of warmth due to the bright exhalation produces summer, whereas the preponderance of moisture due to the dark exhalation brings about winter. His explanations of other phenomena are in harmony with this. He gives no account of the nature of the earth, nor even of the bowls. These, then, were his opinions.

— Diógenes Laértius, *Lives of the Eminent Philosophers*, IX.7-11 (translated by R. D. Hicks)

## Heraclítus Refuses King Daríus

"King Daríus, son of Hystáspes, to Heraclítus the wise man of Éphesus, greeting. You are the author of a treatise *On Nature* that is hard to understand and hard to interpret. In certain parts, if it be interpreted word for word, it seems to contain a power of speculation on the whole universe and all that goes on within it, which depends upon motion most divine; but for the most part judgement is suspended, so that even those who are the most conversant with literature are at a loss to know what is the right interpretation of your work. Accordingly, King Daríus, son of Hystáspes, wishes to enjoy your instruction and Greek culture. Come then with all speed to see me at my palace. For the Greeks as a rule are not prone to mark their wise men; nay, they neglect their excellent precepts which make for good hearing and learning. But at my court there is secured for you every privilege and daily conversation of a good and worthy kind, and a life in keeping with your counsels."

"Heraclítus of Éphesus to King Daríus, son of Hystáspes, greeting. All men upon earth hold aloof from truth and justice, while, by reason of wicked folly, they devote themselves to avarice and thirst for popularity. But I, being forgetful of all wickedness, shunning the general satiety which is closely joined with envy, and because I have a horror of splendor, could not come to Pérsia, being content with little, when that little is to my mind." So independent was he even when dealing with a king.

— Diógenes Laértius, *Lives of the Eminent Philosophers*, IX.13 (translated by R. D. Hicks)

# Parménides of Élea

He was the first to declare that the earth is spherical and is situated in the center of the universe. He held that there were two elements, fire and earth, and that the former discharged the function of a craftsman, the latter of his material. The generation of man proceeded from the sun as first cause; heat and cold, of which all things consist, surpass the sun itself. Again he held that soul and mind are one and the same, as Theophrástus mentions in his Physics, where he is setting forth the tenets of almost all the schools. He divided his philosophy into two parts dealing the one with truth, the other with opinion. Hence he somewhere says:

> Thou must needs learn all things, as well the unshakeable heart of well-rounded truth as the opinions of mortals in which there is no sure trust.

Our philosopher too commits his doctrines to verse just as did Hésiod, Xenóphanes and Empédocles. He made reason the standard and pronounced sensations to be inexact. At all events his words are:

> And let not long-practiced wont force thee to tread this path, to be governed by an aimless eye, an echoing ear and a tongue, but do thou with understanding bring the much-contested issue to decision.

Hence Timon says of him:

> And the strength of high-souled Parménides, of no diverse opinions, who introduced thought instead of imagination's deceit.

It was about him that Pláto wrote a dialogue with the title Parménides or Concerning Ideas.

He flourished in the 69th Olýmpiad. He is believed to have been the first to detect the identity of Hésperus, the evening-star, and Phósphorus, the morning-star; so Favorínus in the fifth book of his *Memorabília*; but others attribute this to Pythágoras, whereas Callímachus holds that the poem in question was not the work of Pythágoras. Parménides is said to have served his native city as a legislator: so we learn from Speusíppus in his book On Philosophers.

— Diógenes Laértius, *Lives of the Eminent Philosophers*, IX.21-23 (translated by R. D. Hicks)

# CHAPTER XVI.

## THE GROWTH OF THE ATHÉNIAN EMPIRE

Themístocles and the Recovery of Áthens, I.—Aristídes and the Confederacy of Délos, II.
Címon and the Growth of Imperialism, III.—Péricles and the Athénian Empire, IV.

## I. THEMÍSTOCLES AND THE RECOVERY OF ÁTHENS

### Themístocles Advances the Cause of Áthens

After these things, he began to rebuild and fortify the city of Áthens, bribing, as Theopómpus reports, the Lacedæmónian Éphors not to be against it, but, as most relate it, overreaching and deceiving them. For, under pretest of an embassy, he went to Spárta, where, upon the Lacedæmónians charging him with rebuilding the walls, and Poliárchus coming on purpose from Ægína to denounce it, he denied the fact, bidding them to send people to Áthens to see whether it were so or no; by which delay he got time for the building of the wall, and also placed these ambassadors in the hands of his countrymen as hostages for him; and so, when the Lacedæmónians knew the truth, they did him no hurt, but, suppressing all display of their anger for the present, sent him away.

Next he proceeded to establish the harbor of Piræus, observing the great natural advantages of the locality and desirous to unite the whole city with the sea, and to reverse, in a manner, the policy of ancient Athénian kings, who, endeavoring to withdraw their subjects from the sea, and to accustom them to live, not by sailing about, but by planting and tilling the earth, spread the story of the dispute between Minérva and Néptune for the sovereignty of Áthens, in which Minérva, by producing to the judges an olive tree, was declared to have won; whereas Themístocles did not only knead up, as Aristóphanes says, the port and the city into one, but made the city absolutely the dependent and the adjunct of the port, and the land of the sea, which increased the power and confidence of the people against the nobility; the authority coming into the hands of sailors and boatswains and pilots. Thus it was one of the orders of the thirty tyrants, that the hustings in the assembly, which had faced towards the sea, should be turned round towards the land; implying their opinion that the empire by sea had been the origin of the democracy, and that the farming population were not so much opposed to oligarchy.

Themístocles, however, formed yet higher designs with a view to naval supremacy. For, after the departure of Xérxes, when the Grécian fleet was arrived at Págasæ, where they wintered, Themístocles, in a public oration to the people of Áthens, told them that he had a design to perform something that would tend greatly to their interests and safety, but was of such a nature, that it could not be made generally public. The Athénians ordered him to impart it to Aristídes only; and, if he approved of it, to put it in practice. And when Themístocles had discovered to him that his design was to burn the Grécian fleet in the haven of Págasæ, Aristídes, coming out to the people, gave this report of the stratagem contrived by Themístocles, that no proposal could be more politic, or more dishonorable; on which the Athénians commanded Themístocles to think no farther of it.

When the Lacedæmónians proposed, at the general council of the Amphictyónians, that the representatives of those cities which were not in the league, nor had fought against the Pérsians, should be excluded, Themístocles, fearing that the Thessálians, with those of Thebes, Árgos, and others, being thrown out of the council, the Lacedæmónians would become wholly masters of the votes, and do what they pleased, supported the deputies of the cities, and prevailed with the members then sitting to alter their opinion in this point, showing them that there were but one and thirty cities which had partaken in the war, and that most of these, also, were very small; how intolerable would it be, if the rest of Greece should be excluded, and the general council should come to be ruled by two or three great cities. By this, chiefly, he incurred the displeasure of the Lacedæmónians, whose honors and favors were now shown to Címon, with a view to making him the opponent of the state policy of Themístocles.

He was also burdensome to the confederates, sailing about the islands and collecting money from them. Heródotus says, that, requiring money of those of the island of Ándros, he told them that he had brought with him two goddesses, Persuasion and Force; and they answered him that they had also two great goddesses, which prohibited them from giving him any money, Poverty and Impossibility.

– Plútarch, Life of Themístocles (translated by John Dryden)

## II. ARISTÍDES AND THE CONFEDERACY OF DÉLOS

## The Spártans Lose Their Hegemony

Meanwhile Pausánias, son of Cleómbrotus, was sent out from Lacedæmon as commander-in-chief of the Héllenes, with twenty ships from Peloponnésus. With him sailed the Athénians with thirty ships, and a number of the other allies. They made an expedition against Cýprus and subdued most of the island, and afterwards against Byzántium, which was in the hands of the Medes, and compelled it to surrender. This event took place while the Spártans were still supreme. But the violence of Pausánias had already begun to be disagreeable to the Héllenes, particularly to the Iónians and the newly liberated populations. These resorted to the Athénians and requested them as their kinsmen to become their leaders, and to stop any attempt at violence on the part of Pausánias. The Athénians accepted their overtures and determined to put down any attempt of the kind and to settle everything else as their interests might seem to demand. In the meantime, the Lacedæmónians recalled Pausánias for an investigation of the reports which had reached them. Manifold and grave accusations had been brought against him by Héllenes arriving in Spárta; and, to all appearance, there had been in him more of the mimicry of a despot than of the attitude of a general.

As it happened, his recall came just at the time when the hatred which he had inspired had induced the allies to desert him, the soldiers from Peloponnésus excepted, and to range themselves by the side of the Athénians. On his arrival at Lacedæmon, he was censured for his private acts of oppression, but was acquitted on the heaviest counts and pronounced not guilty; it must be known that the charge of Médism formed one of the principal, and to all appearance one of the best founded, articles against him. The Lacedæmónians did not, however, restore him to his command, but sent out Dórkis and certain others with a small force; who found the allies no longer inclined to concede to them the supremacy. Perceiving this they departed, and the Lacedæmónians did not send out any to succeed them. They feared for those who went out a deterioration similar to that observable in Pausánias; besides, they desired to be rid of the Médian War, and were satisfied of the competency of the Athénians for the position, and of their friendship at the time towards themselves.

Thucýdides, Peloponnésian War, I.94-95 (translated by Richard Crawley)

## Pausánias Betrays Spárta

The Athénians retorted by ordering the Lacedæmónians to drive out the curse of Tænarus. The Lacedæmónians had once raised up some Hélot suppliants from the temple of Poséidon at Tænarus, led them away and slain them; for which they believe the great earthquake at Spárta to have been a retribution. The Athénians also ordered them to drive out the curse of the goddess of the Brazen House; the history of which is as follows. After Pausánias the Lacedæmónian had been recalled by the Spártans from his command in the Héllespont (this is his first recall), and had been tried by them and acquitted, not being again sent out in a public capacity, he took a galley of Hermíone on his own responsibility, without the authority of the Lacedæmónians, and arrived as a private person in the Héllespont. He came ostensibly for the Hellénic war, really to carry on his intrigues with the King, which he had begun before his recall, being ambitious of reigning over Héllas. The circumstance which first enabled him to lay the King under an obligation, and to make a beginning of the whole design, was this. Some connections and kinsmen of the King had been taken in Byzántium, on its capture from the Medes, when he was first there, after the return from Cýprus. These captives he sent off to the King without the knowledge of the rest of the allies, the account being that they had escaped from him. He managed this with the help of Góngylus, an Erétrian, whom he had placed in charge of Byzántium and the prisoners. He also gave Góngylus a letter for the King, the contents of which were as follows, as was afterwards discovered: "Pausánias, the general of Spárta, anxious to do you a favor, sends you these his prisoners of war. I propose also, with your approval, to marry your daughter, and to make Spárta and the rest of Héllas subject to you. I may say that I think I am able to do this, with your cooperation. Accordingly, if any of this please you, send a safe man to the sea through whom we may in future conduct our correspondence."

This was all that was revealed in the writing, and Xérxes was pleased with the letter. He sent off Artabázus, son of Pharnáces, to the sea with orders to supersede Megabátes, the previous governor in the sátrapy of Daskýlion, and to send over as quickly as possible to Pausánias at Byzántium a letter which he entrusted to him; to show him the royal signet, and to execute any commission which he might receive from Pausánias on the King's matters with all care and fidelity. Artabázus on his arrival carried the King's orders into effect, and sent over the letter, which contained the following answer: "Thus saith King Xérxes to Pausánias. For the men whom you have saved for me across sea from Byzántium, an obligation is laid up for you in our house, recorded for ever; and with your proposals I am well pleased. Let neither night nor day stop you from diligently performing any of your promises to me; neither for cost of gold nor of silver let them be hindered, nor yet for number of troops, wherever it may be that their presence is needed; but with Artabázus, an honorable man whom I send you, boldly advance my objects and yours, as may be most for the honor and interest of us both."

Before held in high honor by the Héllenes as the hero of Platǽa, Pausánias, after the receipt of this letter, became prouder than ever, and could no longer live in the usual style, but went out of Byzántium in a Médian dress, was attended on his march through Thrace by a bodyguard of Medes and Egýptians, kept a Pérsian table, and was quite unable to contain his intentions, but betrayed by his conduct in trifles what his ambition looked one day to enact on a grander scale. He also made himself difficult of access and displayed so violent a temper to every one without exception that no one could come near him. Indeed, this was the principal reason why the confederacy went over to the Athénians.

The above-mentioned conduct, coming to the ears of the Lacedæmónians, occasioned his first recall. And after his second voyage out in the ship of Hermíone, without their orders, he gave proofs of similar behavior. Besieged and expelled from Byzántium by the Athénians, he did not return to Spárta; but news came that he had settled at Cólonæ in the Tróad, and was intriguing with the barbarians, and that his stay there was for no good purpose; and the Éphors, now no longer hesitating, sent him a herald and a scýtale with orders to accompany the herald or be declared a public enemy. Anxious above everything to avoid suspicion, and confident that he could quash the charge by means of money, he returned a second time to Spárta. At first thrown into prison by the Éphors (whose powers enable them to do this to the King), soon compromised the matter and came out again, and offered himself for trial to any who wished to institute an inquiry concerning him.

Now the Spártans had no tangible proof against him—neither his enemies nor the nation—of that indubitable kind required for the punishment of a member of the royal family, and at that moment in high office; he being regent for his first cousin King Plistárchus, Leónidas's son, who was still a minor. But by his contempt of the laws and imitation of the barbarians, he gave grounds for much suspicion of his being discontented with things established; all the occasions on which he had in any way departed from the regular customs were passed in review, and it was remembered that he had taken upon himself to have inscribed on the tripod at Délphi, which was dedicated by the Héllenes as the first-fruits of the spoil of the Medes, the following couplet:

The Mede defeated, great Pausánias raised
This monument, that Phœbus might be praised.

At the time the Lacedæmónians had at once erased the couplet and inscribed the names of the cities that had aided in the overthrow of the barbarian and dedicated the offering. Yet it was considered that Pausánias had here been guilty of a grave offence, which, interpreted by the light of the attitude which he had since assumed, gained a new significance, and seemed to be quite in keeping with his present schemes. Besides, they were informed that he was even intriguing with the Hélots; and such indeed was the fact, for he promised them freedom and citizenship if they would join him in insurrection and would help him to carry out his plans to the end. Even now, mistrusting the evidence even of the Hélots themselves, the Éphors would not consent to take any decided step against him; in accordance with their regular custom towards themselves, namely, to be slow in taking any irrevocable resolve in the matter of a Spártan citizen without indisputable proof. At last, it is said, the person who was going to carry to Artabázus the last letter for the King, a man of Árgilus, once the favorite and most trusty servant of Pausánias, turned informer. Alarmed by the reflection that none of the previous messengers had ever returned, having counterfeited the seal, in order that, if he found himself mistaken in his surmises, or if Pausánias should ask to make some correction, he might not be discovered, he undid the letter, and found the postscript that he had suspected, viz. an order to put him to death.

On being shown the letter, the Éphors now felt more certain. Still, they wished to hear Pausánias commit himself with their own ears. Accordingly, the man went by appointment to Tǽnarus as a suppliant, and there built himself a hut divided into two by a partition; within which he concealed some of the Éphors and let them hear the whole matter plainly. For Pausánias came to him and asked him the reason of his suppliant position; and the man reproached him with the order that he had written concerning him, and one by one declared all the rest of the circumstances, how he who had never yet brought him into any danger, while employed as agent between him and the King, was yet just like the mass of his servants to be rewarded with death. Admitting all this, and telling him not to be angry about the matter, Pausánias gave him the pledge of raising him up from the temple, and begged him to set off as quickly as possible, and not to hinder the business in hand.

The Éphors listened carefully, and then departed, taking no action for the moment, but, having at last attained to certainty, were preparing to arrest him in the city. It is reported that, as he was about to be arrested in the street, he saw from the face of one of the Éphors what he was coming for; another, too, made him a secret signal, and betrayed it to him from kindness. Setting off with a run for the temple of the goddess of the Brazen House, the enclosure of which was near at hand, he succeeded in taking sanctuary before they took him, and entering into a small chamber, which formed part of the temple, to avoid being exposed to the weather, lay still there. The Éphors, for the moment distanced in the pursuit, afterwards took off the roof of the chamber, and having made sure that he was inside, shut him in, barricaded the doors, and staying before the place, reduced him by starvation. When they found that he was on the point of expiring, just as he was, in the chamber, they brought him out of the temple, while the breath was still in him, and as soon as he was brought out he died. They were going to throw him where they cast criminals, but finally decided to inter him somewhere near. But the god at Délphi afterwards ordered the Lacedæmónians to remove the tomb to the place of his death—where he now lies in the consecrated ground, as an inscription on a monument declares—and, as what had been done was a curse to them, to give back two bodies instead of one to the goddess of the Brazen House. So they had two brazen statues made, and dedicated them as a substitute for Pausánias.

Thucýdides, Peloponnésian War, I.128-134 (translated by Richard Crawley)

## The Ostracism of Themístocles

When the citizens of Áthens began to listen willingly to those who traduced and reproached [Themístocles], he was forced, with somewhat obnoxious frequency, to put them in mind of the great services he had performed, and ask those who were offended with him whether they were weary with receiving benefits often from the same person, so rendering himself more odious. And he yet more provoked the people by building a temple to Diána with the epithet of Aristóbule, or Diána of Best Counsel; intimating thereby, that he had given the best counsel, not only to the Athénians, but to all Greece. He built this temple near his own house, in the district called Mélite, where now the public officers carry out the bodies of such as are executed and throw the halters and clothes of those that are strangled or otherwise put to death. There is to this day a small figure of Themístocles in the temple of Diána of Best Counsel, which represents him to be a person, not only of a noble mind, but also of a most heroic aspect. At length the Athénians banished him, making use of the ostracism to humble his eminence and authority, as they ordinarily did with all whom they thought too powerful, or, by their greatness, disproportionable to the equality thought requisite in a popular government. For the ostracism was instituted, not so much to punish the offender, as to mitigate and pacify the violence of the envious, who delighted to humble eminent men, and who, by fixing this disgrace upon them, might vent some part of their rancor.

Themístocles being banished from Áthens, while he stayed at Árgos the detection of Pausánias happened, which gave such advantage to his enemies, that Leóbotes of Agráule, son of Alcmǽon, indicted him of treason, the Spártans supporting him in the accusation.

When Pausánias went about this treasonable design, he concealed it at first from Themístocles, though he were his intimate friend; but when he saw him expelled out of the commonwealth, and how impatiently he took his banishment, he ventured to communicate it to him, and desired his assistance, showing him the king of Pérsia's letters, and exasperating him against the Greeks, as a villainous, ungrateful people. However, Themístocles immediately rejected the proposals of Pausánias, and wholly refused to be a party in the enterprise, though he never revealed his communications, nor disclosed the conspiracy to any man, either hoping that Pausánias would desist from his intentions, or expecting that so inconsiderate an attempt after such chimerical objects would be discovered by other means.

After that Pausánias was put to death, letters and writings being found concerning this matter, which rendered Themístocles suspected, the Lacedæmónians were clamorous against him, and his enemies among the Athénians accused him; when, being absent from Áthens, he made his defense by letters, especially against the points that had been previously alleged against him. In answer to the malicious detractions of his enemies, he merely wrote to the citizens, urging that he who was always ambitious to govern, and not of a character or a disposition to serve, would never sell himself and his country into slavery to a barbarous and hostile nation.

– Plútarch, Life of Themístocles (translated by John Dryden)

## Themístocles and the Great King

After this, Themístocles, going to bed, dreamed that he saw a snake coil itself up upon his belly, and so creep to his neck; then, as soon as it touched his face, it turned into an eagle, which spread its wings over him, and took him up and flew away with him a great distance; then there appeared a herald's golden wand, and upon this at last it set him down securely, after infinite terror and disturbance.

His departure was effected by Nicógenes by the following artifice; the barbarous nations, and amongst them the Pérsians especially, are extremely jealous, severe, and suspicious about their women, not only their wives, but also their bought slaves and concubines, whom they keep so strictly that no one ever sees them abroad; they spend their lives shut up within doors, and, when they take a journey, are carried in close tents, curtained in on all sides, and set upon a wagon. Such a traveling carriage being prepared for Themístocles, they hid him in it, and carried him on his journeys and told those whom they met or spoke with upon the road that they were conveying a young Greek woman out of Iónia to a nobleman at court...

When he was introduced to the king, and had paid his reverence to him, he stood silent, till the king commanding the interpreter to ask him who he was, he replied, "O king, I am Themístocles the Athénian, driven into banishment by the Greeks. The evils that I have done to the Pérsians are numerous; but my benefits to them yet greater, in withholding the Greeks from pursuit, so soon as the deliverance of my own country allowed me to show kindness also to you. I come with a mind suited to my present calamities; prepared alike for favors and for anger; to welcome your gracious reconciliation, and to deprecate your wrath. Take my own countrymen for witnesses of the services I have done for Pérsia and make use of this occasion to show the world your virtue, rather than to satisfy your indignation. If you save me, you will save your suppliant; if otherwise, will destroy an enemy of the Greeks." He talked also of divine admonitions, such as the vision which he saw at Nicógenes's house, and the direction given him by the oracle of Dodóna, where Júpiter commanded him to go to him that had a name like his, by which he understood that he was sent from Júpiter to him, seeing that they both were great, and had the name of kings.

The king heard him attentively, and, though he admired his temper and courage, gave him no answer at that time; but, when he was with his intimate friends, rejoiced in his great good fortune, and esteemed himself very happy in this, and prayed to his god Arimánius, that all his enemies might be ever of the same mind with the Greeks, to abuse and expel the bravest men amongst them. Then he sacrificed to the gods, and presently fell to drinking, and was so well pleased, that in the night, in the middle of his sleep, he cried out for joy three times, "I have Themístocles the Athénian."

In the morning, calling together the chief of his court, he had Themístocles brought before him, who expected no good of it, when he saw, for example, the guards fiercely set against him as soon as they learnt his name, and giving him ill language. As he came forward towards the king, who was seated, the rest keeping silence, passing by Roxánes, a commander of a thousand men, he heard him, with a slight groan, say, without stirring out of his place, "You subtle Greek serpent, the king's good genius hath brought thee hither." Yet, when he came into the presence, and again fell down, the king saluted him, and spoke to him kindly, telling him he was now indebted to him two hundred talents; for it was just and reasonable that he should receive the reward which was proposed to whosoever should bring Themístocles; and promising much more, and encouraging him, he commanded him to speak freely what he would concerning the affairs of Greece. Themístocles replied, that a man's discourse was like to a rich Pérsian carpet, the beautiful figures and patterns of which can only be shown by spreading and extending it out; when it is contracted and folded up, they are obscured and lost; and, therefore, he desired time.

The king being pleased with the comparison, and bidding him take what time he would, he desired a year; in which time, having, learnt the Pérsian language sufficiently, he spoke with the king by himself without the help of an interpreter, it being supposed that he discoursed only about the affairs of Greece; but there happening, at the same time, great alterations at court, and removals of the king's favorites, he drew upon himself the envy of the great people, who imagined that he had taken the boldness to speak concerning them. For the favors shown to other strangers were nothing in comparison with the honors conferred on him; the king invited him to partake of his own pastimes and recreations both at home and abroad, carrying him with him hunting, and made him his intimate so far that he permitted him to see the queen-mother, and converse frequently with her. By the king's command, he also was made acquainted with the Mágian learning.

– Plútarch, *Life of Themístocles* (translated by John Dryden)

## The Political Genius of Themístocles

For Themístocles was a man who exhibited the most indubitable signs of genius; indeed, in this particular he has a claim on our admiration quite extraordinary and unparalleled. By his own native capacity, alike unformed and unsupplemented by study, he was at once the best judge in those sudden crises which admit of little or of no deliberation, and the best prophet of the future, even to its most distant possibilities. An able theoretical expositor of all that came within the sphere of his practice, he was not without the power of passing an adequate judgment in matters in which he had no experience. He could also excellently divine the good and evil which lay hid in the unseen future. In fine, whether we consider the extent of his natural powers, or the slightness of his application, this extraordinary man must be allowed to have surpassed all others in the faculty of intuitively meeting an emergency.

Disease was the real cause of his death; though there is a story of his having ended his life by poison, on finding himself unable to fulfil his promises to the king. However this may be, there is a monument to him in the marketplace of Asiátic Magnésia. He was governor of the district, the King having given him Magnésia, which brought in fifty talents a year, for bread, Lámpsacus, which was considered to be the richest wine country, for wine, and Mýos for other provisions. His bones, it is said, were conveyed home by his relatives in accordance with his wishes and interred in Áttic ground. This was done without the knowledge of the Athénians; as it is against the law to bury in Áttica an outlaw for treason. So ends the history of Pausánias and Themístocles, the Lacedæmónian and the Athénian, the most famous men of their time in Héllas.

Thucýdides, *Peloponnésian War*, I.135-138 (translated by Richard Crawley)

## The Death of Themístocles

But when Égypt revolted, being assisted by the Athénians, and the Greek galleys roved about as far as Cýprus and Cilícia, and Címon had made himself master of the seas, the king turned his thoughts thither, and, bending his mind chiefly to resist the Greeks, and to check the growth of their power against him, began to raise forces, and send out commanders, and to dispatch messengers to Themístocles at Magnésia, to put him in mind of his promise, and to summon him to act against the Greeks. Yet this did not increase his hatred nor exasperate him against the Athénians, neither was he any way elevated with the thoughts of the honor and powerful command he was to have in this war; but judging, perhaps, that the object would not be attained, the Greeks having at that time, beside other great commanders, Címon, in particular, who was gaining wonderful military successes; but chiefly, being ashamed to sully the glory of his former great actions, and of his many victories and trophies, he determined to put a conclusion to his life, agreeable to its previous course. He sacrificed to the gods, and invited his friends; and, having entertained them and shaken hands with them, drank bull's blood, as is the usual story; as others state, a poison producing instant death; and ended his days in the city of Magnésia, having lived sixty-five years, most of which he had spent in politics and in the wars, in government and command. The king, being informed of the cause and manner of his death, admired him more than ever, and continued to show kindness to his friends and relations.

– Plútarch, *Life of Themístocles* (translated by John Dryden)

## Aristídes the Just

Of all his virtues, the common people were most affected with his justice, because of its continual and common use; and thus, although of mean fortune and ordinary birth, he possessed himself of the most kingly and divine appellation of Just—which kings, however, and tyrants have never sought after; but have taken delight to be surnamed besiegers of cities, thunderers, conquerors, or eagles again, and hawks—affecting, it seems, the reputation which proceeds from power and violence, rather than that of virtue. Although the divinity, to whom they desire to compare and assimilate themselves, excels, it is supposed, in three things, immortality, power, and virtue—of which three, the noblest and divinest is virtue. For the elements and vacuum have an everlasting existence; earthquakes, thunders, storms, and torrents have great power; but in justice and equity nothing participates except by means of reason and the knowledge of that which is divine.

And thus, taking the three varieties of feeling commonly entertained towards the deity, the sense of his happiness, fear, and honor of him, people would seem to think him blest and happy for his exemption from death and corruption, to fear and dread him for his power and dominion, but to love, honor, and adore him for his justice. Yet though thus disposed, they covet that immortality which our nature is not capable of, and that power the greatest part of which is at the disposal of fortune; but give virtue, the only divine good really in our reach, the last place, most unwisely; since justice makes the life of such as are in prosperity, power, and authority the life of a god, and injustice turns it to that of a beast.

Aristídes, therefore, had at first the fortune to be beloved for this surname, but at length envied. Especially when Themístocles spread a rumor amongst the people, that, by determining and judging all matters privately, he had destroyed the courts of judicature, and was secretly making way for a monarchy in his own person, without the assistance of guards. Moreover, the spirit of the people, now grown high, and confident with their late victory, naturally entertained feelings of dislike to all of more than common fame and reputation. Coming together, therefore, from all parts into the city, they banished Aristídes by the ostracism, giving their jealousy of his reputation the name of fear of tyranny.

– Plútarch, *Life of Aristídes* (translated by John Dryden)

## Athénian Ostracism

For ostracism was not the punishment of any criminal act, but was speciously said to be the mere depression and humiliation of excessive greatness and power; and was in fact a gentle relief and mitigation of envious feeling, which was thus allowed to vent itself in inflicting no intolerable injury, only a ten years' banishment. But after it came to be exercised upon base and villainous fellows, they desisted from it; Hypérbolus, being the last whom they banished by the ostracism.

The cause of Hypérbolus's banishment is said to have been this. Alcibíades and Nícias, men that bore the greatest sway in the city, were of different factions. As the people, therefore, were about to vote the ostracism, and obviously to decree it against one of them, consulting together and uniting their parties, they contrived the banishment of Hypérbolus. Upon which the people, being offended, as if some contempt or affront was put upon the thing, left off and quite abolished it. It was performed, to be short, in this manner. Everyone taking an óstracon, a sherd, that is, or piece of earthenware, wrote upon it the citizen's name he would have banished, and carried it to a certain part of the marketplace surrounded with wooden rails. First, the magistrates numbered all the sherds in gross (for if there were less than six thousand, the ostracism was imperfect); then, laying every name by itself, they pronounced him whose name was written by the larger number, banished for ten years, with the enjoyment of his estate. As, therefore, they were writing the names on the sherds, it is reported that an illiterate clownish fellow, giving Aristídes his sherd, supposing him a common citizen, begged him to write Aristídes upon it; and he being surprised and asking if Aristídes had ever done him any injury, "None at all," said he, "neither know I the man; but I am tired of hearing him everywhere called the Just." Aristídes, hearing this, is said to have made no reply, but returned the sherd with his own name inscribed.

– Plútarch, *Life of Aristídes* (translated by John Dryden)

## III. CÍMON AND THE GROWTH OF IMPERIALISM

## The Battle at the River Eurýmedon

Éphorus says the admiral of the Pérsian fleet was Tithráustes, and the general of the land army Pherendátes; but Callísthenes is positive that Ariomándes, the son of Góbryas, had the supreme command of all the forces. He lay waiting with the whole fleet at the mouth of the river Eurýmedon, with no design to fight, but expecting a reinforcement of eighty Phœnícian ships on their way from Cýprus. Címon, aware of this, put out to sea, resolved, if they would not fight a battle willingly, to force them to it. The barbarians, seeing this, retired within the mouth of the river to avoid being attacked; but when they saw the Athénians come upon them, notwithstanding their retreat, they met them with six hundred ships, as Phanodémus relates but according to Éphorus, only with three hundred and fifty. However, they did nothing worthy such mighty forces, but immediately turned the prows of their galleys toward the shore, where those that came first threw themselves upon the land, and fled to their army drawn up thereabout, while the rest perished with their vessels, or were taken. By this, one may guess at their number, for though a great many escaped out of the fight, and a great many others were sunk, yet two hundred galleys were taken by the Athénians.

When their land army drew toward the seaside, Címon was in suspense whether he should venture to try and force his way on shore; as he should thus expose his Greeks, wearied with slaughter in the first engagement, to the swords of the barbarians, who were all fresh men, and many times their number. But seeing his men resolute, and flushed with victory, he bade them land, though they were not yet cool from their first battle. As soon as they touched ground, they set up a shout and ran upon the enemy, who stood firm and sustained the first shock with great courage, so that the fight was a hard one, and some principal men of the Athénians in rank and courage were slain. At length, though with much ado, they routed the barbarians, and killing some, took others prisoners, and plundered all their tents and pavilions which were full of rich spoil.

Címon, like a skilled athlete at the games, having in one day carried off two victories, wherein he surpassed that of Sálamis by sea, and that of Platǽa by land, was encouraged to try for yet another success. News being brought that the Phœnícian succors, in number eighty sail, had come in sight at Hýdrum, he set off with all speed to find them, while they as yet had not received any certain account of the larger fleet, and were in doubt what to think; so that thus surprised, they lost all their vessels, and most of their men with them. This success of Címon so daunted the king of Pérsia, that he presently made that celebrated peace, by which he engaged that his armies should come no nearer the Grécian sea than the length of a horse's course; and that none of his galleys or vessels of war should appear between the Cyánean and Chelidónian isles.

– Plútarch, *Life of Címon* (translated by John Dryden)

## The Liberality of Címon

Címon now grew rich, and what he gained from the barbarians with honor, he spent yet more honorably upon the citizens. For he pulled down all the enclosures of his gardens and grounds, that strangers, and the needy of his fellow-citizens, might gather of his fruits freely. At home, he kept

145

a table, plain, but sufficient for a considerable number; to which any poor townsman had free access, and so might support himself without labor, with his whole time left free for public duties. Áristotle states, however, that this reception did not extend to all the Athénians, but only to his own fellow townsmen, the Lacíadæ. Besides this, he always went attended by two or three young companions, very well clad; and if he met with an elderly citizen in a poor habit, one of these would change clothes with the decayed citizen, which was looked upon as very nobly done. He enjoined them, likewise, to carry a considerable quantity of coin about them, which they were to convey silently into the hands of the better class of poor men, as they stood by them in the marketplace. This, Cratínus the poet speaks of in one of his cómedies, the *Archílochi*:

> For I, Metróbius too, the scrivener poor,
> Of ease and comfort in my age secure,
> By Greece's noblest son in life's decline,
> Címon, the generous-hearted, the divine,
> Well-fed and feasted hoped till death to be,
> Death which, alas! has taken him ere me.

Górgias the Léontine gives him this character, that he got riches that he might use them, and used them that he might get honor by them. And Crítias, one of the thirty tyrants, makes it, in his elegies, his wish to have

> The Scópads' wealth, and Címon's nobleness,
> And king Agesiláüs's success.

... Címon's generosity outdid all the old Athénian hospitality and good nature. For though it is the city's just boast that their forefathers taught the rest of Greece to sow grain, and how to use springs of water, and to kindle fire, yet Címon, by keeping open house for his fellow-citizens, and giving travelers liberty to eat the fruits which the several seasons produced in his land, seemed to restore to the world that community of goods, which mythology says existed in the reign of Saturn. Those who object to him that he did this to be popular, and gain the applause of the vulgar, are confuted by the constant tenor of the rest of his actions, which all tended to uphold the interests of the nobility and the Spártan policy, of which he gave instances, when together with Aristídes, he opposed Themístocles, who was advancing the authority of the people beyond its just limits, and resisted Ephiáltes, who to please the multitude, was for abolishing the jurisdiction of the court of Areópagus. And when all of his time, except Aristídes and Ephiáltes, enriched themselves out of the public money, he still kept his hands clean and untainted, and to his last day never acted or spoke for his own private gain or emolument.

– Plútarch, *Life of Címon* (translated by John Dryden)

## Péricles Entertains the People

And the aristocratical party, seeing that Péricles was already before this grown to be the greatest and foremost man of all the city, but nevertheless wishing there should be somebody set up against him, to blunt and turn the edge of his power, that it might not altogether prove a monarchy, put forward Thucýdides of Alópece, a discreet person, and a near kinsman of Címon's, to conduct the opposition against him; who, indeed, though less skilled in warlike affairs than Címon was, yet was better versed in speaking and political business, and keeping close guard in the city, and engaging with Péricles on the hustings, in a short time brought the government to an equality of parties. For he would not suffer those who were called the honest and good (persons of worth and distinction) to be scattered up and down and mix themselves and be lost among the populace, as formerly, diminishing and obscuring their superiority amongst the masses; but taking them apart by themselves and uniting them in one body, by their combined weight he was able, as it were upon the balance, to make a counter-poise to the other party.

For, indeed, there was from the beginning a sort of concealed split, or seam, as it might be in a piece of iron, marking the different popular and aristocratical tendencies; but the open rivalry and contention of these two opponents made the gash deep, and severed the city into the two parties of the people and the few. And so Péricles, at that time more than at any other, let loose the reins to the people, and made his policy subservient to their pleasure, contriving continually to have some great public show or solemnity, some banquet, or some procession or other in the town to please them, coaxing his countrymen like children, with such delights and pleasures as were not, however, unedifying. Besides that every year he sent out threescore galleys, on board of which there went numbers of the citizens, who were in pay eight months, learning at the same time and practicing the art of seamanship.

– Plútarch, *Life of Péricles* (translated by John Dryden)

## The Advance of Athénian Power

The Athénians, having thus succeeded to the supremacy by the voluntary act of the allies through their hatred of Pausánias, fixed which cities were to contribute money against the barbarian, which ships; their professed object being to retaliate for their sufferings by ravaging the King's country. Now was the time that the office of "Treasurers for Héllas" was first instituted by the Athénians. These officers received the tribute, as the money contributed was called. The tribute was first fixed at four hundred and sixty talents. The common treasury was at Délos, and the congresses were held in the temple. Their supremacy commenced with independent allies who acted on the resolutions of a common congress. It was marked by the following undertakings in war and in administration during the interval between the Médian and the present war, against the barbarian, against their own rebel allies, and against the Peloponnésian powers which would come in contact with them on various occasions. My excuse for relating these events, and for venturing on this digression, is that this passage of history has been omitted by all my predecessors, who have confined themselves either to Hellénic history before the Médian War, or the Médian War itself. Hellánicus, it is true, did touch on these events in his Athénian history; but he is somewhat concise and not accurate in his dates. Besides, the history of these events contains an explanation of the growth of the Athénian empire.

First the Athénians besieged and captured Éion on the Strýmon from the Medes, and made slaves of the inhabitants, being under the command of Címon, son of Miltíades. Next they enslaved Scýros, the island in the Ægéan, containing a Dolópian population, and colonized it themselves. This was followed by a war against Carýstus, in which the rest of Eubœa remained neutral, and which was ended by surrender on conditions. After this Náxos left the confederacy, and a war ensued, and she had to return after a siege; this was the first instance of the engagement being broken by the subjugation of an allied city, a precedent which was followed by that of the rest in the order which circumstances prescribed.

Of all the causes of defection, that connected with arrears of tribute and vessels, and with failure of service, was the chief; for the Athénians were very severe and exacting, and made themselves offensive by applying the screw of necessity to men who were not used to and in fact not disposed for any continuous labor. In some other respects the Athénians were not the old popular rulers they had been at first; and if they had more than their fair share of service, it was correspondingly easy for them to reduce any that tried to leave the confederacy. For this the allies had themselves to blame; the wish to get off service making most of them arrange to pay their share of the expense in money instead of in ships, and so to avoid having to leave their homes. Thus while Áthens was increasing her navy with the funds which they contributed, a revolt always found them without resources or experience for war.

Next we come to the actions by land and by sea at the river Eurýmedon, between the Athénians with their allies, and the Medes, when the Athénians won both battles on the same day under the conduct of Címon, son of Miltíades, and captured and destroyed the whole Phœnícian fleet, consisting of two hundred vessels. Some time afterwards occurred the defection of the Thásians, caused by disagreements about the marts on the opposite coast of Thrace, and about the mine in their possession. Sailing with a fleet to Thásos, the Athénians defeated them at sea and effected a landing on the island. About the same time, they sent ten thousand settlers of their own citizens and the allies to settle the place then called Énnea Hódoi or Nine Ways, now Amphípolis. They succeeded in gaining possession of Énnea Hódoi from the Edonians, but on advancing into the interior of Thrace were cut off in Drabéscus, a town of the Edónians, by the assembled Thrácians, who regarded the settlement of the place Énnea Hódoi as an act of hostility.

Meanwhile the Thásians being defeated in the field and suffering siege, appealed to Lacedǽmon, and desired her to assist them by an invasion of Áttica. Without informing Áthens, she promised and intended to do so, but was prevented by the occurrence of the earthquake, accompanied by the secession of the Hélots and the Thúriats and Ǽthæans of the Periœci to Ithóme. Most of the Hélots were the descendants of the old Messénians that were enslaved in the famous war; and so all of them came to be called Messénians. So the Lacedǽmónians being engaged in a war with the rebels in Ithóme, the Thásians in the third year of the siege obtained terms from the Athénians by razing their walls, delivering up their ships, and arranging to pay the moneys demanded at once, and tribute in future; giving up their possessions on the continent together with the mine.

The Lacedǽmónians, meanwhile, finding the war against the rebels in Ithóme likely to last, invoked the aid of their allies, and especially of the Athénians, who came in some force under the command of Címon. The reason for this pressing summons lay in their reputed skill in siege operations; a long siege had taught the Lacedǽmónians their own deficiency in this art, else they would have taken the place by assault. The first open quarrel between the Lacedǽmónians and Athénians arose out of this expedition. The Lacedǽmónians, when assault failed to take the place, apprehensive of the enterprising and revolutionary character of the Athénians, and further looking upon them as of alien extraction, began to fear that, if they remained, they might be tempted by the besieged in Ithóme to attempt some political changes. They accordingly dismissed them alone of the allies, without declaring their suspicions, but merely saying that they had now no need of them. But the Athénians, aware that their dismissal did not proceed from the more honorable reason of the two, but from suspicions which had been conceived, went away deeply offended, and conscious of having done nothing to merit such treatment from the Lacedǽmónians; and the instant that they returned home they broke off the alliance which had been made against the Mede, and allied themselves with Spárta's enemy Árgos; each of the contracting parties taking the same oaths and making the same alliance with the Thessálians.

... The Athénians received another addition to their confederacy in the Megárians; who left the Lacedǽmónian alliance, annoyed by a war about boundaries forced on them by Córinth. The Athénians occupied Mégara and Pégæ and built the Megárians their long walls from the city to Nisǽa, in which they placed an Athénian garrison. This was the principal cause of the Corínthians conceiving such a deadly hatred against Áthens.

Thucýdides, *Peloponnésian War*, 96-103 (translated by Richard Crawley)


## The Earthquake at Spárta and the Ostracism of Címon

In the fourth year of the reign of Archidámus, the son of Zeuxídamus, king of Spárta, there happened in the country of Lacedǽmon, the greatest earthquake that was known in the memory of man; the earth opened into chasms, and the mountain Taýgetus was so shaken, that some of the rocky points of it fell down, and except five houses, all the town of Spárta was shattered to pieces. They say, that a little before any motion was perceived, as the young men and the boys just grown up were exercising themselves together in the middle of the portico, a hare, of a sudden, started out just by them, which the young men, though all naked and daubed with oil, ran after for sport. No sooner were they gone from the place, than the gymnasium fell down upon the boys who had stayed behind, and killed them all. Their tomb is to this day called Sismátias. Archidámus, by the present danger made apprehensive of what might follow, and seeing the citizens intent upon removing the most valuable of their goods out of their houses, commanded an alarm to be sounded, as if an enemy were coming upon them, in order that they should collect about him in a body, with arms. It was this alone that saved Spárta at that time, for the Hélots were got together from the country about, with design to surprise the Spártans, and overpower those whom the earthquake had spared. But finding them armed and well prepared, they retired into the towns and openly made war with them, gaining over a number of the Lacónians of the country districts; while at the same time the Messénians, also, made an attack upon the Spártans, who therefore dispatched Períclidas to Áthens to solicit succors, of whom Aristóphanes says in mockery that he came and

In a red jacket, at the altars seated,
With a white face, for men and arms entreated.

This Ephiáltes opposed, protesting that they ought not to raise up or assist a city that was a rival to Áthens; but that being down, it were best to keep her so, and let the pride and arrogance of Spárta be trodden under. But Címon, as Crítias says, preferring the safety of Lacedæmon to the aggrandizement of his own country, so persuaded the people, that he soon marched out with a large army to their relief. Íon records, also, the most successful expression which he used to move the Athénians. "They ought not to suffer Greece to be lamed, nor their own city to be deprived of her yoke-fellow."

In his return from aiding the Lacedæmónians, he passed with his army through the territory of Córinth; where upon Lachártus reproached him for bringing his army into the country, without first asking leave of the people. For he that knocks at another man's door ought not to enter the house till the master gives him leave. "But you, Corínthians, O Lachártus," said Címon, "did not knock at the gates of the Cleonæans and Megárians, but broke them down, and entered by force, thinking that all places should be open to the stronger." And having thus rallied the Corínthian, he passed on with his army. Some time after this, the Lacedæmónians sent a second time to desire succors of the Athénians against the Messénians and Hélots, who had seized upon Ithóme. But when they came, fearing their boldness and gallantry, of all that came to their assistance, they sent them only back, alleging they were designing innovations. The Athénians returned home, enraged at this usage, and vented their anger upon all those who were favorers of the Lacedæmónians; and seizing some slight occasion, they banished Címon for ten years, which is the time prescribed to those that are banished by the ostracism. In the meantime, the Lacedæmónians, on their return after freeing Délphi from the Phócians, encamped their army at Tánagra, whither the Athénians presently marched with design to fight them.

Címon, also, came thither armed, and ranged himself among those of his own tribe... desirous of fighting with the rest against the Spártans; but the council of five hundred being informed of this, and frighted at it, his adversaries crying out he would disorder the army, and bring the Lacedæmónians to Áthens, commanded the officers not to receive him. Wherefore Címon left the army, conjuring Euthíppus, the Anaphlýstian, and the rest of his companions, who were most suspected as favoring the Lacedæmónians, to behave themselves bravely against their enemies, and by their actions make their innocence evident to their countrymen. These, being in all a hundred, took the arms of Címon and followed his advice; and making a body by themselves, fought so desperately with the enemy, that they were all cut off, leaving the Athénians deep regret for the loss of such brave men, and repentance for having so unjustly suspected them. Accordingly, they did not long retain their severity toward Címon, partly upon remembrance of his former services, and partly, perhaps, induced by the juncture of the times. For being defeated at Tánagra in a great battle and, fearing the Peloponnésians would come upon them at the opening of the spring, they recalled Címon by a decree, of which Péricles himself was author. So reasonable were men's resentments in those times, and so moderate their anger, that it always gave way to the public good. Even ambition, the least governable of all human passions, could then yield to the necessities of the State.

– Plútarch, Life of Címon (translated by John Dryden)

## IV. PÉRICLES AND THE ATHÉNIAN EMPIRE

### Tánagra and the Long Walls

About this time the Athénians began to build the long walls to the sea, that towards Phálerum and that towards Piræus. Meanwhile the Phócians made an expedition against Dóris, the old home of the Lacedæmónians... They had taken one of these towns, when the Lacedæmónians under Nicomédes, son of Cleómbrotus, commanding for King Plistóanax, son of Pausánias, who was still a minor, came to the aid of the Dórians with fifteen hundred heavy infantry of their own, and ten thousand of their allies. After compelling the Phócians to restore the town on conditions, they began their retreat. The route by sea, across the Críssæan Gulf, exposed them to the risk of being stopped by the Athénian fleet; that across Geranéa seemed scarcely safe, the Athénians holding Mégara and Pégæ. For the pass was a difficult one, and was always guarded by the Athénians; and, in the present instance, the Lacedæmónians had information that they meant to dispute their passage. So they resolved to remain in Bœótia, and to consider which would be the safest line of march. They had also another reason for this resolve. Secret encouragement had been given them by a party in Áthens, who hoped to put an end to the reign of democracy and the building of the Long Walls. Meanwhile the Athénians marched against them with their whole levy and a thousand Árgives and the respective contingents of the rest of their allies. Altogether they were fourteen thousand strong. The march was prompted by the notion that the Lacedæmónians were at a loss how to effect their passage, and also by suspicions of an attempt to overthrow the democracy. Some cavalry also joined the Athénians from their Thessálian allies; but these went over to the Lacedæmónians during the battle.

The battle was fought at Tánagra in Bœótia. After heavy loss on both sides, victory declared for the Lacedæmónians and their allies. After entering the Mégarid and cutting down the fruit trees, the Lacedæmónians returned home across Geránia and the Ísthmus. Sixty-two days after the battle the Athénians marched into Bœótia under the command of Myrónides, defeated the Bœótians in battle at Œnóphyta, and became masters of Bœótia and Phócis. They dismantled the walls of the Tanagræans, took a hundred of the richest men of the Opúntian Lócrians as hostages, and finished their own long walls. This was followed by the surrender of the Ægínetans to Áthens on conditions; they pulled down their walls, gave up their ships, and agreed to pay tribute in future. The Athénians sailed round Peloponnésus under Tólmides, son of Tolmæus, burnt the arsenal of Lacedæmon, took Chálcis, a town of the Corínthians, and in a descent upon Sícyon defeated the Sicyónians in battle.

— Thucýdides, Peloponnésian War, 107-108 (translated by Richard Crawley)

# CHAPTER XVII.

## THE ATHÉNIAN CONSTITUTION UNDER PÉRICLES

The Political Organization, I.—The Military Organization, II.—The Financial System, III.

### I. THE POLITICAL ORGANIZATION

### The Areópagus Stripped of Power

The supremacy of the Areópagus lasted for about seventeen years after the Pérsian wars, although gradually declining. But as the strength of the masses increased, Ephiáltes, son of Sophónides, a man with a reputation for incorruptibility and public virtue, who had become the leader of the people, made an attack upon that Council. First of all he ruined many of its members by bringing actions against them with reference to their administration. Then, in the Árchonship of Cónon, he stripped the Council of all the acquired prerogatives from which it derived its guardianship of the constitution and assigned some of them to the Council of Five Hundred, and others to the Assembly and the law-courts. In this revolution he was assisted by Themístocles, who was himself a member of the Areópagus, but was expecting to be tried before it on a charge of treasonable dealings with Pérsia. This made him anxious that it should be overthrown, and accordingly he warned Ephiáltes that the Council intended to arrest him, while at the same time he informed the members of the Areópagus that he would reveal to them certain persons who were conspiring to subvert the constitution. He then conducted the representatives delegated by the Council to the residence of Ephiáltes, promising to show them the conspirators who assembled there, and proceeded to converse with them in an earnest manner. Ephiáltes, seeing this, was seized with alarm and took refuge in suppliant guise at the altar. Everyone was astounded at the occurrence, and presently, when the Council of Five Hundred met, Ephiáltes and Themístocles together proceeded to denounce the Areópagus to them. This they repeated in similar fashion in the Assembly, until they succeeded in depriving it of its power. Not long afterwards, however, Ephiáltes was assassinated by Aristódicus of Tánagra. In this way was the Council of Areópagus deprived of its guardianship of the state.

— School of Áristotle, *Athénian Constitution*, 25 (translated by Frederic G. Kenyon)

### Political Changes Under Péricles

After this revolution the administration of the state became more and more lax, in consequence of the eager rivalry of candidates for popular favor. During this period the moderate party, as it happened, had no real chief, their leader being Címon son of Miltíades, who was a comparatively young man, and had been late in entering public life; and at the same time the general populace suffered great losses by war. The soldiers for active service were selected at that time from the roll of citizens, and as the generals were men of no military experience, who owed their position solely to their family standing, it continually happened that some two or three thousand of the troops perished on an expedition; and in this way the best men alike of the lower and the upper classes were exhausted. Consequently, in most matters of administration less heed was paid to the laws than had formerly been the case. No alteration, however, was made in the method of election of the nine Árchons, except that five years after the death of Ephiáltes it was decided that the candidates to be submitted to the lot for that office might be selected from the Zéugitæ as well as from the higher classes. Up to this time all the Árchons had been taken from the Pentacósio-medímni and Híppeis, while the Zéugitæ were confined to the ordinary magistracies, save where an evasion of the law was overlooked. Four years later, in the Árchonship of Lysícrates, the thirty 'local justices', as they were called, were re-established; and two years afterwards, in the Árchonship of Antídotus, in consequence of the great increase in the number of citizens, it was resolved, on the motion of Péricles, that no one should be admitted to the franchise who was not of citizen birth by both parents.

— School of Áristotle, *Athénian Constitution*, 26 (translated by Frederic G. Kenyon)

## II. THE MILITARY ORGANIZATION

## Címon's Policy Toward the Délian League

The allies of the Athénians began now to be weary of war and military service, willing to have repose, and to look after their husbandry and traffic. For they saw and did not fear any new vexations from them. They still paid the tax they were assessed at, but did not send men and galleys, as they had done before. This the other Athénian generals wished to constrain them to, and by judicial proceedings against defaulters, and penalties which they inflicted on them, made the government uneasy, and even odious. But Címon practiced a contrary method; he forced no man to go that was not willing, but of those that desired to be excused from service he took money and vessels unmanned, and let them yield to the temptation of staying at home, to attend to their private business. Thus they lost their military habits, and luxury and their own folly quickly changed them into unwarlike husbandmen and traders, while Címon, continually embarking large numbers of Athénians on board his galleys, thoroughly disciplined them in his expeditions, their enemies driven out of the country, and ere long made them the lords of their own paymasters. The allies, whose indolence maintained them, while they thus went sailing about everywhere, and incessantly bearing arms and acquiring skill, began to fear and flatter then, and found themselves after a while allies no longer, but unwittingly become tributaries and slaves.

– Plútarch, *Life of Címon* (translated by John Dryden)

## III. THE FINANCIAL SYSTEM

## Dícasts (Jurors) Receive Pay

Péricles was also the first to institute pay for service in the law-courts, as a bid for popular favor to counterbalance the wealth of Címon. The latter, having private possessions on a regal scale, not only performed the regular public services magnificently, but also maintained a large number of his fellow demesmen. Any member of the deme of Lacíadæ could go every day to Címon's house and there receive a reasonable provision; while his estate was guarded by no fences, so that anyone who liked might help himself to the fruit from it. Péricles' private property was quite unequal to this magnificence and accordingly he took the advice of Damónides of Óia, which was that, as he was beaten in the matter of private possessions, he should make gifts to the people from their own property; and accordingly he instituted pay for the members of the juries. Some critics accuse him of thereby causing a deterioration in the character of the juries, since it was always the common people who put themselves forward for selection as jurors, rather than the men of better position. Moreover, bribery came into existence after this, the first person to introduce it being Ánytus, after his command at Pýlos. He was prosecuted by certain individuals on account of his loss of Pýlos, but escaped by bribing the jury.

— School of Áristotle, *Athénian Constitution*, 27 (translated by Frederic G. Kenyon)

# CHAPTER XVIII.

## ÁTHENS AND ATHÉNIAN ART UNDER PÉRICLES

The Topography of Áthens, I.—The Acrópolis and its Buildings, II.
Athénian Sculpture and Painting, III.—Influence of Athénian Art, IV.

### I. THE TOPOGRAPHY OF ÁTHENS

## A Description of Áthens

The city itself is a rock situated in a plain and surrounded by dwellings. On the rock is the sacred precinct of Athéna, comprising both the old temple of Athéna Pólias, in which is the lamp that is never quenched, and the Párthenon built by Ictínus, in which is the work in ivory by Phídias, the Athéna. However, if I once began to describe the multitude of things in this city that are lauded and proclaimed far and wide, I fear that I should go too far, and that my work would depart from the purpose I have in view. For the words of Hegésias occur to me: "I see the Acrópolis, and the mark of the huge trident there. I see Eléusis, and I have become an initiate into its sacred mysteries; yonder is the Leocórium, here is the Theséum; I am unable to point them all out one by one; for Áttica is the possession of the gods, who seized it as a sanctuary for themselves, and of the ancestral heroes." So this writer mentioned only one of the significant things on the Acrópolis; but Pólemon Periegétes wrote four books on the dedicatory offerings on the Acrópolis alone. Hegésias is proportionately brief in referring to the other parts of the city and to the country; and though he mentions Eléusis, one of the one hundred and seventy demes (or one hundred and seventy-four, as the number is given), he names none of the others.

Most of the demes, if not all, have numerous stories of a character both mythical and historical connected with them; Aphídna, for example, has the snatching of Hélen by Théseus, the sacking of the place by the Dioscúri and their recovery of their sister; Márathon has the Pérsian battle; Rhámnus has the statue of Némesis, ... a work which both in grandeur and in beauty is a great success and rivals the works of Phídias; and so with Decélea, the base of operations of the Peloponnésians in the Decélean War; and Phýle, whence Thrasýbulus brought the popular party back to the Piræus and then to the city. And so, also, in the case of several other demes there are many historical incidents to tell... and so has the Lycéum, and the Olympiéum, which the king who dedicated it left half finished at his death. And in like manner also the Academy, and the gardens of the philosophers, and the Odéum, and the colonnade called "Pœcile," and the temples in the city containing very many marvelous works of different artists.

The greater men's fondness for learning about things that are famous and the greater the number of men who have talked about them, the greater the censure, if one is not master of the historical facts. For example, in his *Collection of the Rivers*, Callímachus says that it makes him laugh if anyone makes bold to write that the Athénian maids "draw pure liquid from the Erídanus," from which even cattle would hold aloof. Its sources are indeed existent now, with pure and potable water, as they say, outside the Gates of Dióchares, as they are called, near the Lycéum; but in earlier times there was also a fountain nearby which was constructed by man, with abundant and excellent water; and even if the water is not so now, why should it be a thing to wonder at, if in early times the water was abundant and pure, and therefore also potable, but in later times underwent a change?

– Strábo, *Geography*, IX.1.16-17,19 (translated by H. L. Jones)

## The Bones of Théseus

But in succeeding ages, beside several other circumstances that moved the Athénians to honor Théseus as a demigod, in the battle which was fought at Márathon against the Medes, many of the soldiers believed they saw an apparition of Théseus in arms, rushing on at the head of them against the barbarians. And after the Médian war, Phæedo being Árchon of Áthens, the Athénians, consulting the oracle at Délphi, were commanded to gather together the bones of Théseus, and, laying them in some honorable place, keep them as sacred in the city. But it was very difficult to recover these relics, or so much as to find out the place where they lay, on account of the inhospitable and savage temper of the barbarous people that inhabited the island. Nevertheless, afterwards, when Címon took the island (as is related in his life), and had a great ambition to find out the place where Théseus was buried, he, by chance, spied an eagle upon a rising ground pecking with her beak and tearing up the earth with her talons, when on the sudden it came into his mind, as it were by some divine inspiration, to dig there, and search for the bones of Théseus. There were found in that place a coffin of a man of more than ordinary size, and a brazen spearhead, and a sword lying by it, all which he took aboard his galley and brought with him to Áthens. Upon which the Athénians, greatly delighted, went out to meet and receive the relics with splendid processions and with sacrifices, as if it were Théseus himself returning alive to the city.

He lies interred in the middle of the city, near the present gymnasium. His tomb is a sanctuary and refuge for slaves, and all those of mean condition that fly from the persecution of men in power, in memory that Théseus while he lived was an assister and protector of the distressed, and never refused the petitions of the afflicted that fled to him.

– Plútarch, *Life of Théseus* (translated by John Dryden)

## II. THE ACRÓPOLIS AND ITS BUILDINGS

# On Magnificence

It would seem proper to discuss magnificence next. For this also seems to be a virtue concerned with wealth; but it does not like liberality extend to all the actions that are concerned with wealth, but only to those that involve expenditure; and in these it surpasses liberality in scale. For, as the name itself suggests, it is a fitting expenditure involving largeness of scale. But the scale is relative; for the expense of equipping a tríreme is not the same as that of heading a sacred embassy. It is what is fitting, then, in relation to the agent, and to the circumstances and the object. The man who in small or middling things spends according to the merits of the case is not called magnificent (e.g. the man who can say 'many a gift I gave the wanderer'), but only the man who does so in great things. For the magnificent man is liberal, but the liberal man is not necessarily magnificent. The deficiency of this state of character is called niggardliness, the excess vulgarity, lack of taste, and the like, which do not go to excess in the amount spent on right objects, but by showy expenditure in the wrong circumstances and the wrong manner; we shall speak of these vices later.

The magnificent man is like an artist; for he can see what is fitting and spend large sums tastefully. For, as we said at the beginning, a state of character is determined by its activities and by its objects. Now the expenses of the magnificent man are large and fitting. Such, therefore, are also his results; for thus there will be a great expenditure and one that is fitting to its result. Therefore the result should be worthy of the expense, and the expense should be worthy of the result, or should even exceed it. And the magnificent man will spend such sums for honor's sake; for this is common to the virtues. And further he will do so gladly and lavishly; for nice calculation is a niggardly thing. And he will consider how the result can be made most beautiful and most becoming rather than for how much it can be produced and how it can be produced most cheaply.

It is necessary, then, that the magnificent man be also liberal. For the liberal man also will spend what he ought and as he ought; and it is in these matters that the greatness implied in the name of the magnificent man—his bigness, as it were—is manifested, since liberality is concerned with these matters; and at an equal expense he will produce a more magnificent work of art. For a possession and a work of art have not the same excellence. The most valuable possession is that which is worth most, e.g. gold, but the most valuable work of art is that which is great and beautiful (for the contemplation of such a work inspires admiration, and so does magnificence); and a work has an excellence—viz. magnificence—which involves magnitude. Magnificence is an attribute of expenditures of the kind which we call honorable, e.g. those connected with the gods—votive offerings, buildings, and sacrifices—and similarly with any form of religious worship, and all those that are proper objects of public-spirited ambition, as when people think they ought to equip a chorus or a tríreme, or entertain the city, in a brilliant way. But in all cases, as has been said, we have regard to the agent as well and ask who he is and what means he has; for the expenditure should be worthy of his means, and suit not only the result but also the producer. Hence a poor man cannot be magnificent, since he has not the means with which to spend large sums fittingly; and he who tries is a fool, since he spends beyond what can be expected of him and what is proper, but it is right expenditure that is virtuous. But great expenditure is becoming to those who have suitable means to start with, acquired by their own efforts or from ancestors or connections, and to people of high birth or reputation, and so on; for all these things bring with them greatness and prestige.

– Áristotle, *Nicomáchean Ethics*, IV.2 (translated by D. P. Chase)

## Péricles Lavishly Adorns the City of Áthens

That which gave most pleasure and ornament to the city of Áthens, and the greatest admiration and even astonishment to all strangers, and that which now is Greece's only evidence that the power she boasts of and her ancient wealth are no romance or idle story, was his construction of the public and sacred buildings. Yet this was that of all his actions in the government which his enemies most looked askance upon and caviled at in the popular assemblies, crying out how that the commonwealth of Áthens had lost its reputation and was ill-spoken of abroad for removing the common treasure of the Greeks from the isle of Délos into their own custody; and how that their fairest excuse for so doing, namely, that they took it away for fear the barbarians should seize it, and on purpose to secure it in a safe place, this Péricles had made unavailable, and how that "Greece cannot but resent it as an insufferable affront, and consider herself to be tyrannized over openly, when she sees the treasure, which was contributed by her upon a necessity for the war, wantonly lavished out by us upon our city, to gild her all over, and to adorn and set her forth, as it were some vain woman, hung round with precious stones and figures and temples, which cost a world of money."

Péricles, on the other hand, informed the people, that they were in no way obliged to give any account of those moneys to their allies, so long as they maintained their defense, and kept off the barbarians from attacking them; while in the meantime they did not so much as supply one horse or man or ship, but only found money for the service; "which money," said he, "is not theirs that give it, but theirs that receive it, if they perform the conditions upon which they receive it." And that it was good reason, now that the city was sufficiently provided and stored with all things necessary for the war, that they should convert the overplus of its wealth to such undertakings, as would hereafter, when completed, give them eternal honor, and, for the present, while in process, freely supply all the inhabitants with plenty. With their variety of workmanship and of occasions for service, which summon all arts and trades and require all hands to be employed about them, they do actually put the whole city, in a manner, into state-pay; while at the same time she is both beautified and maintained by herself. For as those who are of age and strength for war are provided for and maintained in the armaments abroad by their pay out of the public stock, so, it being his desire and design that the undisciplined mechanic multitude that stayed at home should not go without their share of public salaries, and yet should not have them given them for sitting still and doing nothing, to that end he thought fit to bring in among them, with the approbation of the people, these vast projects of buildings and designs of works, that would be of some continuance before they were finished, and would give employment to numerous arts, so that the part of the people that stayed at home might, no less than those that were at sea or in garrisons or on expeditions, have a fair and just occasion of receiving the benefit and having their share of the public moneys.

The materials were stone, brass, ivory, gold, ebony cypress-wood; and the arts or trades that wrought and fashioned them were smiths and carpenters, molders, founders and braziers, stone-cutters, dyers, goldsmiths, ivory-workers, painters, embroiderers, turners; those again that conveyed them to the town for use, merchants and mariners and ship-masters by sea, and by land, cartwrights, cattle-breeders, wagoners, rope-makers, flax-workers, shoe-makers and leather-dressers, road makers, miners. And every trade in the same nature, as a captain in an army has his particular company of soldiers under him, had its own hired company of journeymen and laborers belonging to it banded together as in array, to be as it were the instrument and body for the performance of the service. Thus, to say all in a word, the occasions and services of these public works distributed plenty through every age and condition.

As then grew the works up, no less stately in size than exquisite in form, the workmen striving to outvie the material and the design with the beauty of their workmanship, yet the most wonderful thing of all was the rapidity of their execution. Undertakings, any one of which singly might have required, they thought, for their completion, several successions and ages of men, were every one of them accomplished in the height and prime of one man's political service. Although they say, too, that Zéuxis once, having heard Agathárchus the painter boast of dispatching his work with speed and ease, replied, "I take a long time." For ease and speed in doing a thing do not give the work lasting solidity or exactness of beauty; the expenditure of time allowed to a man's pains beforehand for the production of a thing is repaid by way of interest with a vital force for its preservation when once produced. For which reason Péricles's works are especially admired, as having been made quickly, to last long. For every particular piece of his work was immediately, even at that time, for its beauty and elegance, antique; and yet in its vigor and freshness looks to this day as if it were just executed. There is a sort of bloom of newness upon those works of his, preserving them from the touch of time, as if they had some perennial spirit and undying vitality mingled in the composition of them.

Phídias had the oversight of all the works, and was surveyor-general, though upon the various portions other great masters and workmen were employed. For Callícrates and Ictínus built the Párthenon; the chapel at Eléusis, where the mysteries were celebrated, was begun by Corœbus, who erected the pillars that stand upon the floor or pavement, and joined them to the architraves; and after his death Metágenes of Xýpete added the frieze and the upper line of columns; Xénocles of Cholárgus roofed or arched the lantern on the top of the temple of Cástor and Póllux; and the long wall, which Sócrates says he himself heard Péricles propose to the people, was undertaken by Callícrates.

The Odéum, or music-room, which in its interior was full of seats and ranges of pillars, and outside had its roof made to slope and descend from one single point at the top, was constructed, we are told, in imitation of the king of Pérsia's Pavilion; this likewise by Péricles's order...

Péricles, also, eager for distinction, then first obtained the decree for a contest in musical skill to be held yearly at the Panathenǽa, and he himself, being chosen judge, arranged the order and method in which the competitors should sing and play on the flute and on the harp. And both at that time, and at other times also, they sat in this music-room to see and hear all such trials of skill.

The Propylæa, or entrances to the Acrópolis, were finished in five years' time, Mnésicles being the principal architect. A strange accident happened in the course of building, which showed that the goddess was not averse to the work, but was aiding and cooperating to bring it to perfection. One of the artificers, the quickest and the handiest workman among them all, with a slip of his foot fell down from a great height, and lay in a miserable condition, the physicians having no hopes of his recovery. When Péricles was in distress about this, Minérva appeared to him at night in a dream, and ordered a course of treatment, which he applied, and in a short time and with great ease cured the man. And upon this occasion it was that he set up a brass statue of Minérva, surnamed Health, in the citadel near the altar, which they say was there before. But it was Phídias who wrought the goddess's image in gold, and he has his name inscribed on the pedestal as the workman of it; and indeed the whole work in a manner was under his charge, and he had, as we have said already, the oversight over all the artists and workmen, through Péricles's friendship for him; and this, indeed, made him much envied, and his patron shamefully slandered with stories...

When the orators, who sided with Thucýdides and his party, were at one time crying out, as their custom was, against Péricles, as one who squandered away the public money, and made havoc of the state revenues, he rose in the open assembly and put the question to the people, whether they thought that he had laid out much; and they saying, "Too much, a great deal." "Then," said he, "Since it is so, let the cost not go to your account, but to mine; and let the inscription upon the buildings stand in my name." When they heard him say thus, whether it were out of a surprise to see the greatness of his spirit, or out of emulation of the glory of the works, they cried aloud, bidding him to spend on, and lay out what he thought fit from the public purse, and to spare no cost, till all were finished.

– Plútarch, *Life of Péricles* (translated by John Dryden)

## III. ATHÉNIAN SCULPTURE AND PAINTING

## The Excellence of Phídias

Among all nations which the fame of the Olýmpian Júpiter has reached, Phídias is looked upon, beyond all doubt, as the most famous of artists: but to let those who have never even seen his works, know how deservedly he is esteemed, we will take this opportunity of adducing a few slight proofs of the genius which he displayed. In doing this, we shall not appeal to the beauty of his Olýmpian Júpiter, nor yet to the vast proportions of his Athénian Minérva, six and twenty cúbits in height, and composed of ivory and gold; but it is to the shield of this last statue that we shall draw attention; upon the convex face of which he has chased a combat of the Ámazons, while, upon the concave side of it, he has represented the battle between the Gods and the Giants. Upon the sandals again, we see the wars of the Lápithæ and Céntaurs, so careful has he been to fill every smallest portion of his work with some proof or other of his artistic skill. To the story chased upon the pedestal of the statue, the name of the "Birth of Pandóra" has been given; and the figures of new-born gods to be seen upon it are no less than twenty in number. The figure of Victory, in particular, is most admirable, and connoisseurs are greatly struck with the serpent and the sphinx in bronze lying beneath the point of the spear. Let thus much be said incidentally in reference to an artist who can never be sufficiently praised; if only to let it be understood that the richness of his genius was always equal to itself, even in the very smallest details.

– Plíny the Elder, *The Natural History*, 36.4 (translated by John Bostock and H. T. Riley)

157

# The Death of Phídias

Phídias the Sculptor had, as has before been said, undertaken to make the statue of Minérva. Now he, being admitted to friendship with Péricles, and a great favorite of his, had many enemies upon this account, who envied and maligned him; who also, to make trial in a case of his, what kind of judges the commons would prove, should there be occasion to bring Péricles himself before them, having tampered with Ménon, one who had been a workman with Phídias, stationed him ill the market-place, with a petition desiring public security upon his discovery and impeachment of Phídias. The people admitting the man to tell his story, and the prosecution proceeding in the assembly, there was nothing of theft or cheat proved against him; for Phídias, from the very first beginning, by the advice of Péricles, had so wrought and wrapt the gold that was used in the work about the statue, that they might take it all off and make out the just weight of it, which Péricles at that time bade the accusers do. But the reputation of his works was what brought envy upon Phídias, especially that where he represents the fight of the Ámazons upon the goddesses' shield, he had introduced a likeness of himself as a bald old man holding up a great stone with both hands, and had put in a very fine representation of Péricles fighting with an Ámazon. And the position of the hand, which holds out the spear in front of the face, was ingeniously contrived to conceal in some degree the likeness, which, meantime, showed itself on either side.

Phídias then was carried away to prison, and there died of a disease; but, as some say, of poison, administered by the enemies of Péricles, to raise a slander, or a suspicion, at least, as though he had procured it.

– Plútarch, *Life of Péricles* (translated by John Dryden)

# IV. INFLUENCE OF ATHÉNIAN ART

# The Olýmpian Zeus of Phídias

But the greatest of these was the image of Zeus made by Phídias of Áthens, son of Chármides; it was made of ivory, and it was so large that, although the temple was very large, the artist is thought to have missed the proper symmetry, for he showed Zeus seated but almost touching the roof with his head, thus making the impression that if Zeus arose and stood erect he would unroof the temple. Certain writers have recorded the measurements of the image, and Callímachus has set them forth in an iámbic poem. Panǽnus the painter, who was the nephew and collaborator of Phídias, helped him greatly in decorating the image, particularly the garments, with colors. And many wonderful paintings, works of Panǽnus, are also to be seen round the temple. It is related of Phídias that, when Panǽnus asked him after what model he was going to make the likeness of Zeus, he replied that he was going to make it after the likeness set forth by Hómer in these words "Crónion spake, and nodded assent with his dark brows, and then the ambrósial locks flowed streaming from the lord's immortal head, and he caused great Olýmpus to quake." A noble description indeed, as appears not only from the "brows" but from the other details in the passage, because the poet provokes our imagination to conceive the picture of a mighty personage and a mighty power worthy of a Zeus, just as he does in the case of Héra, at the same time preserving what is appropriate in each; for of Héra he says, "she shook herself upon the throne, and caused lofty Olýmpus to quake." What in her case occurred when she moved her whole body, resulted in the case of Zeus when he merely "nodded with his brows," although his hair too was somewhat affected at the same time. This, too, is a graceful saying about the poet, that "he alone has seen, or else he alone has shown, the likenesses of the gods."

– Strábo, *Geography*, VIII.3.30 (translated by H. L. Jones)

# CHAPTER XIX.

## INTELLECTUAL CULTURE IN THE AGE OF PÉRICLES

The Theater as a Means of Culture, I.—The Drama and the Great Tragedians, II.
The Progress of Philosophy and Education, III.—Beginnings of Prose Literature, IV.

## I. THE THEATER AS A MEANS OF CULTURE

### The Contest Between Æschylus and Sóphocles

Sóphocles, still a young man, had just brought forward his first plays; opinions were much divided, and the spectators had taken sides with some heat. So, to determine the case, Apséphion, who was at that time Árchon, would not cast lots who should be judges; but when Címon, and his brother commanders with him, came into the theater, after they had performed the usual rites to the god of the festival, he would not allow them to retire, but came forward and made them swear, (being ten in all, one from each tribe,) the usual oath; and so being sworn judges, he made them sit down to give sentence. The eagerness for victory grew all the warmer, from the ambition to get the suffrages of such honorable judges. And the victory was at last adjudged to Sóphocles, which Æschylus is said to have taken so ill, that he left Áthens shortly after, and went in anger to Sícily, where he died, and was buried near the city of Géla.

– Plútarch, *Life of Címon* (translated by John Dryden)

## II. THE DRAMA AND THE GREAT TRAGEDIANS

### Trágic Plots

These principles being established, let us now discuss the proper structure of the plot, since this is the first and most important thing in Tragedy.

Now, according to our definition Tragedy is an imitation of an action that is complete, and whole, and of a certain magnitude; for there may be a whole that is wanting in magnitude. A whole is that which has a beginning, a middle, and an end. A beginning is that which does not itself follow anything by causal necessity, but after which something naturally is or comes to be. An end, on the contrary, is that which itself naturally follows some other thing, either by necessity, or as a rule, but has nothing following it. A middle is that which follows something as some other thing follows it. A well constructed plot, therefore, must neither begin nor end at haphazard, but conform to these principles.

Again, a beautiful object, whether it be a living organism or any whole composed of parts, must not only have an orderly arrangement of parts, but must also be of a certain magnitude; for beauty depends on magnitude and order. Hence a very small animal organism cannot be beautiful; for the view of it is confused, the object being seen in an almost imperceptible moment of time. Nor, again, can one of vast size be beautiful; for as the eye cannot take it all in at once, the unity and sense of the whole is lost for the spectator; as for instance if there were one a thousand miles long. As, therefore, in the case of animate bodies and organisms a certain magnitude is necessary, and a magnitude which may be easily embraced in one view; so in the plot, a certain length is necessary, and a length which can be easily embraced by the memory...

... Unity of plot does not, as some persons think, consist in the unity of the hero. For infinitely various are the incidents in one man's life which cannot be reduced to unity; and so, too, there are many actions of one man out of which we cannot make one action. Hence the error, as it appears, of all poets who have composed a Herácleid, a Théseid, or other poems of the kind. They imagine that as Héracles was one man, the story of Héracles must also be a unity. But Hómer, as in all else he is of surpassing merit, here too—whether from art or natural genius—seems to have happily discerned the truth. In composing the Ódyssey he did not include all the adventures of Odýsseus—such as his wound on Parnássus, or his feigned madness at the mustering of the host—incidents between which there was no necessary or probable connection: but he made the Ódyssey, and likewise the Íliad, to center round an action that in our sense of the word is one.

It is, moreover, evident from what has been said, that it is not the function of the poet to relate what has happened, but what may happen—what is possible according to the law of probability or necessity. The poet and the historian differ not by writing in verse or in prose. The work of Heródotus might be put into verse, and it would still be a species of history, with meter no less than without it. The true difference is that one relates what has happened, the other what may happen. Poetry, therefore, is a more philosophical and a higher thing than history: for poetry tends to express the universal, history the particular. By the universal I mean how a person of a certain type on occasion speak or act, according to the law of probability or necessity; and it is this universality at which poetry aims in the names she attaches to the personages. The particular is—for example—what Alcibíades did or suffered...

Reversal of the Situation is a change by which the action veers round to its opposite, subject always to our rule of probability or necessity. Thus in the Œdipus, the messenger comes to cheer Œdipus and free him from his alarms about his mother, but by revealing who he is, he produces the opposite effect...

... Recognition, as the name indicates, is a change from ignorance to knowledge, producing love or hate between the persons destined by the poet for good or bad fortune. The best form of recognition is coincident with a Reversal of the Situation, as in the Œdipus.

Two parts, then, of the plot—Reversal of the Situation and Recognition—turn upon surprises. A third part is the Scene of Suffering. The Scene of Suffering is a destructive or painful action, such as death on the stage, bodily agony, wounds, and the like.

As the sequel to what has already been said, we must proceed to consider what the poet should aim at, and what he should avoid, in constructing his plots; and by what means the specific effect of Tragedy will be produced.

A perfect tragedy should ... imitate actions which excite pity and fear, this being the distinctive mark of tragic imitation. It follows plainly, in the first place, that the change of fortune presented must not be the spectacle of a virtuous man brought from prosperity to adversity: for this moves neither pity nor fear; it merely shocks us. Nor, again, that of a bad man passing from adversity to prosperity: for nothing can be more alien to the spirit of Tragedy; it possesses no single tragic quality; it neither satisfies the moral sense nor calls forth pity or fear. Nor, again, should the downfall of the utter villain be exhibited. A plot of this kind would, doubtless, satisfy the moral sense, but it would inspire neither pity nor fear; for pity is aroused by unmerited misfortune, fear by the misfortune of a man like ourselves. Such an event, therefore, will be neither pitiful nor terrible. There remains, then, the character between these two extremes: that of a man who is not eminently good and just, yet whose misfortune is brought about not by vice or depravity, but by some error or frailty. He must be one who is highly renowned and prosperous—a personage like Œdipus, Thyéstes, or other illustrious men of such families.

– Áristotle, Poetics, VI-IX,XI,XIII (translated by S. H. Butcher)

# The Education of Péricles

The master that taught him music, most authors are agreed, was Dámon (whose name, they say, ought to be pronounced with the first syllable short). Though Áristotle tells us that he was thoroughly practiced in all accomplishments of this kind by Pythóclides. Dámon, it is not unlikely, being a sóphist, out of policy, sheltered himself under the profession of music to conceal from people in general his skill in other things, and under this pretense attended Péricles, the young athlete of politics, so to say, as his training-master in these exercises. Dámon's lyre, however, did not prove altogether a successful blind; he was banished from the country by ostracism for ten years as a dangerous intermeddler and a favorer of arbitrary power, and, by this means, gave the stage occasion to play upon him. As, for instance, Pláto, the comic poet, introduces a character, who questions him:

Tell me, if you please,
Since you're the Chíron who taught Péricles.

Péricles, also, was a hearer of Zéno, the Eleátic, who treated of natural philosophy in the same manner as Parménides did, but had also perfected himself in an art of his own for refuting and silencing opponents in argument; as Tímon of Phlíus describes it:

The two-edged tongue of mighty Zéno, who,
what one would, could argue it untrue.

But he that saw most of Péricles, and furnished him most especially with a weight and grandeur of sense, superior to all arts of popularity, and in general gave him his elevation and sublimity of purpose and of character, was Anaxágoras of Clazómenæ; whom the men of those times called by the name of Nous, that is, mind, or intelligence, whether in admiration of the great and extraordinary gift he displayed for the science of nature, or because that he was the first of the philosophers who did not refer the first ordering of the world to fortune or chance, nor to necessity or compulsion, but to a pure, unadulterated intelligence, which acts as a principle of discrimination, and of combination of like with like, in all other existing mixed and compound things.

For this man, Péricles entertained an extraordinary esteem and admiration, and, filling himself with this lofty, and, as they call it, up-in-the-air sort of thought, derived hence not merely, as was natural, elevation of purpose and dignity of language, raised far above the base and dishonest buffooneries of mob-eloquence, but, besides this, a composure of countenance, and a serenity and calmness in all his movements, which no occurrence whilst he was speaking could disturb, a sustained and even tone of voice, and various other advantages of a similar kind, which produced the greatest effect on his hearers. Once, after being reviled and ill-spoken of all day long in his own hearing by some vile and abandoned fellow in the open marketplace, where he was engaged in the dispatch of some urgent affair, he continued his business in perfect silence, and in the evening returned home composedly, the man still dogging him at the heels, and pelting him all the way with abuse and foul language; and stepping into his house, it being by this time dark, he ordered one of his servants to take a light, and to go along with the man and see him safe home. Ion, it is true, the dramatic poet, says that Péricles's manner in company was somewhat over-assuming and pompous; and that into his high bearing there entered a good deal of slightingness and scorn of others; he reserves his commendation for Címon's ease and pliancy and natural grace in society. Íon, however, who must needs make virtue, like a show of tragedies, include some comic scenes, we shall not altogether rely upon; Zéno used to bid those who called Péricles's gravity the affectation of a charlatan, to go and affect the like themselves; inasmuch as this mere counterfeiting might in time insensibly instill into them a real love and knowledge of those noble qualities.

Nor were these the only advantages which Péricles derived from Anaxágoras's acquaintance; he seems also to have become, by his instructions, superior to that superstition with which an ignorant wonder at appearances, for example, in the heavens possesses the minds of people unacquainted with their causes, eager for the supernatural, and excitable through an inexperience which the knowledge of natural causes removes, replacing wild and timid superstition by the good hope and assurance of an intelligent piety.

– Plútarch, Life of Péricles (translated by John Dryden)

## The Public Life of Péricles

Péricles, while yet but a young man, stood in considerable apprehension of the people, as he was thought in face and figure to be very like the tyrant Pisístratus, and those of great age remarked upon the sweetness of his voice, and his volubility and rapidity in speaking, and were struck with amazement at the resemblance. Reflecting, too, that he had a considerable estate, and was descended of a noble family, and had friends of great influence, he was fearful all this might bring him to be banished as a dangerous person; and for this reason meddled not at all with state affairs, but in military service showed himself of a brave and intrepid nature. But when Aristídes was now dead, and Themístocles driven out, and Címon was for the most part kept abroad by the expeditions he made in parts out of Greece, Péricles, seeing things in this posture, now advanced and took his side, not with the rich and few, but with the many and poor, contrary to his natural bent, which was far from democratical; but, most likely, fearing he might fall under suspicion of aiming at arbitrary power, and seeing Címon on the side of the aristocracy, and much beloved by the better and more distinguished people, he joined the party of the people, with a view at once both to secure himself and procure means against Címon.

He immediately entered, also, on quite a new course of life and management of his time. For he was never seen to walk in any street but that which led to the marketplace and the council-hall, and he avoided invitations of friends to supper, and all friendly visiting and intercourse whatever; in all the time he had to do with the public, which was not a little, he was never known to have gone to any of his friends to a supper, except that once when his near kinsman Euryptólemus married, he remained present till the ceremony of the drink-offering, and then immediately rose from table and went his way. For these friendly meetings are very quick to defeat any assumed superiority, and in intimate familiarity an exterior of gravity is hard to maintain. Real excellence, indeed, is most recognized when most openly looked into; and in really good men, nothing which meets the eyes of external observers so truly deserves their admiration, as their daily common life does that of their nearer friends. Péricles, however, to avoid any feeling of commonness, or any satiety on the part of the people, presented himself at intervals only, not speaking to every business, nor at all times coming into the assembly, but, as Critoláüs says, reserving himself, like the Salamínian galley, for great occasions, while matters of lesser importance were dispatched by friends or other speakers under his direction...

The style of speaking most consonant to his form of life and the dignity of his views he found, so to say, in the tones of that instrument with which Anaxágoras had furnished him; of his teaching he continually availed himself, and deepened the colors of rhetoric with the dye of natural science. For having, in addition to his great natural genius, attained, by the study of nature, to use the words of the divine Pláto, this height of intelligence, and this universal consummating power, and drawing hence whatever might be of advantage to him in the art of speaking, he showed himself far superior to all others. Upon which account, they say, he had his nickname given him, though some are of opinion he was named the Olýmpian from the public buildings with which he adorned the city; and others again, from his great power in public affairs, whether of war or peace. Nor is it unlikely that the confluence of many attributes may have conferred it on him. However, the cómedies represented at the time, which, both in good earnest and in merriment, let fly many hard words at him, plainly show that he got that appellation especially from his speaking; they speak of his "thundering and lightning" when he harangued the people, and of his wielding a dreadful thunderbolt in his tongue.

A saying also of Thucýdides, the son of Melésias, stands on record, spoken by him by way of pleasantry upon Péricles's dexterity. Thucýdides was one of the noble and distinguished citizens, and had been his greatest opponent; and, when Archidámus, the king of the Lacedæmónians, asked him whether he or Péricles were the better wrestler, he made this answer: "When I," said he, "have thrown him and given him a fair fall, by persisting that he had no fall, he gets the better of me, and makes the bystanders, in spite of their own eyes, believe him." The truth, however, is, that Péricles himself was very careful what and how he was to speak, insomuch that, whenever he went up to the hustings, he prayed the gods that not one word might unawares slip from him unsuitable to the matter and the occasion.

– Plútarch, *Life of Péricles* (translated by John Dryden)

## The Complaint of Anaxágoras

Nor was all this the luck of some happy occasion; nor was it the mere bloom and grace of a policy that flourished for a season. Having for forty years together maintained the first place among statesmen—such as Ephiáltes, Leócrates, Myrónides, Címon, Tólmides and Thucýdides—after the defeat and banishment of Thucýdides, he preserved his integrity unspotted for no less than fifteen years longer in the exercise of one continuous command in the office of General, to which he was annually reelected. Though otherwise he was not altogether idle or careless in looking after his pecuniary advantage. His paternal estate, which of right belonged to him, he so ordered that it might neither through negligence be wasted or lessened, nor yet, being so full of business as he was, cost him any great trouble or time with taking care of it. He put it into such a way of management as he thought to be the most easy for himself, and the most exact. All his yearly products and profits he sold together in a lump, and supplied his household needs afterward by buying everything that he or his family wanted out of the market. Upon which account, his children, when they grew to age, were not well pleased with his management, and the women that lived with him were treated with little cost, and complained of this way of housekeeping, where everything was ordered and set down from day to day, and reduced to the greatest exactness; since there was not there, as is usual in a great family and a plentiful estate, any thing to spare, or over and above. But all that went out or came in, all disbursements and all receipts, proceeded as it were by number and measure. His manager in all this was a single servant, Evángelus by name, a man either naturally gifted or instructed by Péricles so as to excel everyone in this art of domestic economy.

All this, in truth, was very little in harmony with Anaxágoras's wisdom; if, indeed, it be true that he, by a kind of divine impulse and greatness of spirit, voluntarily quitted his house, and left his land to lie fallow and to be grazed by sheep like a common. But the life of a contemplative philosopher and that of an active statesman are, I presume, not the same thing. For the one merely employs upon great and good objects of thought an intelligence that requires neither aid of instruments nor supply of any external materials. Whereas the other, who tempers and applies his virtue to human uses, may have occasion for affluence, not as a matter of mere necessity, but as a noble thing; which was Péricles's case, who relieved numerous poor citizens.

However, there is a story that Anaxágoras himself, while Péricles was taken up with public affairs, lay neglected, and that, now being grown old, he wrapped himself up with a resolution to die for want of food. This being by chance brought to Péricles's ear, he was horror-struck, and instantly ran thither, and used all the arguments and entreaties he could to him, lamenting not so much Anaxágoras's condition as his own, should he lose such a counselor as he had found him to be; and that, upon this, Anaxágoras unfolded his robe, and showing himself, made answer: "Péricles," said he, "even those who have occasion for a lamp supply it with oil."

– Plútarch, *Life of Péricles* (translated by John Dryden)

## Anaxágoras

Anaxágoras ... was a native of Clazómenæ. He was a pupil of Anaximenes, and was the first who set mind above matter, for at the beginning of his treatise, which is composed in attractive and dignified language, he says, "All things were together; then came Mind and set them in order." This earned for Anaxágoras himself the nickname of Nous or Mind...

He was eminent for wealth and noble birth, and furthermore for magnanimity, in that he gave up his patrimony to his relations. For, when they accused him of neglecting it, he replied, "Why then do you not look after it?" And at last he went into retirement and engaged in physical investigation without troubling himself about public affairs. When some one inquired, "Have you no concern in your native land?" Gently, he replied, "I am greatly concerned with my fatherland," and pointed to the sky. He is said to have been twenty years old at the invasion of Xérxes and to have lived seventy-two years.

He declared the sun to be a mass of red-hot metal and to be larger than the Peloponnésus, though others ascribe this view to Tántalus; he declared that there were dwellings on the moon, and moreover hills and ravines. He took as his principles the homœomeries or homogeneous molecules; for just as gold consists of fine particles which are called gold-dust, so he held the whole universe to be compounded of minute bodies having parts homogeneous to themselves. His moving principle was Mind; of bodies, he said, some, like earth, were heavy, occupying the region below, others, light like fire, held the region above, while water and air were intermediate in position. For in this way over the earth, which is flat, the sea sinks down after the moisture has been evaporated by the sun. In the beginning the stars moved in the sky as in a revolving dome, so that the celestial pole which is always visible was vertically overhead; but subsequently the pole took its inclined position. He held the Milky Way to be a reflection of the light of stars which are not shone upon by the sun; comets to be a conjunction of planets which emit flames; shooting-stars to be a sort of sparks thrown off by the air. He held that winds arise when the air is rarefied by the sun's heat; that thunder is a clashing together of the clouds, lightning their violent friction; an earthquake a subsidence of air into the earth.

Animals were produced from moisture, heat, and an earthy substance; later the species were propagated by generation from one another, males from the right side, females from the left.

There is a story that he predicted the fall of the meteoric stone at Ægospótami, which he said would fall from the sun. Hence Eurípides, who was his pupil, in the Pháthon calls the sun itself a "golden clod." Furthermore, when he went to Olýmpia, he sat down wrapped in a sheep-skin cloak as if it were going to rain; and the rain came. When some one asked him if the hills at Lámpsacus would ever become sea, he replied, "Yes, it only needs time." Being asked to what end he had been born, he replied, "To study sun and moon and heavens." To one who inquired, "Do you miss the society of the Athénians?" his reply was, "Not I, but they miss mine." When he saw the tomb of Mausólus, he said, "A costly tomb is an image of an estate turned into stone." To one who complained that he was dying in a foreign land, his answer was, "The descent to Hádes is much the same from whatever place we start."

Favorínus in his *Miscellaneous History* says Anaxágoras was the first to maintain that Hómer in his poems treats of virtue and justice, and that this thesis was defended at greater length by his friend Metrodórus of Lámpsacus, who was the first to busy himself with Hómer's physical doctrine. Anaxágoras was also the first to publish a book with diagrams. Silénus in the first book of his *History* gives the Árchonship of Démylus as the date when the meteoric stone fell, and says that Anaxágoras declared the whole firmament to be made of stones; that the rapidity of rotation caused it to cohere; and that if this were relaxed it would fall.

Of the trial of Anaxágoras different accounts are given. Sótion in his *Succession of the Philosophers* says that he was indicted by Cléon on a charge of impiety, because he declared the sun to be a mass of red-hot metal; that his pupil Péricles defended him, and he was fined five talents and banished. Sátyrus in his *Lives* says that the prosecutor was Thucýdides, the opponent of Péricles, and the charge one of treasonable correspondence with Pérsia as well as of impiety; and that sentence of death was passed on Anaxágoras by default. When news was brought him that he was condemned and his sons were dead, his comment on the sentence was, "Long ago nature condemned both my judges and myself to death"; and on his sons, "I knew that my children were born to die." Some, however, tell this story of Sólon, and others of Xénophon. That he buried his sons with his own hands is asserted by Demétrius of Phálerum in his work *On Old Age*. Hermíppus in his *Lives* says that he was confined in the prison pending his execution; that Péricles came forward and asked the people whether they had any fault to find with him in his own public career; to which they replied that they had not. "Well," he continued, "I am a pupil of Anaxágoras; do not then be carried away by slanders and put him to death. Let me prevail upon you to release him." So he was released; but he could not brook the indignity he had suffered and committed suicide. Hierónymus in the second book of his *Scattered Notes* states that Péricles brought him into court so weak and wasted from illness that he owed his acquittal not so much to the merits of his case as to the sympathy of the judges.

— Diógenes Laértius, *Lives of the Eminent Philosophers*, II.6-14 (translated by R. D. Hicks)

## Anaxágoras on Lunar Eclipses

That the sun might be darkened about the close of the month, this even ordinary people now understood pretty well to be the effect of the moon; but the moon itself to be darkened, how that could come about, and how, on the sudden, a broad full moon should lose her light, and show such various colors, was not easy to be comprehended; they concluded it to be ominous, and a divine intimation of some heavy calamities. For he who the first, and the most plainly of any, and with the greatest assurance committed to writing how the moon is enlightened and overshadowed, was Anaxágoras; and he was as yet but recent, nor was his argument much known, but was rather kept secret, passing only amongst a few, under some kind of caution and confidence. People would not then tolerate natural philosophers, and theorists, as they then called them, about things above; as lessening the divine power, by explaining away its agency into the operation of irrational causes and senseless forces acting by necessity, without anything of Providence, or a free agent. Hence it was that Protágoras was banished, and Anaxágoras cast in prison, so that Péricles had much difficulty to procure his liberty; and Sócrates, though he had no concern whatever with this sort of learning, yet was put to death for philosophy. It was only afterwards that the reputation of Pláto, shining forth by his life, and because he subjected natural necessity to divine and more excellent principles, took away the obloquy and scandal that had attached to such contemplations, and obtained these studies currency among all people.

– Plútarch, *Life of Nícias* (translated by John Dryden)

## Fragment of Anaxágoras on "Nous" or Mind

All other things partake in a portion of everything, while Nous is infinite and self-ruled, and is mixed with nothing, but is alone itself by itself. For if it were not by itself, but were mixed with anything else, it would partake in all things if it were mixed with any; for in everything there is a portion of everything, as has been said by me in what goes before, and the things mixed with it would hinder it, so that it would have power over nothing in the same way that it has now being alone by itself. For it is the thinnest of all things and the purest, and it has all knowledge about everything and the greatest strength; and Nous has power over all things, both greater and smaller, that have life. And Nous had power over the whole revolution, so that it began to revolve in the beginning. And it began to revolve first from a small beginning; but the revolution now extends over a larger space and will extend over a larger still. And all the things that are mingled together and separated off and distinguished are all known by Nous. And Nous set in order all things that were to be, and all things that were and are not now and that are, and this revolution in which now revolve the stars and the sun and the moon, and the air and the æther that are separated off. And this revolution caused the separating off, and the rare is separated off from the dense, the warm from the cold, the light from the dark, and the dry from the moist. And there are many portions in many things. But no thing is altogether separated off nor distinguished from anything else except Nous. And all Nous is alike, both the greater and the smaller; while nothing else is like anything else, but each single thing is and was most manifestly those things of which it has most in it.

— Anaxágoras, *Fragments*, 12 (translated by John Burnet)

## Protágoras the Sóphist

Protágoras was the first to maintain that there are two sides to every question, opposed to each other, and he even argued in this fashion, being the first to do so. Furthermore, he began a work thus: "Man is the measure of all things, of things that are that they are, and of things that are not that they are not." He used to say that soul was nothing apart from the senses, as we learn from Pláto in the Theætetus, and that everything is true. In another work he began thus: "As to the gods, I have no means of knowing either that they exist or that they do not exist. For many are the obstacles that impede knowledge, both the obscurity of the question and the shortness of human life." For this introduction to his book the Athénians expelled him; and they burnt his works in the marketplace, after sending round a herald to collect them from all who had copies in their possession.

He was the first to exact a fee of a hundred mínas and the first to distinguish the tenses of verbs, to emphasize the importance of seizing the right moment, to institute contests in debating, and to teach rival pleaders the tricks of their trade. Furthermore, in his dialectic he neglected the meaning in favor of verbal quibbling, and he was the father of the whole tribe of eristical disputants now so much in evidence... He too first introduced the method of discussion which is called Socrátic. Again, as we learn from Pláto in the *Euthydémus*, he was the first to use in discussion the argument of Antísthenes which strives to prove that contradiction is impossible, and the first to point out how to attack and refute any proposition laid down: so says Artemidórus the dialectician in his treatise *In Reply to Chrysíppus*.

— Diógenes Laértius, *Lives of the Eminent Philosophers*, IX.50-53 (translated by R. D. Hicks)

## IV. BEGINNINGS OF PROSE LITERATURE

## Introduction to Heródotus's *History*

These are the researches of Heródotus of Halicarnássus, which he publishes, in the hope of thereby preserving from decay the remembrance of what men have done, and of preventing the great and wonderful actions of the Greeks and the Barbarians from losing their due meed of glory; and withal to put on record what were their grounds of feud.

— Heródotus, *History*, Preface to I (translated by George Rawlinson)

# CHAPTER XX.

## SOCIAL CULTURE, LIFE AND MANNERS

Industrial Life in Áthens, I.—Domestic Life in Áthens, II.—Social Life in Áthens, III.

## I. INDUSTRIAL LIFE IN ÁTHENS

### The Resources of Áthens

I had no sooner begun my investigation than one fact presented itself clearly to my mind, which is that the country itself is made by nature to provide the amplest resources. And with a view to establishing the truth of this initial proposition I will describe the physical features of Áttica.

In the first place, the extraordinary mildness of the climate is proved by the actual products of the soil. Numerous plants which in many parts of the world appear as stunted leafless growths are here fruit-bearing. And as with the soil so with the sea indenting our coasts, the varied productivity of which is exceptionally great. Again with regard to those kindly fruits of earth which Providence bestows on man season by season, one and all they commence earlier and end later in this land. Nor is the supremacy of Áttica shown only in those products which year after year flourish and grow old, but the land contains treasures of a more perennial kind. Within its folds lies imbedded by nature an unstinted store of marble, out of which are chiseled temples and altars of rarest beauty and the glittering splendor of images sacred to the gods. This marble, moreover, is an object of desire to many foreigners, Héllenes and barbarians alike. Then there is land which, although it yields no fruit to the sower, needs only to be quarried in order to feed many times more mouths than it could as grain-land. Doubtless we owe it to a divine dispensation that our land is veined with silver; if we consider how many neighboring states lie round us by land and sea and yet into none of them does a single thinnest vein of silver penetrate.

Indeed, it would be scarcely irrational to maintain that the city of Áthens lies at the navel, not of Héllas merely, but of the habitable world. So true is it, that the farther we remove from Áthens the greater the extreme of heat or cold to be encountered; or to use another illustration, the traveler who desires to traverse the confines of Héllas from end to end will find that, whether he voyages by sea or by land, he is describing a circle, the center of which is Áthens.

Once more, this land though not literally sea-girt has all the advantages of an island, being accessible to every wind that blows, and can invite to its bosom or waft from its shore all products, since it is peninsular; whilst by land it is the emporium of many markets, as being a portion of the continent.

Lastly, while the majority of states have barbarian neighbors, the source of many troubles, Áthens has as her next-door neighbors civilized states which are themselves far remote from the barbarians.

– Xénophon, *Ways and Means*, I. (translated by H. G. Dakyns)

### The Commercial Advantages of Áthens

At this point I propose to offer some remarks in proof of the attractions and advantages of Áthens as a center of commercial enterprise. In the first place, it will hardly be denied that we possess the finest and safest harborage for shipping, where vessels of all sorts can come to moorings and be laid up in absolute security as far as stress of weather is concerned. But further than that, in most states the trader is under the necessity of lading his vessel with some merchandise or other in exchange for his cargo, since the current coin has no circulation beyond the frontier. But at Áthens he has a choice: he can either in return for his wares export a variety of goods, such as human beings seek after, or, if he does not desire to take goods in exchange for goods, he has simply to export silver, and he cannot have a more excellent freight to export, since wherever he likes to sell it he may look to realize a large percentage on his capital.

– Xénophon, *Ways and Means*, III. (translated by H. G. Dakyns)

## The Silver Mines at Láurium

I come to a new topic. I am persuaded that the establishment of the silver mines on a proper footing would be followed by a large increase in wealth apart from the other sources of revenue. And I would like, for the benefit of those who may be ignorant, to point out what the capacity of these mines really is. You will then be in a position to decide how to turn them to better account. It is clear, I presume, to everyone that these mines have for a very long time been in active operation; at any rate no one will venture to fix the date at which they first began to be worked. Now in spite of the fact that the silver ore has been dug and carried out for so long a time, I would ask you to note that the mounds of rubbish so shoveled out are but a fractional portion of the series of hillocks containing veins of silver, and as yet unquarried. Nor is the silver-bearing region gradually becoming circumscribed. On the contrary it is evidently extending in wider area from year to year. That is to say, during the period in which thousands of workers have been employed within the mines no hand was ever stopped for want of work to do.

– Xénophon, *Ways and Means*, IV. (translated by H. G. Dakyns)

## The Art of Money-Making

... The uses of every possession are two, both dependent upon the thing itself, but not in the same manner, the one supposing an inseparable connection with it, the other not. A shoe, for instance, ... may be either worn, or exchanged for something else. Both of these are the uses of the shoe. For he who exchanges a shoe with some man who wants one, for money or provisions, uses the shoe as a shoe, but not according to the original intention, for shoes were not at first made to be exchanged. The same thing holds true of all other possessions. For barter, in general, had its original beginning in nature, some men having a surplus, others too little of what was necessary for them. Hence it is evident that selling provisions for money is not according to the natural use of things, for they were obliged to use barter for those things which they wanted. But it is plain that barter could have no place in the first, that is to say, in family society; but must have begun when the number of those who composed the community was enlarged. For the first of these had all things in common, but when they came to be separated they were obliged to exchange with each other many different things which both parties wanted. This custom of barter is still preserved amongst many barbarous nations, who procure one necessary with another, but never sell anything, as giving and receiving wine for grain and the like.

This sort of barter is not contradictory to nature, nor is it any species of money-getting; but is necessary in procuring that subsistence which is so consonant to it. But this barter introduced the use of money, as might be expected. For a convenient place from whence to import what you wanted, or to export what you had a surplus of, being often at a great distance, money necessarily made its way into commerce. For it is not everything which is naturally most useful that is easiest of carriage, for which reason they invented something to exchange with each other which they should mutually give and take, that being really valuable itself, should have the additional advantage of being of easy conveyance, for the purposes of life—as iron and silver, or anything else of the same nature. And this at first passed in value simply according to its weight or size; but in process of time it had a certain stamp, to save the trouble of weighing, which stamp expressed its value.

Money being established as the necessary medium of exchange, another species of money-getting soon took place, namely, by buying and selling, probably at first in a simple manner, afterwards with more skill and experience, where and how the greatest profits might be made. For which reason the art of money-getting seems to be chiefly conversant about trade, and the business of it to be able to tell where the greatest profits can be made, being the means of procuring abundance of wealth and possessions. And thus wealth is very often supposed to consist in the quantity of money which any one possesses, as this is the medium by which all trade is conducted and a fortune made, others again regard it as of no value, as being of none by nature, but arbitrarily made so by compact; so that if those who use it should alter their sentiments, it would be worth nothing, as being of no service for any necessary purpose.

Besides, he who abounds in money often wants necessary food, and it is impossible to say that any person is in good circumstances when with all his possessions he may perish with hunger, like Mídas in the fable, who from his insatiable wish had everything he touched turned into gold. For which reason others endeavor to procure other riches and other property, and rightly. For there are other riches and property in nature, and these are the proper objects of economy; while trade only procures money, not by all means, but by the exchange of it, and for that purpose it is this which it is chiefly employed about. For money is the first principle and the end of trade. Nor are there any bounds to be set to what is thereby acquired. Thus also there are no limits to the art of medicine, with respect to the health which it attempts to procure. The same also is true of all other arts; no line can be drawn to terminate their bounds, the several professors of them being desirous to extend them as far as possible. (But still the means to be employed for that purpose are limited; and these are the limits beyond which the art cannot proceed.)

Thus in the art of acquiring riches there are no limits, for the object of that is money and possessions. But economy has a boundary, though [acquiring riches] has not ... for which reason it should seem that some boundary should be set to riches—though we see the contrary to this is what is practiced. For all those who get riches add to their money without end, the cause of which is the near connection of these two arts with each other, which sometimes occasions the one to change employments with the other, as getting of money is their common object. For economy requires the possession of wealth, but not on its own account but with another view, to purchase necessary things. But the other procures it merely to increase it, so that some persons are confirmed in their belief that this is the proper object of economy and think that for this purpose money should be saved and hoarded up without end. The reason for this disposition is that they are intent upon living, but not upon living well. This desire being boundless in its extent, the means which they aim at for that purpose are boundless also. Those who propose to live well often confine that to the enjoyment of the pleasures of sense. So that, as this also seems to depend upon what a man has, all their care is to get money. And hence arises the other cause for this art, for as this enjoyment is excessive in its degree, they endeavor to procure means proportionate to supply it. And if they cannot do this merely by the art of dealing in money, they will endeavor to do it by other ways, and apply all their powers to a purpose they were not by nature intended for. Thus, for instance, courage was intended to inspire fortitude, not to get money. Neither is this the end of the soldier's or the physician's art, but victory and health. But such persons make everything subservient to money-getting, as if this was the only end; and to the end everything ought to refer.

We have now considered that art of money-getting which is not necessary, and have seen in what manner we became in want of it, and also that which is necessary, which is different from it. For that economy which is natural, and whose object is to provide food, is not like this unlimited in its extent, but has its bounds.

We have now determined what was before doubtful, whether or not the art of getting money is his business who is at the head of a family or a state, and though not strictly so, it is however very necessary. For a politician does not make men, but receiving them from the hand of nature employs them to proper purposes. Thus the earth, or the sea, or something else ought to supply them with provisions, and this it is the business of the master of the family to manage properly... Now money-making, as we say, being twofold, may be applied to two purposes, the service of the house or retail trade, of which the first is necessary and commendable, the other justly censurable. For it has not its origin in nature, but by it men gain from each other. Usury is most reasonably detested, as it is increasing our fortune by money itself, and not employing it for the purpose it was originally intended, namely exchange.

And this is the explanation of the name τόκος (tókos), which means the breeding of money. For as offspring resemble their parents, so usury is money bred of money. Whence of all forms of money-making it is most against nature.

– Áristotle, *Politics*, I.9-10 (translated by William Ellis)


## II. DOMESTIC LIFE IN ÁTHENS

## Sócrates on Economy

I once heard him discuss the topic of economy after the following manner. Addressing Critóbulus, he said: Tell me, Critóbulus, is "economy," like the words "medicine," "carpentry," "building," "smithying," "metal-working," and so forth, the name of a particular kind of knowledge or science?

*Critóbulus*. Yes, I think so.

*Sócrates*. And as, in the case of the arts just named, we can state the proper work or function of each, can we (similarly) state the proper work and function of economy?

*Critóbulus*. It must, I should think, be the business of the good economist at any rate to manage his own house or estate well.

*Sócrates*. And supposing another man's house to be entrusted to him, he would be able, if he chose, to manage it as skillfully as his own, would he not? since a man who is skilled in carpentry can work as well for another as for himself: and this ought to be equally true of the good economist?

*Critóbulus*. Yes, I think so, Sócrates.

*Sócrates*. Then there is no reason why a proficient in this art, even if he does not happen to possess wealth of his own, should not be paid a salary for managing a house, just as he might be paid for building one?

*Critóbulus*. None at all: and a large salary he would be entitled to earn if, after paying the necessary expenses of the estate entrusted to him, he can create a surplus and improve the property.

*Sócrates*. Well! and this word "house," what are we to understand by it? the domicile merely? or are we to include all a man's possessions outside the actual dwelling-place?

*Critóbulus*. Certainly, in my opinion at any rate, everything which a man has got, even though some portion of it may lie in another part of the world from that in which he lives, forms part of his estate.

*Sócrates*. "Has got"? but he may have got enemies?

*Critóbulus*. Yes, I am afraid some people have got a great many.

*Sócrates.* Then shall we say that a man's enemies form part of his possessions?

*Critóbulus.* A comic notion indeed! that some one should be good enough to add to my stock of enemies, and that in addition he should be paid for his kind services.

*Sócrates.* Because, you know, we agreed that a man's estate was identical with his possessions?

*Critóbulus.* Yes, certainly! the good part of his possessions; but the evil portion! no, I thank you, that I do not call part of a man's possessions.

*Sócrates.* As I understand, you would limit the term to what we may call a man's useful or advantageous possessions?

*Critóbulus.* Precisely; if he has things that injure him, I should regard these rather as a loss than as wealth.

*Sócrates.* It follows apparently that if a man purchases a horse and does not know how to handle him, but each time he mounts he is thrown and sustains injuries, the horse is not part of his wealth?

*Critóbulus.* Not, if wealth implies weal, certainly.

*Sócrates.* And by the same token land itself is no wealth to a man who so works it that his tillage only brings him loss?

*Critóbulus.* True; mother earth herself is not a source of wealth to us if, instead of helping us to live, she helps us to starve.

*Sócrates.* And by a parity of reasoning, sheep and cattle may fail of being wealth if, through want of knowledge how to treat them, their owner loses by them; to him at any rate the sheep and the cattle are not wealth?

*Critóbulus.* That is the conclusion I draw.

*Sócrates.* It appears, you hold to the position that wealth consists of things which benefit, while things which injure are not wealth?

*Critóbulus.* Just so.

*Sócrates.* The same things, in fact, are wealth or not wealth, according as a man knows or does not know the use to make of them? To take an instance, a flute may be wealth to him who is sufficiently skilled to play upon it, but the same instrument is no better than the stones we tread under our feet to him who is not so skilled . . . unless indeed he chose to sell it?

— Xénophon, *Œconómicus*, I. (translated by H. G. Dakyns)

## Marriage and Economy

It chanced, one day I saw him seated in the portico of Zeus Eleuthérios, and as he appeared to be at leisure, I went up to him and, sitting down by his side, accosted him: How is this, Ischómachus? you seated here, you who are so little wont to be at leisure? As a rule, when I see you, you are doing something, or at any rate not sitting idle in the marketplace.

Nor would you see me now so sitting, Sócrates (he answered), but that I promised to meet some strangers, friends of mine, at this place.

And when you have no such business on hand (I said) where in heaven's name do you spend your time and how do you employ yourself? I will not conceal from you how anxious I am to learn from your lips by what conduct you have earned for yourself the title "beautiful and good." It is not by spending your days indoors at home, I am sure; the whole habit of your body bears witness to a different sort of life.

Then Ischómachus, smiling at my question, but also, as it seemed to me, a little pleased to be asked what he had done to earn the title "beautiful and good," made answer: Whether that is the title by which folk call me when they talk to you about me, I cannot say; all I know is, when they challenge me to exchange properties, or else to perform some service to the state instead of them, the fitting out of a tríreme, or the training of a chorus, nobody thinks of asking for the beautiful and good gentleman, but it is plain Ischómachus, the son of So-and-so, on whom the summons is served. But to answer your question, Sócrates (he proceeded), I certainly do not spend my days indoors, if for no other reason, because my wife is quite capable of managing our domestic affairs without my aid.

Ah! (said I), Ischómachus, that is just what I should like particularly to learn from you. Did you yourself educate your wife to be all that a wife should be, or when you received her from her father and mother was she already a proficient well skilled to discharge the duties appropriate to a wife?

Well skilled! (he replied). What proficiency was she likely to bring with her, when she was not quite fifteen at the time she wedded me, and during the whole prior period of her life had been most carefully brought up to see and hear as little as possible, and to ask the fewest questions? or do you not think one should be satisfied, if at marriage her whole experience consisted in knowing how to take the wool and make a dress, and seeing how her mother's handmaidens had their daily spinning-tasks assigned them? For (he added), as regards control of appetite and self-indulgence, she had received the soundest education, and that I take to be the most important matter in the bringing-up of man or woman.

Then all else (said I) you taught your wife yourself, Ischómachus, until you had made her capable of attending carefully to her appointed duties?

That did I not (replied he) until I had offered sacrifice and prayed that I might teach and she might learn all that could conduce to the happiness of us twain.

*Sócrates*. And did your wife join in sacrifice and prayer to that effect?

*Ischómachus*. Most certainly, with many a vow registered to heaven to become all she ought to be; and her whole manner showed that she would not be neglectful of what was taught her.

*Sócrates*. Pray narrate to me, Ischómachus, I beg of you, what you first essayed to teach her. To hear that story would please me more than any description of the most splendid gymnastic contest or horse-race you could give me.

Why, Sócrates (he answered), when after a time she had become accustomed to my hand, that is, was tamed sufficiently to play her part in a discussion, I put to her this question: "Did it ever strike you to consider, dear wife, what led me to choose you as my wife among all women, and your parents to entrust you to me of all men? ... It was with deliberate intent to discover, I for myself and your parents in behalf of you, the best partner of house and children we could find, that I sought you out, and your parents, acting to the best of their ability, made choice of me. If at some future time God grant us to have children born to us, we will take counsel together how best to bring them up, for that too will be a common interest, and a common blessing if haply they shall live to fight our battles and we find in them hereafter support and succor when we ourselves are old. But at present there is our house here, which belongs like to both. It is common property, for all that I possess goes by my will into the common fund, and in the same way all that you deposited was placed by you to the common fund. We need not stop to calculate in figures which of us contributed most, but rather let us lay to heart this fact that whichever of us proves the better partner, he or she at once contributes what is most worth having."

Thus I addressed her, Sócrates, and thus my wife made answer: "But how can I assist you? what is my ability? Nay, everything depends on you. My business, my mother told me, was to be sober-minded!"

"Most true, my wife," I replied, "and that is what my father said to me. But what is the proof of sober-mindedness in man or woman? Is it not so to behave that what they have of good may ever be at its best, and that new treasures from the same source of beauty and righteousness may be most amply added?"

"But what is there that I can do," my wife inquired, "which will help to increase our joint estate?"

"Assuredly," I answered, "you may strive to do as well as possible what Heaven has given you a natural gift for and which the law approves."

"And what may these things be?" she asked.

"To my mind they are not the things of least importance," I replied, "unless the things which the queen bee in her hive presides over are of slight importance to the bee community; for the gods" (so Ischómachus assured me, he continued), "the gods, my wife, would seem to have exercised much care and judgment in compacting that twin system which goes by the name of male and female, so as to secure the greatest possible advantage to the pair. Since no doubt the underlying principle of the bond is first and foremost to perpetuate through procreation the races of living creatures; and next, as the outcome of this bond, for human beings at any rate, a provision is made by which they may have sons and daughters to support them in old age.

"And again, the way of life of human beings, not being maintained like that of cattle in the open air, obviously demands roofed homesteads. But if these same human beings are to have anything to bring in under cover, someone to carry out these labors of the field under high heaven must be found them, since such operations as the breaking up of fallow with the plough, the sowing of seed, the planting of trees, the pasturing and herding of flocks, are one and all open-air employments on which the supply of products necessary to life depends.

"As soon as these products of the field are safely housed and under cover, new needs arise. There must be someone to guard the store and someone to perform such necessary operations as imply the need of shelter. Shelter, for instance, is needed for the rearing of infant children; shelter is needed for the various processes of converting the fruits of earth into food, and in like manner for the fabrication of clothing out of wool.

"But whereas both of these, the indoor and the outdoor occupations alike, demand new toil and new attention, to meet the case," I added, "God made provision from the first by shaping, as it seems to me, the woman's nature for indoor and the man's for outdoor occupations. Man's body and soul He furnished with a greater capacity for enduring heat and cold, wayfaring and military marches; or, to repeat, He laid upon his shoulders the outdoor works.

"While in creating the body of woman with less capacity for these things," I continued, "God would seem to have imposed on her the indoor works; and knowing that He had implanted in the woman and imposed upon her the nurture of new-born babies, He endowed her with a larger share of affection for the new-born child than He bestowed upon man. And since He imposed on woman the guardianship of the things imported from without, God, in His wisdom, perceiving that a fearful spirit was no detriment to guardianship, endowed the woman with a larger measure of timidity than He bestowed on man. Knowing further that he to whom the outdoor works belonged would need to defend them against malign attack, He endowed the man in turn with a larger share of courage.

"And seeing that both alike feel the need of giving and receiving, He set down memory and carefulness between them for their common use, so that you would find it hard to determine which of the two, the male or the female, has the larger share of these. So, too, God set down between them for their common use the gift of self-control, where needed, adding only to that one of the twain, whether man or woman, which should prove the better, the power to be rewarded with a larger share of this perfection. And for the very reason that their natures are not alike adapted to like ends, they stand in greater need of one another; and the married couple is made more useful to itself, the one fulfilling what the other lacks.

"Now, being well aware of this, my wife," I added, "and knowing well what things are laid upon us twain by God Himself, must we not strive to perform, each in the best way possible, our respective duties? Law, too, gives her consent — law and the usage of mankind, by sanctioning the wedlock of man and wife; and just as God ordained them to be partners in their children, so the law establishes their common ownership of house and estate. Custom, moreover, proclaims as beautiful those excellences of man and woman with which God gifted them at birth. Thus for a woman to bide tranquilly at home rather than roam abroad is no dishonor; but for a man to remain indoors, instead of devoting himself to outdoor pursuits, is a thing discreditable. But if a man does things contrary to the nature given him by God, the chances are, such insubordination escapes not the eye of Heaven: he pays the penalty, whether of neglecting his own works, or of performing those appropriate to woman."

I added: "Just such works, if I mistake not, that same queen-bee we spoke of labors hard to perform, like yours, my wife, enjoined upon her by God Himself."

"And what sort of works are these?" she asked; "what has the queen-bee to do that she seems so like myself, or I like her in what I have to do?"

"Why," I answered, "she too stays in the hive and suffers not the other bees to idle. Those whose duty it is to work outside she sends forth to their labors; and all that each of them brings in, she notes and receives and stores against the day of need; but when the season for use has come, she distributes a just share to each. Again, it is she who presides over the fabric of choicely woven cells within. She looks to it that warp and woof are wrought with speed and beauty. Under her guardian eye the brood of young is nursed and reared; but when the days of rearing are past and the young bees are ripe for work, she sends them out as colonists with one of the seed royal to be their leader."

"Shall I then have to do these things?" asked my wife.

"Yes," I answered, "you will need in the same way to stay indoors, dispatching to their toils without those of your domestics whose work lies there. Over those whose appointed tasks are wrought indoors, it will be your duty to preside; yours to receive the stuffs brought in; yours to apportion part for daily use, and yours to make provision for the rest, to guard and garner it so that the outgoings destined for a year may not be expended in a month. It will be your duty, when the wools are introduced, to see that clothing is made for those who need; your duty also to see that the dried grain is rendered fit and serviceable for food.

"There is just one of all these occupations which devolve upon you," I added, "you may not find so altogether pleasing. Should any one of our household fall sick, it will be your care to see and tend them to the recovery of their health."

"Nay," she answered, "that will be my pleasantest of tasks, if careful nursing may touch the springs of gratitude and leave them friendlier than before."

And I (continued Ischómachus) was struck with admiration at her answer, and replied: "Think you, my wife, it is through some such traits of forethought seen in their mistress-leader that the hearts of bees are won, and they are so loyally affectioned towards her that, if ever she abandon her hive, not one of them will dream of being left behind; but one and all must follow her."

And my wife made answer to me: "It would much astonish me (said she) did not these leader's works, you speak of, point to you rather than myself. Methinks mine would be a pretty guardianship and distribution of things indoors without your provident care to see that the importations from without were duly made."

"Just so," I answered, "and mine would be a pretty importation if there were no one to guard what I imported. Do you not see," I added, "how pitiful is the case of those unfortunates who pour water in their sieves for ever, as the story goes, and labor but in vain?"

Work without hope draws nectar in a sieve, And hope without an object cannot live.

"Pitiful enough, poor souls," she answered, "if that is what they do."

"But there are other cares, you know, and occupations," I answered, "which are yours by right, and these you will find agreeable. This, for instance, to take some maiden who knows naught of carding wool and to make her proficient in the art, doubling her usefulness; or to receive another quite ignorant of housekeeping or of service, and to render her skillful, loyal, serviceable, till she is worth her weight in gold; or again, when occasion serves, you have it in your power to requite by kindness the well-behaved whose presence is a blessing to your house; or maybe to chasten the bad character, should such an one appear. But the greatest joy of all will be to prove yourself my better; to make me your faithful follower; knowing no dread lest as the years advance you should decline in honor in your household, but rather trusting that, though your hair turn gray, yet, in proportion as you come to be a better helpmate to myself and to the children, a better guardian of our home, so will your honor increase throughout the household as mistress, wife, and mother, daily more dearly prized. Since," I added, "it is not through excellence of outward form, but by reason of the luster of virtues shed forth upon the life of man, that increase is given to things beautiful and good."

That, Sócrates, or something like that, as far as I may trust my memory, records the earliest conversation which I held with her.

— Xénophon, *Œconómicus*, VII. (translated by H. G. Dakyns)

## Ischómachus on Household Management

"So, too, an army," I said, "my wife, an army destitute of order is confusion worse confounded: to enemies an easy prey, courting attack; to friends a bitter spectacle of wasted power; a mingled mob of asses, heavy infantry, and baggage-bearers, light infantry, cavalry, and wagons. Now, suppose they are on the march; how are they to get along? In this condition everybody will be a hindrance to everybody: 'slow march' side by side with 'double quick,' 'quick march' at cross purposes with 'stand at ease'; wagons blocking cavalry and asses fouling wagons; baggage-bearers and hoplites jostling together: the whole a hopeless jumble. And when it comes to fighting, such an army is not precisely in condition to deliver battle. The troops who are compelled to retreat before the enemy's advance are fully capable of trampling down the heavy infantry detachments in reserve.

"How different is an army well organized in battle order: a splendid sight for friendly eyes to gaze at, albeit an eyesore to the enemy. For who, being of their party, but will feel a thrill of satisfaction as he watches the serried masses of heavy infantry moving onwards in unbroken order? who but will gaze with wonderment as the squadrons of the cavalry dash past him at the gallop? And what of the foeman? will not his heart sink within him to see the orderly arrangements of the different arms: here heavy infantry and cavalry, and there again light infantry, there archers and there slingers, following each their leaders, with orderly precision. As they tramp onwards thus in order, though they number many myriads, yet even so they move on and on in quiet progress, stepping like one man, and the place just vacated in front is filled up on the instant from the rear.

175

"Or picture a tríreme, crammed choke-full of mariners; for what reason is she so terror-striking an object to her enemies, and a sight so gladsome to the eyes of friends? is it not that the gallant ship sails so swiftly? And why is it that, for all their crowding, the ship's company cause each other no distress? Simply that there, as you may see them, they sit in order; in order bend to the oar; in order recover the stroke; in order step on board; in order disembark. But disorder is, it seems to me, precisely as though a man who is a husbandman should stow away together in one place wheat and barley and pulse, and by and by when he has need of barley meal, or wheaten flour, or some condiment of pulse, then he must pick and choose instead of laying his hand on each thing separately sorted for use.

"And so with you too, my wife, if you would avoid this confusion, if you would fain know how to administer our goods, so as to lay your finger readily on this or that as you may need, or if I ask you for anything, graciously to give it me: let us, I say, select and assign the appropriate place for each set of things. This shall be the place where we will put the things; and we will instruct the housekeeper that she is to take them out thence, and mind to put them back again there; and in this way we shall know whether they are safe or not. If anything is gone, the gaping space will cry out as if it asked for something back. The mere look and aspect of things will argue what wants mending; and the fact of knowing where each thing is will be like having it put into one's hand at once to use without further trouble or debate."

— Xénophon, Œconómicus, VIII. (translated by H. G. Dakyns)

III. SOCIAL LIFE IN ÁTHENS

## Sócrates Arrives at the Sympósium

He said that he met Sócrates fresh from the bath and sandaled; and as the sight of the sandals was unusual, he asked him whither he was going that he had been converted into such a beau.

To a banquet at Ágathon's, he replied, whose invitation to his sacrifice of victory I refused yesterday, fearing a crowd, but promising that I would come today instead; and so I have put on my finery, because he is such a fine man. What say you to going with me unasked?

I will do as you bid me, I replied.

Follow then, he said, and let us demolish the proverb: 'To the feasts of inferior men the good unbidden go.' Instead of which our proverb will run: 'To the feasts of the good the good unbidden go.' And this alteration may be supported by the authority of Hómer himself, who not only demolishes but literally outrages the proverb. For, after picturing Agamémnon as the most valiant of men, he makes Meneláüs, who is but a fainthearted warrior, come unbidden to the banquet of Agamémnon, who is feasting and offering sacrifices, not the better to the worse, but the worse to the better.

I rather fear, Sócrates, said Aristodémus, lest this may still be my case; and that, like Meneláüs in Hómer, I shall be the inferior person, who 'To the feasts of the wise unbidden goes.' But I shall say that I was bidden of you, and then you will have to make an excuse.

'Two going together,' he replied, in Hómeric fashion, one or other of them may invent an excuse by the way.

This was the style of their conversation as they went along. Sócrates dropped behind in a fit of abstraction, and desired Aristodémus, who was waiting, to go on before him. When he reached the house of Ágathon he found the doors wide open, and a comical thing happened. A servant coming out met him, and led him at once into the banqueting-hall in which the guests were reclining, for the banquet was about to begin. Welcome, Aristodémus, said Ágathon, as soon as he appeared—you are just in time to sup with us; if you come on any other matter put it off, and make one of us, as I was looking for you yesterday and meant to have asked you, if I could have found you. But what have you done with Sócrates?

I turned round, but Sócrates was nowhere to be seen; and I had to explain that he had been with me a moment before, and that I came by his invitation to the supper.

You were quite right in coming, said Ágathon; but where is he himself?

He was behind me just now, as I entered, he said, and I cannot think what has become of him.

Go and look for him, boy, said Ágathon, and bring him in; and do you, Aristodémus, meanwhile take the place by Eryxímachus.

The servant then assisted him to wash, and he lay down, and presently another servant came in and reported that our friend Sócrates had retired into the portico of the neighboring house. 'There he is fixed,' said he, 'and when I call to him he will not stir.'

How strange, said Ágathon; then you must call him again, and keep calling him.

Let him alone, said my informant; he has a way of stopping anywhere and losing himself without any reason. I believe that he will soon appear; do not therefore disturb him.

Well, if you think so, I will leave him, said Ágathon. And then, turning to the servants, he added, 'Let us have supper without waiting for him. Serve up whatever you please, for there is no one to give you orders; hitherto I have never left you to yourselves. But on this occasion imagine that you are our hosts, and that I and the company are your guests; treat us well, and then we shall commend you.' After this, supper was served, but still no Sócrates; and during the meal Ágathon several times expressed a wish to send for him, but Aristodémus objected; and at last when the feast was about half over—for the fit, as usual, was not of long duration—Sócrates entered. Ágathon, who was reclining alone at the end of the table, begged that he would take the place next to him; that 'I may touch you,' he said, 'and have the benefit of that wise thought which came into your mind in the portico, and is now in your possession; for I am certain that you would not have come away until you had found what you sought.'

How I wish, said Sócrates, taking his place as he was desired, that wisdom could be infused by touch, out of the fuller into the emptier man, as water runs through wool out of a fuller cup into an emptier one; if that were so, how greatly should I value the privilege of reclining at your side! For you would have filled me full with a stream of wisdom plenteous and fair; whereas my own is of a very mean and questionable sort, no better than a dream. But yours is bright and full of promise and was manifested forth in all the splendor of youth the day before yesterday, in the presence of more than thirty thousand Héllenes.

You are mocking, Sócrates, said Ágathon, and ere long you and I will have to determine who bears off the palm of wisdom—of this Dionýsus shall be the judge; but at present you are better occupied with supper.

Sócrates took his place on the couch, and supped with the rest; and then libations were offered, and after a hymn had been sung to the god, and there had been the usual ceremonies, they were about to commence drinking, when Pausánias said, And now, my friends, how can we drink with least injury to ourselves? I can assure you that I feel severely the effect of yesterday's potations, and must have time to recover; and I suspect that most of you are in the same predicament, for you were of the party yesterday. Consider then: How can the drinking be made easiest?

I entirely agree, said Aristóphanes, that we should, by all means, avoid hard drinking, for I was myself one of those who were yesterday drowned in drink.

I think that you are right, said Eryxímachus, the son of Acuménus; but I should still like to hear one other person speak: Is Ágathon able to drink hard?

I am not equal to it, said Ágathon.

Then, said Eryxímachus, the weak heads like myself, Aristodémus, Phædrus, and others who never can drink, are fortunate in finding that the stronger ones are not in a drinking mood. (I do not include Sócrates, who is able either to drink or to abstain, and will not mind, whichever we do.) Well, as of none of the company seem disposed to drink much, I may be forgiven for saying, as a physician, that drinking deep is a bad practice, which I never follow, if I can help, and certainly do not recommend to another, least of all to any one who still feels the effects of yesterday's carouse.

I always do what you advise, and especially what you prescribe as a physician, rejoined Phædrus the Myrrhinúsian, and the rest of the company, if they are wise, will do the same.

It was agreed that drinking was not to be the order of the day, but that they were all to drink only so much as they pleased.

Then, said Eryxímachus, as you are all agreed that drinking is to be voluntary, and that there is to be no compulsion, I move, in the next place, that the flute-girl, who has just made her appearance, be told to go away and play to herself, or, if she likes, to the women who are within. Today let us have conversation instead; and, if you will allow me, I will tell you what sort of conversation. This proposal having been accepted, Eryxímachus proceeded as follows:

I will begin, he said, after the manner of Melaníppe in Eurípides, 'Not mine the word' which I am about to speak, but that of Phædrus. For often he says to me in an indignant tone, 'What a strange thing it is, Eryxímachus, that, whereas other gods have poems and hymns made in their honor, the great and glorious god, Love, has no encomiast among all the poets who are so many. There are the worthy sóphists too—the excellent Pródicus for example, who have descanted in prose on the virtues of Héracles and other heroes; and, what is still more extraordinary, I have met with a philosophical work in which the utility of salt has been made the theme of an eloquent discourse; and many other like things have had a like honor bestowed upon them. And only to think that there should have been an eager interest created about them, and yet that to this day no one has ever dared worthily to hymn Love's praises! So entirely has this great deity been neglected.' Now in this Phædrus seems to me to be quite right, and therefore I want to offer him a contribution; also I think that at the present moment we who are here assembled cannot do better than honor the god Love. If you agree with me, there will be no lack of conversation; for I mean to propose that each of us in turn, going from left to right, shall make a speech in honor of Love. Let him give us the best which he can; and Phædrus, because he is sitting first on the left hand, and because he is the father of the thought, shall begin.

No one will vote against you, Eryxímachus, said Sócrates. How can I, who profess to understand nothing but matters of love oppose, your motion; nor, I presume, will Ágathon and Pausánias; and there can be no doubt of Aristóphanes, whose whole concern is with Dionýsus and Aphrodíte; nor will any one disagree of those whom I see around me. The proposal, as I am aware, may seem rather hard upon us whose place is last; but we shall be contented if we hear some good speeches first. Let Phædrus begin the praise of Love, and good luck to him. All the company expressed their assent and desired him to do as Sócrates bade him.

— Pláto, *Sympósium* (translated by Benjamin Jowett)

## Aristóphanes Speaks at the Sympósium

Mankind, he said, judging by their neglect of him, have never, as I think, at all understood the power of Love. For if they had understood him they would surely have built noble temples and

178

altars, and offered solemn sacrifices in his honor; but this is not done, and most certainly ought to be done: since of all the gods he is the best friend of men, the helper and the healer of the ills which are the great impediment to the happiness of the race. I will try to describe his power to you, and you shall teach the rest of the world what I am teaching you.

In the first place, let me treat of the nature of man and what has happened to it; for the original human nature was not like the present, but different. The sexes were not two as they are now, but originally three in number; there was man, woman, and the union of the two, having a name corresponding to this double nature, which had once a real existence, but is now lost, and the word 'androgynous' is only preserved as a term of reproach. In the second place, the primeval man was round, his back and sides forming a circle; and he had four hands and four feet, one head with two faces, looking opposite ways, set on a round neck and precisely alike; also four ears, two privy members, and the remainder to correspond. He could walk upright as men now do, backwards or forwards as he pleased, and he could also roll over and over at a great pace, turning on his four hands and four feet, eight in all, like tumblers going over and over with their legs in the air; this was when he wanted to run fast.

Now the sexes were three, and such as I have described them; because the sun, moon, and earth are three; and the man was originally the child of the sun, the woman of the earth, and the man-woman of the moon, which is made up of sun and earth, and they were all round and moved round and round like their parents. Terrible was their might and strength, and the thoughts of their hearts were great, and they made an attack upon the gods; of them is told the tale of Ótys and Ephiáltes who, as Hómer says, dared to scale heaven, and would have laid hands upon the gods. Doubt reigned in the celestial councils. Should they kill them and annihilate the race with thunderbolts, as they had done the giants, then there would be an end of the sacrifices and worship which men offered to them; but, on the other hand, the gods could not suffer their insolence to be unrestrained. At last, after a good deal of reflection, Zeus discovered a way. He said: 'Methinks I have a plan which will humble their pride and improve their manners; men shall continue to exist, but I will cut them in two and then they will be diminished in strength and increased in numbers; this will have the advantage of making them more profitable to us. They shall walk upright on two legs, and if they continue insolent and will not be quiet, I will split them again and they shall hop about on a single leg.'

He spoke and cut men in two, like a sorb-apple which is halved for pickling, or as you might divide an egg with a hair; and as he cut them one after another, he bade Apóllo give the face and the half of the neck a turn in order that the man might contemplate the section of himself: he would thus learn a lesson of humility. Apóllo was also bidden to heal their wounds and compose their forms. So he gave a turn to the face and pulled the skin from the sides all over that which in our language is called the belly, like the purses which draw in, and he made one mouth at the center, which he fastened in a knot (the same which is called the navel); he also molded the breast and took out most of the wrinkles, much as a shoemaker might smooth leather upon a last; he left a few, however, in the region of the belly and navel, as a memorial of the primeval state. After the division the two parts, each desiring his other half, came together, and throwing their arms about one another, entwined in mutual embraces, longing to grow into one, they were on the point of dying from hunger and self-neglect, because they did not like to do anything apart; and when one of the halves died and the other survived, the survivor sought another mate, man or woman as we call them,—being the sections of entire men or women,—and clung to that.

— Pláto, *Sympósium* (translated by Benjamin Jowett)

## Sócrates Speaks at the Sympósium

'He who has been instructed thus far in the things of love, and who has learned to see the beautiful in due order and succession, when he comes toward the end will suddenly perceive a nature of wondrous beauty (and this, Sócrates, is the final cause of all our former toils)—a nature which in the first place is everlasting, not growing and decaying, or waxing and waning; secondly, not fair in one point of view and foul in another, or at one time or in one relation or at one place fair, at another time or in another relation or at another place foul, as if fair to some and foul to others, or in the likeness of a face or hands or any other part of the bodily frame, or in any form of speech or knowledge, or existing in any other being, as for example, in an animal, or in heaven, or in earth, or in any other place; but beauty absolute, separate, simple, and everlasting, which without diminution and without increase, or any change, is imparted to the ever-growing and perishing beauties of all other things.

He who from these ascending under the influence of true love, begins to perceive that beauty, is not far from the end. And the true order of going, or being led by another, to the things of love, is to begin from the beauties of earth and mount upwards for the sake of that other beauty, using these as steps only, and from one going on to two, and from two to all fair forms, and from fair forms to fair practices, and from fair practices to fair notions, until from fair notions he arrives at the notion of absolute beauty, and at last knows what the essence of beauty is. This, my dear Sócrates,' said the stranger of Mantinéa, 'is that life above all others which man should live, in the contemplation of beauty absolute; a beauty which if you once beheld, you would see not to be after the measure of gold, and garments, ... and youths, whose presence now entrances you; and you and many a one would be content to live seeing them only and conversing with them without meat or drink, if that were possible—you only want to look at them and to be with them. But what if man had eyes to see the true beauty—the divine beauty, I mean, pure and clear and unalloyed, not clogged with the pollutions of mortality and all the colors and vanities of human life—thither looking, and holding converse with the true beauty simple and divine? Remember how in that communion only, beholding beauty with the eye of the mind, he will be enabled to bring forth, not images of beauty, but realities (for he has hold not of an image but of a reality), and bringing forth and nourishing true virtue to become the friend of God and be immortal, if mortal man may. Would that be an ignoble life?'

Such, Phædrus—and I speak not only to you, but to all of you—were the words of Diotíma; and I am persuaded of their truth. And being persuaded of them, I try to persuade others, that in the attainment of this end human nature will not easily find a helper better than love: And therefore, also, I say that every man ought to honor him as I myself honor him, and walk in his ways, and exhort others to do the same, and praise the power and spirit of love according to the measure of my ability now and ever.

— Pláto, *Sympósium* (translated by Benjamin Jowett)

## Alcibíades Arrives at the Sympósium

When Sócrates had done speaking, the company applauded, and Aristóphanes was beginning to say something in answer to the allusion which Sócrates had made to his own speech, when suddenly there was a great knocking at the door of the house, as of revelers, and the sound of a flute-girl was heard. Ágathon told the attendants to go and see who were the intruders. 'If they are friends of ours,' he said, 'invite them in, but if not, say that the drinking is over.' A little while afterwards they heard the voice of Alcibíades resounding in the court; he was in a great state of intoxication, and kept roaring and shouting 'Where is Ágathon? Lead me to Ágathon,' and at length, supported by the flute-girl and some of his attendants, he found his way to them. 'Hail, friends,' he said, appearing at the door crowned with a massive garland of ivy and violets, his head flowing with ribands. 'Will you have a very drunken man as a companion of your revels? Or shall I crown Ágathon, which was my intention in coming, and go away? For I was unable to come yesterday, and therefore I am here today, carrying on my head these ribands, that taking them from my own head, I may crown the head of this fairest and wisest of men, as I may be allowed to call him. Will you laugh at me because I am drunk? Yet I know very well that I am speaking the truth, although you may laugh. But first tell me; if I come in shall we have the understanding of which I spoke? Will you drink with me or not?'

The company were vociferous in begging that he would take his place among them, and Ágathon specially invited him. Thereupon he was led in by the people who were with him; and as he was being led, intending to crown Ágathon, he took the ribands from his own head and held them in front of his eyes; he was thus prevented from seeing Sócrates, who made way for him, and Alcibíades took the vacant place between Ágathon and Sócrates, and in taking the place he embraced Ágathon and crowned him. Take off his sandals, said Ágathon, and let him make a third on the same couch.

By all means; but who makes the third partner in our revels? said Alcibíades, turning round and starting up as he caught sight of Sócrates. By Héracles, he said, what is this? here is Sócrates always lying in wait for me, and always, as his way is, coming out at all sorts of unsuspected places: and now, what have you to say for yourself, and why are you lying here, where I perceive that you have contrived to find a place, not by a joker or lover of jokes, like Aristóphanes, but by the fairest of the company?

— Pláto, *Sympósium* (translated by Benjamin Jowett)

# PUBLIC DOMAIN TRANSLATION CREDITS

*Analects*, students of Confucius, translated by James Legge in *Chinese Classics* (London: Trubner and Co., 1861)

*Aristotle's Ethics*, Aristotle, translated by D. P. Chase (London: J. M. Dent, 1911)

*Athenian Constitution*, School of Aristotle, translated by Frederic G. Kenyon (Oxford: Clarendon Press, 1921)

*Code of Hammurabi*, Hammurabi, translated by Leonard William King (1910)

*Description of Greece*, Pausanias, translated by W. H. S. Jones, *Loeb Classical Library* (Cambridge, MA: Harvard University Press, 1917-1926)

*Dialogues of Plato*, Plato, translated by Benjamin Jowett (Oxford: Clarendon Press, 1892)

*Early Greek Philosophy*, John Burnet (London: Adam and Charles Black, 1892)

*Greek Poets in English Verse*, edited by William Hyde Appleton (Cambridge: Riverside Press, 1893)

*History of Herodotus*, Herodotus, translated by George Rawlinson, (London: John Murray, 1859)

*History of the Peloponnesian Wars*, Thucydides, translated by Richard Crawley (New York: E. P. Dutton and Co., 1910)

*Iliad*, Homer, translated by Augustus Taber Murray, *Loeb Classical Library* (Cambridge, MA: Harvard University Press, 1924)

*Inscription of Tiglath-Pileser I.*, translated by Sir Henry Rawlinson, Royal Asiatic Society (London: J. W. Parker and Son: 1857)

*Library of History*, Diodorus Siculus, translated by C. H. Oldfather, *Loeb Classical Library* (Cambridge, MA: Harvard University Press, 1933)

*Life of Pythagoras*, Porphyry, Iamblichus, translated by Kenneth Sylvan Guthrie (Alpine, NJ: Platonist Press, 1919)

*Lives*, Plutarch, translated by John Dryden, edited by A.H. Clough (Boston: Little Brown and Co., 1906)

*Lives of the Eminent Philosophers*, Diogenes Laertius, translated by Robert Drew Hicks, *Loeb Classical Library* (Cambridge, MA: Harvard University Press, 1925)

*Masterpieces of Greek Literature*, edited by John Henry Wright (Cambridge: Riverside Press, 1902)

*Pastorals, Epistles, Odes, and Other Poems*, Ambrose Philips (London: Tonson and Draper, 1748)

*Poetical Works of Thomas Moore*, Thomas Moore (Philadelphia: J. B. Lippincott and Co., 1856)

*Poetics*, Aristotle, translated by Samuel Henry Butcher (New York: Macmillan and Co., 1902)

*The Dhammapada*, translated by Friedrich Max Müller in *Sacred Books of the East*, Volume X, Part I (Oxford: Clarendon Press, 1881)

*The Fall of Troy*, Quintus of Smyrna, translated by Arthur S. Way (London: William Heinemann, 1913)

*The Geography of Strabo*, Strabo, translated by Horace Leonard Jones (London: William Heinemann, 1917-1932)

*The Homeric Hymns and Homerica*, Hesiod, translated by H. G. Evelyn-White (New York: G. P. Putman and Sons, 1920)

*The Natural History, Pliny the Elder,* translated by John Bostock and H. T. Riley (London: Taylor and Francis, Red Lion Court, Fleet Street, 1855)

*Theogony*, Hesiod, translated by H. G. Evelyn-White (New Haven: Harvard University Press 1920)

*The Papyrus of Ani*, translated by E. A. Wallace Budge (London: The Medici Society Ltd.: 1913)

*The Sayings of Lao-Tse*, Lao-Tse, translated by Lionel Giles from the *Tao Te Ching* (London: The Orient Press, 1904)

*The Ten Books on Architecture*, Vitruvius, translated by Morris Hickey Morgan (Cambridge: Harvard University Press, 1914)

*The Works of Flavius Josephus*, Flavius Josephus, translated by William Whiston, A.M. (Auburn and Buffalo: John E. Beardsley, 1895)

*The Writings of Henry David Thoreau*, Henry David Thoreau, Volume V (Boston, MA: Houghton Mifflin, 1906)

*Works of Xenophon*, Xenophon, translated by H. G. Dakyns (London: Macmillan and Co., 1890)

Made in the USA
Columbia, SC
17 May 2020